A LINE OUT
FOR A WALK

8/26/01

Katie,

I read the beginning of
the first essay to it made
me laugh. Hope you like them.

Happy 25th Birthday!

Love,

Sarah

A LINE OUT FOR A WALK

Familiar Essays by

JOSEPH EPSTEIN

W·W·NORTON & COMPANY

NEW YORK   LONDON

The text of this book is composed in 11/14 Janson Alternate, with the display set
in Weiss Initial. Composition and manufacturing by the Haddon Craftsmen, Inc.

First Edition

Library of Congress Cataloging-in-Publication Data
Epstein, Joseph, 1937–
A line out for a walk : familiar essays / by Joseph Epstein.
p. cm.
I. Title.
AC8.E664 1991
081—dc20   90-44698
ISBN 0-393-30854-5

W.W. Norton & Company, Inc., 500 Fifth Avenue, New York, N.Y. 10110
W.W. Norton & Company, Ltd., 10 Coptic Street, London WC1A 1PU

4 5 6 7 8 9 0

Burton Epstein
(1962–1990)

"I TAKE A LINE OUT FOR A WALK."

—PAUL KLEE

Contents

A Note on the Title

A NUMBER OF YEARS AGO a reviewer of an earlier book of mine, writing in *The New Republic*, remarked that the genre of the familiar essay was best defined by the painter Paul Klee's explanation of how his own art worked. "I take a line out for a walk," said Klee. As time went by, I forgot the name of the reviewer, and for a while even mis-attributed the quotation to Kandinsky, but "I take a line out for a walk" remained with me. I have thought of it afresh each time I began a new essay; it describes exactly, precisely, absolutely what I do.

The "line" is of course my subject. A subject is all the familiar essayist needs. Character, point of view, observation, past reading, these he has, or ought already to have, in his kit. But where his subject will take him he is unlikely to know in advance, just as Paul Klee did not know where his line would take him. "I am writing a Theme and Variations," the composer William Walton wrote to Herbert von Karajan. "I've written the Variations but I don't yet have the Theme." The familiar essayist knows whereof William Walton speaks. The chanciness of the enterprise, the element of discovery and surprise in it, are among the pleasures of writing the familiar

essay—and I can only hope that something like the same pleasures come through in reading these particular essays.

Yet again I owe more thanks than I can recount to my
friends Jean Stipicevic, Sandra Costich, and Thomas Nieman,
all of *The American Scholar,* for their help with these essays.

A LINE OUT
FOR A WALK

You Probably Don't Know Me

I USED OCCASIONALLY to play racquetball with Saul Bellow, the Nobel Prize–winning novelist. I was then in my late thirties, Bellow in his late fifties. To offer an athletic as distinct from an aesthetic criticism, if a Nobel Prize were offered for racquetball, Saul Bellow would not have won it. He was a middling player, I a bit above middling, but the difference in our ages made our games, to me at any rate, a touch frightening. The problem was that Bellow knew only one way to play, and that was full-out, which at his age was dangerous. To be "in the pink" is thought to be a fine thing; but on the racquetball court it didn't take Saul Bellow long to be somewhere in between the vermilion and the magenta. Sometimes, after a particularly vigorous point, I would inquire the score from my place at the service line and hear it come back to me in the piping, rather quavering voice of a man physically *in extremis*. My God, I thought, what if he drops dead right here on this racquetball court! And then, tenderheartedly, near bursting with compassion, I proceeded to think—of myself.

In particular, I began to imagine how I might be treated by the press in the event of such an unpleasant happenstance. Suddenly I saw a headline that read, "Nobel Novelist Goes Down for Final Count as Essayist Looks On." I imagined a grainy photograph taken inside the racquetball court, in whose caption I am mentioned as "Man at left in shorts unidentified." Spinning an unascertainable number of years forward into the future, I espied my own two-inch-long obituary, in the dolorous typeface of the *New York Times,* carrying the small-type headline "Man Who Served Death to Nobel Writer Dies Out of Court." Whew! A damn near thing and luckily avoided, not only for Saul Bellow but for me.

I am not certain why I seem naturally to identify with men and women who in newspaper photographs are themselves unidentified, but I do. I find my heart also going out to those who are given brief obituaries for playing cameo roles in history through their relation to the lives of the truly famous: the ex-wife of the third son of an American president, a lawyer who represented celebrities, a half sister to a shah, a brother-in-law to a well-known comedian, a violinist who toured with Caruso, a Hollywood voice coach, the owner of an umbrella and cane shop that catered to politicians, the widow of a cellist, the father of an all-American basketball player, the great-grandson of Karl Marx. So, too, am I taken by people who have limited, if not to say severely restricted, claims to fame, such as the man who took the famous photograph of the raising of the American flag on Iwo Jima, one partner of a famous bridge team, the first black federal bankruptcy judge, a prominent hand surgeon, an expert on jaw malfunctions, the lyricist for "If You Knew Susie," or the creator of the first Orange Julius. The late M. Doug Wood, a name unknown to almost everyone, provides a perfect example of what I have in mind. His obituary in the *New York Times* of May 7, 1987, reads *in toto:*

M. Doug Wood

Salt Lake City, May 5 (AP)—M. Doug Wood, a co-founder of Evelyn Wood Reading Dynamics, died Saturday at the age of 83.

Besides his wife, his survivors include his daughter, Carol Davis
Evans of Tucson, Ariz., and four grandchildren.

The briefest possible obituary for one of the founders of speed-
reading—has the punishment ever more snugly fit the crime?
Well, I recall thinking, reading this pared-down obit on the
day it appeared, at least it won't take anyone too long to read
about his demise. Doubtless, Doug would have wanted it that
way.

I wonder, too, if when alive, Mr. M. Doug Wood did not
feel a slight but fairly frequent twinge of resentment over the
greater fame enjoyed by Evelyn Wood, his wife, whose name
has become synonymous with the dubious invention of reading so fast that one ignores style, nuance, and irony. Did Ira
Gershwin, who wrote all those lovely lyrics, feel a similar
resentment at the greater fame of his brother George? Doug
Wood and Ira Gershwin, though they may have shared naught
else, share the status, at least so far as the public knew, of being
sidekicks, right-hand men, secondo dons. Of honorable sidekicks, there has been no paucity: the Lone Ranger had Tonto,
Roy Rogers had the untidy Gabby Hayes, Wonder Woman
had a pudgy, bonbon-chomping pal named Tootsie. At a
higher literary level, Sancho Panza and Falstaff are second
bananas, packing as much if not more potassium as the first
bananas with whom their creators bunched them.

To play the role of sidekick, to accept the status of second
banana, however substantial the rewards, nonetheless requires
certain gifts of temperament: one must be prepared to subsume
one's interest to those of another, to settle for less in the way
of attention and glory and other of those prizes that men and
women, in their well-advertised vanity, have always striven
for. One must, in short, be ready to let go one's ego.

Many jobs—in fact, most jobs—demand the submergence

of one's own interests. In literary life, an editor, a biographer, a translator, an anthologist, a bibliographer—all are indispensable, yet all are second, some even third, bananas. Journalists used to be third, possibly fourth, bananas, but no longer. Journalists, especially television journalists, are usually among the best-known local people in any city; and my guess is that most of us can name our local anchorman much more readily than our congressman. Any good Marxist would take all this as self-evidently true; after all, journalists control the means of production—and what is being produced is, of course, fame.

Ah, fame, which Milton (neither Berle nor Friedman) called "that last infirmity of noble mind," is far from afflicting only the noble-minded. The desire for fame was once thought to be, along with the love of truth, a sign of great character. But today everyone knows that a proper attitude toward fame requires that one disregard it, or at least look askance at it. Fame, it is understood, is as ephemeral as a suntan—perhaps more so. Fame is tinny, fame is bogus, fame is ultimately empty. In the future everyone will be famous for fifteen minutes, or so said a man so famous that I think I shall not even bother to give his name. Fame is a shuck and a crock, humbug and poppycock. Who needs it?

Sorry to have to report, I believe I do. If needing fame is perhaps putting it a bit strongly, let me revise that statement and say that, at a minimum, I know I should rather like it. As a general rule, I would add that, unless you happen to be cheating on your husband or wife, or are employed as a spy, it is usually nicer to be known than not. One of the few ways that I failed to mis-spend my youth was sitting in bars, but I clearly recall, in my early twenties, the glow of appreciation I felt when, awaiting a table in a popular Italian restaurant I had been to the week before, the bartender, a middle-aged man of grave mien (he was probably ten years younger than I am now), remembered what I drank. "It's scotch and water, isn't it, sir?" he said. My heart leapt the bar and landed in his pocket. In remembering what I drank, he seemed to discern that I was not of the mass, to lift me above the ruck of ordinary suckers, and to make plain that I was a young man of rare quality whose very drinking habits were worth noting. Had we been in France, I should have grasped the lapels of his short red bartender's jacket and kissed him on both cheeks. Instead, in my more measured Midwestern manner, I merely lavishly over-tipped him.

If it is nice to be known, it is even nicer, for one who has a taste for fame, to be talked about. In contemporary life, being famous may be no more complicated than being talked about. Of course, the way one is talked about is decisive. My own first small bout of fame—that is to say, of arranging to have myself talked about—came in high school when I turned down membership in a senior boys' honorary society for students who had been on the school's athletic teams or active in extracurricular activities. I was passed over the first time new members were taken in, as was a friend of mine who was also a likely candidate for membership. One day, talking about it, we resolved that, should we be asked to join on the second round of invitations, we would tell the members of this honorary society to stow it in Ashtabula.

The morning I was informed that I had been elected, I told the two boys who had come to break the happy news to me that I was sorry but I must refuse membership, owing to my having so many other activities. Later that morning my friend, who had also been elected, asked, in a worried voice, if I would mind greatly if he went back on his pledge, broke our compact, and accepted membership. I told him that of course it was fine with me, that I quite understood his position, that he was not to worry about it in the slightest. What I really felt was delight to be doing this alone, so that I wouldn't have to share the distinction of being the first boy in the school's history to refuse membership in this generally admired society. The limelight, such as it was, would be mine and mine alone. It would be I, and I alone, who would be talked about. And so I was— for about two or three days, after which everyone lost interest. But while it lasted, I have to add, I enjoyed it immensely.

No doubt about it, fame was jolly, but as with many another of the jolly items on life's menu—food and sex jump to mind—it didn't last very long. As with food and sex, so with fame: one couldn't subsist very long on the mere memory of it. Himself no stranger to fame, Freud once said that the artist gives up fame, money, and the love of beautiful women for his art, through which he hopes to win fame, money, and the love of beautiful women. His subject was sublimation, a point on which I have never been quite convinced: Is Aleksandr Solzhenitsyn, for example, sublimating through his writing? To ask the question is to ridicule it. Although fame is one of those things one is not supposed to want, most people nonetheless seem to. "I'm really a very private person," many a starlet has told ten or twenty million people on many a talk show. Even quite bashful people, when it is available to them, do not altogether shun fame; they merely prefer that people talk about them when they are not present.

A desire for fame, and of a quite crude kind, was certainly among the motives of my own incipient urge to become a writer. When, at roughly the age of twenty, I thought I might one day be able to write, I did not wish to do so because I felt I possessed powerful truths that only I was capable of formulating for the world. Nor was I driven to work free, as the boys in the head trades might put it, from a terrible childhood that left me many a ghost to bury in one or another kind of writing. True, I adored the sound, shape, and feel of words and was much taken with the superior game of lining them up in sentences and paragraphs, but I cannot really say that I was impelled to write out of aesthetic necessity. Something far simpler and rather more embarrassing to report was at work; this was that I felt a tremendous desire, ardor, make that sheer heat, to see my name in print. I would dreamily imagine it in different typefaces: in the Caslon Old Face of *The New Yorker*, in the all-caps Bembo of *Poetry*, in the Times Roman of the *Times Literary Supplement*. Just my name, you understand; what appeared under or over it mattered scarcely at all. Bodoni bold of me to admit to this coarse vanity, but I tell you, sans serif, that I would have willingly exchanged a toe or an appendix to find my name in any of those or many another magazine. In listing the motives for writing that Orwell set down in his famous essay "Why I Write," he put first, "Sheer egotism." No dope that George.

"You remind me of a famous actor," said the young man checking me out in the express lane at the supermarket on a steamy Sunday evening, "but I can't remember his name." "How can you be sure I'm not that famous actor?" I asked. "Because you wouldn't be here," he replied—quite rightly, too. He never was able to recall the actor's name, and I left hoping that the actor wasn't, say, Ernest Borgnine. Looking like someone famous can carry its own comic ironies. One summer I saw a man at the Ravinia Music Festival outside Chicago wearing a bright red T-shirt across whose front large white letters proclaimed, "I Am Not Cesar Romero." Of course, he looked exactly like Cesar Romero, a condition he must have enjoyed hugely; for if he didn't, why was he wearing a mustache and hairdo altogether similar to "the old Latin lover's," as the gutter press might describe him. Which reminds me that it was in the gutter press—the *National Enquirer?* the *Star?*— that I noted an item about the actress

Farrah Fawcett wishing to make a movie in which she plays
Fawn Hall, Colonel Oliver North's assistant, who rather looks
like Farrah Fawcett and may even have been consciously imi-
tating the actress's looks. What we have here, then, is an actress
wanting to play the part of someone who, in so-called real life,
may have been modeling herself on that actress to begin with.
Rich stuff. Where did you say you wanted that mirror put up,
Señor Borges?

To look like someone who is famous is one thing; to be the
child of someone who is famous is quite another, much more
difficult thing. There is an amusing story about the son of
Arnold Schoenberg reprimanding his father for scolding him,
arguing that he is after all the son of a great composer and
hence someone rather better born than Schoenberg himself.
But most stories about the children of the famous, especially
the artistically famous, are stories of sadness, squalor, and defeat. Nathan Asch, the son of the once world-famous novelist
Sholem Asch, in a heartbreaking memoir, "My Father and I,"
wrote: "There is more apostasy, suicide, homosexuality, fraud,
and lying as well as plain ne'er-do-wellism among [the children
of famous artists] than among the children of other kinds of
people." Without knowing the first fact of their actual lives,
one's sympathies immediately go out to the daughter of Rita
Hayworth and Orson Welles, the son of Mary McCarthy and
Edmund Wilson, all the children of Picasso. And one silently
thanks one's own parents for the unconscious kindness implied
in their remaining, outside their circle of friends and business
acquaintances, happily obscure.

Once, when working as a publisher's editor, I was told that
a man with a manuscript wished to see me. Small, red-haired,
with refined features, he set his manuscript upon my desk
before introducing himself. On a white card pasted to a black
plastic manuscript cover was typed an academic-sounding title

and under it the name, followed by the suffix "Jr.," of the most famous producer in the history of Hollywood. "Are you . . ." I began, about to ask the question he had doubtless been asked hundreds, perhaps thousands of times already. His eyelids drooped over his eyes, he nodded his head slightly, and there was no need to finish my question. In the brief droop of those eyelids I saw a life haunted by the ghost of a famous father, Irving Thalberg.

If one has drawn a ticket in life's lottery as the son or daughter of someone famous, it is probably a good idea to go into a line of work other than that of one's famous parent. This is so because the competition against a famous parent is so unfair, the odds so stacked against the child, the chill of constant comparison so likely to freeze him up. Some, true enough, win through. But for every Pliny and Pitt the Younger there must be uncounted Plinys and Pitts the Worse and the Sadder. Some of us take a not-so-secret pleasure in learning about the failures of the children of the famous. When we hear that the great writer's daughter has had a nervous breakdown, or that the famous actress's son is a drug addict, we do a half gainer, double somersault in the dark pool of our souls. Such is the cost of fame, we conclude about these family tragedies, and it isn't worth it. And for the nonce we feel justified in our own obscurity.

Better luck, perhaps, to have been born more distantly related to someone famous. In my time I have known a nephew of the Notre Dame football coach Frank Leahy, a cousin of the television comedian Morey Amsterdam, a sister of the boxer Barney Ross—as an exercise in name-dropping, I must confess, this is pitiful—and all seemed quite pleased with their connections with the famous in their families. Their relatives' fame didn't weigh down on them, but, on the contrary, seemed to buoy them up a bit. Even remote association with the famous tends to do that for people. This is a lesson I learned fairly early in life, and I put it to use as an adolescent attempting, almost always vainly, to pick up girls in a large and now long-defunct amusement park in Chicago called Riverview. My modus operandi in those days was to ask any gaggle of girls—on behalf of my pals and myself—if they went, say, to Schurz High School. When they replied, usually rather curtly, that in fact they went to Roosevelt, I would jump in with, "Ah, then you must know my cousin, Louie Landt," who just happened to be the star of the Roosevelt High basketball team. Whatever school a group of girls claimed to go to, I claimed cousinage with that school's current basketball or football star. It generally worked, at least to break the ice. I accumulated a lot of broken ice, those summers of my adolescence. Such is the strange power of fame.

And such is the oddity of fame that the first thing most people who achieve it try to do with it is avoid it or, at any rate, complain about its encumbrances. One tends to think of fame in this connection with dark glasses, darting into limousines, screaming at press photographers who have gone too far, hiding away in villas on the Dalmatian coast to which the pestering bloody public cannot gain entry. Fame, in this reading, is a bed of thorns in which no one can hope to get any rest. In extreme cases, such as that of J. D. Salinger or Howard Hughes or Greta Garbo, reclusiveness is the usually unsatisfactory answer. Carried out on a grand or zany enough scale, one is only likely to become—as did Salinger, Hughes, Garbo—even more famous for wishing to avoid fame. Perhaps the desire for fame is one of those tricky wishes that one does best not to mention to your local djinn.

Others toss and roll in their fame, lapping it up, loving every minute of it. The interview, the press conference, the talk show—bring 'em on! The woman from the *New York*

Times on the phone, the photographer from *People* setting up in the living room, the dork with the Minicam from the local television station ringing the doorbell—hey, as they say in the beer ads, go for it! The best tables in the best restaurants, mail filled with offers and invitations, the feeling that the world really is at one's feet, such can be among the high, heady delights that accompany fame. "Where to?" a cab driver in Paris is said once to have asked Herbert von Karajan. "It doesn't matter," the famous conductor is said to have replied. "They want me everywhere."

I have never come near to having been wanted everywhere, but I have from time to time been permitted to potter a bit about the purlieus where contemporary fame is manufactured. Usually in connection with books I have published, I have been interviewed by *Vogue* and *W,* I have been the subject of three dreary pages in *People,* and I was once a solo guest on *The Phil Donahue Show* (surely you remember, it was the same splendid week that he had the transsexuals and Kareem Abdul-Jabbar). I tell you this to establish that I am a man who has had his foot past the bordello door. Didn't much like it in there, I have to confess. The air was fetid with fraudulence. Taking part in an exercise so essentially phony depressed me.

As for the exercise itself, it might be called Killing Time and Filling Space. Or so at least I thought of my job a number of years ago when, on a tour to promote a book, I visited seven cities in six days, gassing away on various radio and television talk shows and lending the details of my private life for eight or nine newspaper feature stories all about me. Not long afterward, on television before an audience of I don't know how many millions, I gazed deep into the blue eyes of Phil Donahue to discover that they resembled the city of Oakland in Gertrude Stein's youth in that there was "no there there." Did I, as a result of these efforts at self-promotion, become famous?

Not very. Did I at least sell vast quantities of my book? Not many. Still, I like to look fondly back upon that time and think of all the friendships I didn't make.

"Do you know me?" ran the tag line from an American Express television commercial. Whenever it played on my television set, I found myself muttering in response, "No, sir, nor do I wish to." I always thought that the advertising agency that staged those commercials missed a fine opportunity by not having the man who says "Do you know me?" turn out to be Martin Bormann, or Josef Mengele, or some still-at-large mad, serial killer in California, but then those ad boys do tend to play it safe.

If I were in such a commercial, I should like my own tag line to be "You probably don't know me, and, if it is all the same to you, why don't we just leave it that way." By which I mean that, however passionate the hunger for fame on the part of writers, it is doubtless best that they not be too well known. Although there have been writers of great celebrity in America, from Mark Twain through Ernest Hemingway to Truman Capote, and although toward the end of his life Leo Tolstoy may have been the most famous man in Russia, as a general rule it is better that writers be observers but not ob- served, as close to ringside as they can get but not themselves in the ring. Yet writers may hunger more for fame than other artists do because, first, people do not see them performing their art, as they do dancers and actors and musicians; and, second, writers do not see their audience actually enjoying their work, as do painters and playwrights and composers. Only once have I seen a stranger reading something I had written; this happened on a New York subway where a woman standing alongside me was reading an essay I had in the current month's issue of *Harper's*. It was all that I could do not to tell her that I was the author of the essay she was reading.

I surely would have done so had she not read with so clearly disapproving a look upon her face that my taking a bow just then seemed a serious error.

"You probably don't know me, and it is driving me nuts" is another view of fame, and one that tends to be held by people who have had fame, took much delight in it, and now sense it is leaving them. I have a friend who until recently was a member of the City Council in Chicago; he is a man with strong opinions, which he expresses well. Because for the better part of his time on the council he was in opposition to the faction in power, he was frequently called upon to criticize the mayor on the six and ten o'clock news shows. This has made him locally famous; in Chicago his had become a household face. I hope he will not mind my saying that he rather enjoys this fame. I note that whenever we enter a restaurant or other public place, he checks the room to see if he is recognized. He usually is. A waiter or the owners of the restaurant or a customer will ask him if he isn't the fellow they suspect he is. Although he is not made rapturously happy by this, it is plain that he is pleased to be recognized. He has not made anywhere near as much money in politics as he could have made as a lawyer, and he may well view such fame as he has earned as a sufficient substitute (psychic) income, which seems to me fair enough.

But should he stay out of politics, and hence out of television camera range, his local fame—the political consultants, I believe, call it his "recognition factor"—will no doubt quickly diminish. In a year, people will strain to recall his name; in eighteen months he may well be taken for a weekend weatherman; in two years—oblivion. I remember reading a journalist's account of going into the Sans Souci restaurant in Washington, D.C., with a man who had only a few years before left a job as a chief political correspondent with one of the major networks. The Sans Souci was then said to be the favorite restaurant of Henry Kissinger—this was late in the second Nixon administration—and hence a politically potent place. The former network correspondent checked the room and, the journalist recounted, no one in the joint recognized him—and it was as if someone had poured machine oil over the food. Those who live by the kind of large, lumpish fame made possible only by the television camera often die without it.

Not everyone is so piggish in his appetite for fame as to require it in the heavy portions dispensed by television. I not long ago visited an old friend awaiting surgery in a once grand but now slightly dilapidated Jewish hospital—"Kings have lain here," wrote Karl Shapiro of such an institution, "And fabulous small Jews / And actresses whose legs were always news"—and noted countless memorial plaques. Every wing, section, surgical theater, waiting room, patient room, elevator—everything, in short, but the ashtrays, urinals, and toilets was dedicated to the memory of someone or other. Some donated money to memorialize parents or dead children; others doubtless left money behind in their wills to memorialize themselves. You can't take your money with you into death, but you can leave enough behind to allow the memory of yourself to linger awhile. In his autobiography, Irving Howe reports that Abram Sacher, then president of Brandeis, used to tell potential donors to the university the story of the Widener family giving money to Harvard to honor the memory of their son Henry, who went down with the *Titanic*, so that today students at Harvard rarely say "Let's go to the library" but instead say "Let's go to Widener." Howe writes: "A hush fell across the room. One could almost see quivers of emotion journeying from soul to soul, as if the assembled manufacturers and real estate men were ruminating, 'Someday maybe they'll say, "Let's go to Shapiro!" ' "

To have a major university library named after you, to be recognized in a fashionable restaurant, to have a plaque bearing your name in the elevator of a fading hospital, to have a local bartender know your drink—obviously, there are degrees of fame, yet no clear measure to gauge it. When the bill was presented from Père-Lachaise cemetery for burying Balzac, whose entire life was a struggle for fame, the great writer's name was spelled "Balsaque." (Surely there is a moral there somewhere.) I have always been partial to the definition of fame that holds you are only famous when someone who is crazy imagines he is you. I tried to remember who said that, and when I finally found it in *The Viking Book of Aphorisms*, I discovered that it was that prolific author who goes by the name of Anonymous. (Can there be a moral here, too?)

Thirty or so years ago, one might have argued that fame was being on the cover of *Time*, but now that is no longer true, nor does being on the cover of any magazine, or the subject of an ornate scandal, or the winner of honors and prizes. All these things, it is now commonly understood, render one a celebrity, and celebrity, it is also understood, is seasonal. In medicine, in fashion, in art, Proust once remarked, "there must be new names." That one of the new names this week, or month, or year happens to be yours shouldn't be taken too seriously.

Yet, as is not quite the case with money and power, the only people who can authoritatively dismiss fame are those who either have it or have walked away from a solid opportunity for attaining it. As coolheaded a man as Spinoza said he thought that those who cried out most loudly against fame were probably themselves most desirous of it. In order to despise fame properly one really must have it, and being in the superior position of despising it may even be worth the effort of achieving it. I wouldn't know; I would, however, like to know.

Everyone who writes, I have no doubt, would like to be famous, and not only famous now, while on this earth, but, embarrassing enough to admit given the odds, famous after he has departed the earth. And this, I believe, is true of serious and frivolous writers alike. All of us would like to have said about us what I heard a eulogist say of the songwriter Yip Harburg: "He is survived by his words." A certain absurdity is built into this desire, to be sure, and this is that death presents at least three distinct possibilities—heaven, hell, or sheer oblivion— none of which is a condition likely to be improved upon by posthumous fame. Still, every writer likes to think that posterity will take his proper measure, which also means that he hopes posterity will esteem him as he wishes to be esteemed. Given the general level of vanity among writers, it is fair to say that contemporary society has not arrived at the stage of development where this is possible.

Yet there is a serious distinction between wanting fame and wanting recognition for one's accomplishments. Edward Gibbon, for example, upon completion of his great history, noted: "I will not dissemble the firm emotions of joy on the recovery of my freedom, and, perhaps, the establishment of my fame." As is now known, about Gibbons's fame there was no "perhaps" whatsoever. Gibbons's fame arrived on schedule, remained, lived after him, endures today more than two centuries later, and, based on solid achievement as it is, is entirely deserved. Without such fame, based on true accomplishment, there can be no tradition, no worthy models, no passing on of high achievement across generations and down through centuries. In this sense fame is no trivial matter.

Yet it sometimes seems as if fame is all a writer can think about—his reputation, his ranking among other writers, and the rest of it—and yet it is probably the worst thing for him to think about. To think about posthumous fame is still worse.

As soon as he begins to direct his writing to future generations, it is almost certain to become portentous and empty. As soon as he begins to think of his own fame in comparison with that of his contemporaries, his mood figures to turn rivalrous and mean. Fame, for a writer, is very difficult to control. If he writes too little, his fame is endangered; if he writes too much, it is also endangered. The appetite for money or power can be slaked; I at any rate have seen people once quite mad for money or power be calmed after they had achieved an ample portion of either. I cannot say the same for those with a strong taste for fame. *"La gloire et le repos sont choses qui ne peuvent loger en même gîte,"* wrote Montaigne, which I should loosely translate, "You want fame, kid, kiss tranquility good-bye."

In a certain kind of stupid, falsely sincere television interview, there comes a moment toward the end when the interviewer leans in and, in a serious and intimate tone of voice, asks, "How do you wish to be remembered?" To which the person being interviewed usually responds, "As a person who always cared deeply for quality," or "As a good parent to my children," or "For my work with animal shelters," or some such self-congratulatory lie. To the question "How do you wish to be remembered?" my own, simpler answer is "For as long as possible."

The Gentle Art of the Resounding Put-Down

THERE I SIT, calm as you please, about to lay into a nicely underdone and ample portion of leg of lamb in an expensive and quite good restaurant called Jean-Louis at the Watergate for which a large organization is to pay what in my youth in Chicago used to be called "the damages," when the young woman seated next to me inquires after the salt. I search for a saltshaker among the plate and crystal, flowers and candles, but none is to be found. A small oversight, doubtless. I ask our waiter, a tall and rather well-set-up fellow, for salt for our table, and, in a somewhat dubious foreign accent, he replies, "I am sorry, sir, but Jean-Louis does not permit salt at the table." If I were quicker than I am, I should have replied, "Very well, then, bring us a bottle of chili sauce." If I were cleverer, I should have repaired to a public telephone, there to order a pizza to be delivered to me at table in time for the arrival of Jean-Louis's dessert. But on this occasion, as on many another, I was neither quick nor clever enough. When told that Jean-Louis does not permit salt at the table, I replied, in italics, *"Oh,"* my face, I rather suspect, matching the lamb upon my plate.

My condition reminded me of a skit that the comedian Danny Thomas used to do in which he played a little man who is told off by his boss, or a bureaucrat, or his mother-in-law, and somewhat mousily takes it. But as soon as his tormentor departs, scores of brilliant, even excoriating responses occur to him. Contemplating his recent degradation, the little man, doing a slow burn that heats up fast, says, "Why, I should've said to him, I should've said . . . ," and then there issues from him a cascade of funny remarks, each more devastating than the one that preceded it, and the only appropriate response to which would be for his tormentor, were he still on the premises, to beg forgiveness before finding a tidy way to take his life. Then, as I recall, the boss, or bureaucrat, or mother-in-law returns, and our man, so courageously witty when alone, once more turns into a Milquetoast.

I am by no means the Mittyesque figure of Danny Thomas's imagining, but, I must confess, I have spent my share of time in the activity that I think of as malign afterthought. Although I seem to be able to write my mind fairly well, I have not always spoken it with the same ease and confidence. Part of the problem may be insufficient quickness; even when it comes to insults, I need time to revise and polish. Part of the problem, too, is that I don't have much appetite for face-to-face confrontation, at least not confrontation of a combative kind. I don't wish to imply natural sweetness of temper. I don't mind expressing my dissatisfaction at egregiously bad service, or hopeless bureaucratic snaggle, or the attempt on the part of someone to deal unfairly with me, but usually I go a bit too far, my gorge rises too quickly, I waste wit on someone who turns out not to know English well, or I blast someone else for some mishap in terms that would be more appropriate for telling off, say, Hermann Göring.

But, to return to my man Jean-Louis, permit me to make

a quick paranoia check. Ought I to have been insulted by Jean-Louis's de-salinization program? I do not think an insult was intended. Certainly there was nothing personal about it; I, after all, didn't require any salt, but found the food splendid as it came to the table. No, I took it, if not as a personal insult, then as a strong gesture—even, it does not seem to me going too far to say, a somewhat bullying gesture—that called for a strong response. When a chef tells you, in effect, that his food is so perfectly prepared that only a man with an aluminum palate could possibly need to add salt to it, well, in my view, that chef should have something said to him that is direct and a bit peppery.

"Don't make a scene," a voice of reason calls out at such moments. "Ah, but it was not you who set this scene," another, rather more aggressive voice responds. I used to hate what people of my parents' generation call "making a scene." I do not love doing so now. But with the passing of years, and the acquisition of greater confidence (or is it the simple loss of tact?), my feeling is that certain scenes are unavoidable, some absolutely cry out to be played, and still others are eluded only at the cost of self-contempt. Lots of rudeness, nastiness, touchiness in the world; it's all part, I fear, of city living. So when a cab driver attempts to cheat me on a fare, or an academic behaves snobbishly, or a person in a position of temporary power over me acts badly, I take a deep breath, exhale slowly, and to myself mutter, "Ready when you are, C.B."

As in another age one needed to know how to wield a weapon if one traveled the highways, so today one needs to acquire the ability to wield the put-down if one is to be assured reasonably safe passage in the contemporary world. Many of us doubtless prefer to think otherwise—to think that good manners and goodwill shall win the day. Yet wasn't Santayana correct when he wrote: "In solitude it is possible to love mankind; in the world, for one who knows the world, there can be nothing but secret or open war." Detached philosopher that he was, practitioner of old-world courtesies that he also was, Santayana knew and understood the need for the put-down in modern life. The put-down is, of course, an imaginative insult, and Santayana, in his autobiography, confessed to having a strong taste in this line; and he even noted: "The habit of scribbling mocking epigrams has accompanied me through life and invaded the margins of my most serious authors."

As an admirer of Santayana, it pleased me enormously to learn this, for I, too, have this habit, and sometimes go about in a perfectly jolly mood formulating what I think are imaginative insults. When I learned that the literary critic Harold Bloom claimed, in *Time* magazine, to be able to read one thousand pages an hour, for example, it occurred to me to ask, What possible value can this have, except to permit one to read everything that Harold Bloom has written in fewer than two hours? Reading yet another interview with the novelist Philip Roth, I thought that over the years Roth has made himself into more and more of a minor writer, but without one of the principal charms of the minor writer: modesty. Formulating put-downs when alone may seem an odd activity for a man of middle years, but it does pass the time.

As put-downs go, these aren't bad, but they do suffer from not having been delivered in person. Malice formulated in tranquillity is art of a lower kind than that exercised, so to speak, on site. I do not think of myself as slow-witted, but I do, apparently, need time to compose. It wasn't always thus. Although the term *put-down* had not yet been invented, the activity was widely practiced among the adolescent boys with whom I grew up on the far north side of Chicago. I hope I do not seem unduly vain—"duly vain" I will settle for—when I say that in the realm of put-downs, I was one of the fastest guns in the West. Where I grew up, wit was valued much more than learning; in the list of masculine virtues, wit followed only physical courage and athletic prowess. In those days, with a tongue quicker than an iguana's, I could destroy a bully in under thirty words, leaving him stammering in his own verbal ineptitude. In its way, it was a feeling of power.

Which reminds me to ask if the perfectly aimed put-down isn't the civilized person's equivalent of the perfectly aimed knockout punch. Perhaps "civilized person" isn't the precise phrase; "smallish person," by which I mean physically small, may be more precise. I read somewhere not long ago that the preponderant number of poisoners have been small men, and I am inclined to think that the same applies to the preponderant number of put-down artists. When I think over the history of insult, the splendid put-down artists seem mostly to have been smallish men and women, of the general size and frame of Dorothy Parker and Evelyn Waugh. The only notable exception that comes to mind is Oscar Wilde, whom I have always assumed to be more than six feet tall. Generally, though, the best height for a put-down artist is somewhere between five-five and five-ten for a man, five feet and five-four for a woman. Delicate work calls for a delicate touch, and too much bulk can only get in the way.

As for bulk, I have often tried to imagine how different my own life would have been—and would continue to be—if I were, say, a foot taller and seventy or so pounds heavier. If so, when in a traffic jam the man in the car behind my own who presses his heavy hand on his horn might be subjected to something more than my privately formulated put-downs— "Your low intelligence, sir, is only exceeded by your high boorishness"—which he will never have to hear anyway. But if I were six-seven or so, I think I might, in such a circumstance, be inclined to put on my emergency brake, slip out from behind the steering wheel, and have a word or two with the gentleman on what the late President Eisenhower called "a person-to-person basis." Or I might cut out the middleman— in this case, the English language—and instead hold him aloft for a spell, shaking him gingerly to determine if his upper and lower teeth are making good contact with each other. Better, perhaps, not to have that additional foot.

A certain portliness, however, does not seem out of place in a put-down artist. It lends ballast and can make one seem vaguely menacing, a person clearly not to be trifled with. Among Englishmen, Maurice Bowra, Evelyn Waugh, and the older Kingsley Amis all had (in Amis's case, still has) good put-down weight. So did Edmund Wilson, who had not the lightness of touch required of the supreme put-down artist but who, through conveying a general atmosphere of belligerence, could make plain that he was not a man who took kindly to being put down. Still, in these matters the best defense remains a strong offense, and no one could be more offensive, in an artful way, than Evelyn Waugh.

As the armadillo is built for defense, so was Waugh for offense. He even put his deafness (which some people believed he exaggerated) to good purpose by acquiring an ear trumpet, which caused anyone who wished to speak to him to feel he had to speak very loudly in his presence—and it is difficult to be clever let alone subtle when practically shouting. Once, at a banquet in Waugh's honor, when Malcolm Muggeridge rose to speak in tribute to him, Waugh, sitting upon the raised dais, rather emphatically removed his ear trumpet, setting it well in front of him, a gesture that made it all too plain that Muggeridge could not possibly say anything worth hearing. Yet this is rather crude when set beside Waugh's powers of incisive formulation, a brief sample of which is his remark to the effect that now that the Church no longer defrocks priests for sodomy, it is impossible to get decent proofreading.

Why would someone wish to say anything so outrageous? Chiefly, I should guess, because it happens to be terribly funny—that is, if you don't happen to be a liberal cleric, a homosexual, or in publishing. Without the wit, of course, such sentiments would be construed as deeply insulting, not to say bigoted. One is no longer permitted straight-out insults in contemporary society, at least not in public, if only because it is no longer clear how a straight-out insult ought to be dealt with. To cite a personal instance, as a result of an editorial contretemps, I once had an author accuse me of nothing less than "moral cowardice," which I felt pushed the stakes up too high too fast, for all it left me in the way of a return was open conjecture about his mother's profession. Instead I wrote back suggesting a duel when next he was in town. So far I have heard nothing further from him.

An insult is a blatant, coarse, ugly thing. "You emanate hopelessness and resentment and boredom and death," says a woman to her husband in Kingsley Amis's novel *The Old Devils*. Earlier she had addressed herself to his physical repulsiveness. Such insults don't leave a man much. A put-down at least gives its target a fighting chance. Thus George Bernard Shaw once sent Winston Churchill two tickets for the opening night of one of his new plays, noting, "Bring a friend—if you have one"; to which Churchill wrote back to say that he was otherwise engaged opening night, but would appreciate tickets for the second performance—"if there is one." What makes a put-down an insult with imagination is its high style; a put-down is an insult delivered with style. It is only the force of style that permits even the most outrageous put-down to elude the charge of pettiness, bad taste, or viciousness.

Saying something well may not be the best revenge, but it tends to be the most effective revenge. It can also be a reasonably enduring revenge. A serious put-down is under the obligation not only to sting but to leave a scar—that is, to be memorable. As Jorge Luis Borges remarks in his all-too-brief essay "The Art of Verbal Abuse," a put-down (he does not use this term) is an exercise in wrath and not in reason. Yet a winning put-down is wrath under absolute control, using whatever methods—irony, hyperbole, understatement—are at one's disposal, and not sticking around to talk logic. "My prayer to God is a very short one," wrote Voltaire. " 'O Lord, make my enemies ridiculous.' God has granted it." No, what God granted was the power of style to Voltaire, who used it to make them appear so through eternity.

In a better world, the need for put-downs would vanish, and skill at this deadly art would be equivalent in its utility to skill today with the net and trident. But until such a world arrives—and no time of arrival is yet listed, no gate posted—the art of the put-down remains, well, I would not say indispensable but highly useful. At the same time, this art of verbal abuse must not itself be abused through overuse. To have the reputation for being too strong in this line is not, I think, on the whole advisable, though Alexander Pope, one of the best in the business, clearly reveled in his own high reputation as a verbal killer:

> Yes, I am proud; and must be proud, to see
> Men not afraid of God afraid of me.

Such a boast set up its own natural rejoinder, and in a bit of put-down Ping-Pong, Lord Hervey, whom Pope had cut up in "An Epistle to Dr. Arbuthnot," picked up a paddle and shot back:

> The great honour of that boast is such
> That hornets and mad dogs may boast as much.

Samuel Johnson said of Pope that "he hardly drank tea without a strategem," a thing of which no one would ever have accused Johnson, who lowered the boom, my guess is, without rehearsal and whenever the mood was upon him. Shouldn't have liked to have been Boswell when Johnson served up the following put-down to him: "Sir, you have but two topics, yourself and me. I am sick of both." Posterity, or at least that part of it that remains interested in bookish things, has of course grown sick of neither. Yet I am reminded of my recently telling a young literary journalist, whose interview and portrait of a contemporary novelist had been rejected by a magazine, that, apart from the loss of the fee, perhaps it was just as well. "What do you want to be a Boswell for," I said, "in an age without any Johnsons?" As put-downs of an age go, that isn't too bad, but I have to admit that it wasn't altogether spontaneous. I had thought it a number of times before, folded it away, and now unfurled it in the breeze of this particular conversation.

Yet it is the spontaneous put-down, the well-turned jibe that rolls off on the spur of the moment and meets the opportunity exactly, that seems to me most impressive. A truly spontaneous put-down artist resembles the gunfighter in his need for speedy response. Such an artist must not only have wit but have ready wit. Your second-line put-down artists—among whom, perhaps rather generously, I am inclined to place myself—keep a certain amount of material stored up for use when needed. Your first-line artist, however, is inspired by the moment or occasion and lets the chips, chaps, and slaps fall where they may. I once introduced the late Henry Fairlie, the British journalist, to Edward Shils, who, upon introduction, complimented Fairlie on his past writings, but added that he was sorry to learn that he had recently declared himself a socialist and asked how this had come about. "Very simple," said Fairlie. "I

happened to hear Michael Harrington lecture in Chicago."
"Hmmm," said Shils. "Michael Harrington lecturing in Chicago—surely a case of worst comes to worst." There it was;
one shot and you could hear at least two bodies and a city fall.

Not all put-downs are best delivered face-to-face. Some are
too cruel to deliver before their targets, lest they maim them
psychologically for life. Some come up by the way and are not
the result of any dramatic encounter. A friend of mine once
concluded a general attack on a rather well known sociologist
by saying, "Well, at least he has never taken undue advantage
of being Jewish"—the point here being that the target of this
attack, though indeed Jewish, has kept that fact fairly well
hidden throughout a long career. A story is told about two
women, one of whom reports to the other that a particularly
dull newspaper columnist is supposed to marry a famous and
beautiful movie actress, causing the second woman to remark,
"I suppose I'd rather sleep with him than actually have to read
him"—which seems to me as rough a put-down of a writer as
I have heard. I once heard someone describe a man who had
only recently walked away after what appeared a friendly
enough exchange as "obviously suffering from delusions of
equality," which would have been vicious, even delivered out
of earshot of the victim, had not the latter himself been a great
snob. The force of the slap in the face, the French philosopher
Alain said, is best registered by the one who receives it, yet
these behind-the-back put-downs are slaps delivered but never
received.

Does the taste for put-downs—not enjoying hearing them
but actually delivering them—imply a certain appetite for the
jugular, a certain surliness, perhaps a meanness of spirit? Horace
Walpole said of Samuel Johnson that he "made the most
brutal speeches to living persons; for though he was good-natured
at bottom, he was ill-natured at top." Some put-down

artists seem to be motivated chiefly by a kind of self-defensive petulance (Dorothy Parker, S. J. Perelman), some by an enthusiasm for destructive criticism (Mary McCarthy, Dwight Macdonald), some by simple anger at shoddiness, fraudulence, falsity generally (fill in your own candidates here). Some are menthol-cool in their disdain, some red-hot in their rage; some are amused by the folly of their targets, some are outraged in their hatred. At a minimum, all, I believe it can safely be said, tend to concur that the world is in need of a few adjustments.

Gertrude Stein announced—Gertrude Stein never merely "said" anything—that "remarks are not literature," and yet literature is studded with splendid remarks, many of them fine put-downs. Many of Oscar Wilde's best put-downs occur in his plays, though two of my favorites—his remark about George Meredith being "a prose Browning, and so is Browning" and his remark that Bernard Shaw "hasn't an enemy in the world, and none of his friends like him"—do not. In "Him with His Foot in His Mouth," Saul Bellow has a narrator-hero who, seemingly out of sheer playfulness, cannot resist the impulse to let fly with put-downs, often when they are quite uncalled-for and even when they work against his own best interests. In Kingsley Amis's novels there is a general crackle of put-down in the air, relieved only by occasional flashes of genuine bad feeling. Ah, me, I believe I have just committed a put-down of my own, and I rather like Kingsley Amis's novels.

Name-dropping is generally a form of one-upmanship (itself a variant of put-downmanship), but there are some who have not minded being put down by people of sufficient fame. About a most rambunctious homosexual member of Parliament named Tom Driberg, Winston Churchill reportedly said, "He is the man who brought pederasty into disrepute." Driberg is supposed to have been rather proud of this remark;

he was, after all, put down by no less a figure than the greatest political leader of the twentieth century. The poet John Frederick Nims, a man with a lovely, sly sense of humor, once told me that while visiting Bernard Berenson at I Tatti, he was asked by his host what he was doing in Europe. Nims explained that he was on a Fulbright Fellowship to lecture on contemporary poetry. "Oh," replied Berenson, "you mean that squiggly stuff." There are limits, though. I shouldn't at all care to be the subject of a Vladimir Nabokov put-down, especially of the not-at-all-witty but quite efficient kind he dealt out to Norman Mailer by way of a journalist for *Time:* "I detest everything in American life that he stands for."

To be put down by one's putative inferiors can be a more complicated affair. Max Beerbohm told a story about his efforts to win the regard of the rather elegant hall porter at the Athenaeum Club. Then one day he left at the club a rare copy of a brochure his friend Logan Pearsall Smith's mother had written titled *How Little Logan Was Brought to Jesus,* which Smith had given him to read for his amusement. Beerbohm didn't want the lofty hall porter to think he read such stuff, yet, the copy of the brochure being so rare, he had no choice but to try to rescue it. With some trepidation, he asked the porter if anyone had found the brochure, whose title he had to report to the porter. A few days later the porter returned the brochure to him in a wrapped and tied package. Beerbohm felt he had forever after lost status in the hall porter's eyes, and that the fact that the brochure was wrapped as it was, suggesting that no serious person would want it known he read such drivel, itself constituted a powerful put-down.

Max Beerbohm had social antennae too sensitive to mistake the intent of such a gesture. But with only a touch of paranoia in one's makeup one can discover intent to put down everywhere. Often there is no question. Years ago I recall meeting an acquaintance from army days; he was twenty-seven, Jewish, and unmarried. He told me that he had just gone to the wedding of a nineteen-year-old female cousin at which he was seated at the children's table—a gesture in which he discovered dissatisfaction at his unmarried state of a kind that constituted a strong general put-down. More recently I attended a gala at which many a political celebrity was present: a big-city mayor, a United States senator, a couple of ambassadors, the current secretary of state. The number of security men almost equaled the number of guests. At my own table there were no politicians, but instead musicians, writers, and critics; I found it delightful. A few days later it was reported to me that someone had said that, in this setting, ours was clearly "the children's table." An amusing remark, but since I should rather dine among artists than among all but a very small number of politicians—most of them, now that I think about it, dead—I continue not to find anything of the put-down in our seating arrangements that night.

Many a put-down is engendered in a sticky fluid of ambiguity. An example of what I have in mind is the remark of the man or woman who said that "Wagner's music is better than it sounds." Or Peter Ustinov's comment on the embarrassing candor of Laurence Olivier's memoirs: "I wish he'd put on a false nose and be himself again." Henry James's conversation had something of this quality; it was stippled, as Edith Wharton noted, with "merry malice." Weldon Kees reported that Marianne Moore was capable of a similar merry maliciousness, and often used the words *generous* and *courageous* to mean the reverse of what they are supposed to mean.

Here the put-down slides into that marshier terrain known as the put-on. If the put-down is an imaginative insult, the put-on tends to be an ambiguous one—so much so that the insulted party often isn't even aware that he is being insulted.

The word *put-on* derives from the notion of putting something over *on* somebody. "To put someone on is, almost by definition, to rob him of his cool," writes Jacob Brackman in *The Put-On,* a slender volume that carries the splendidly put-on-ish dedication "To my mother and father, right?" The put-on has an air of tongue-in-cheek about it; it attempts, in E. E. Cummings's phrase, to "pull the wool over your toes."

I am myself made edgy in the company of a put-on artist. Cutting through the clouds of ambiguity, the mists of irony, the vapors of conversational strategy leaves me a bit weary. I prefer to retain what little cool remains to me. Before a talk I gave some while ago in Denver, though, I nearly lost it when, over drinks, I was introduced to a rather open-faced man with a rather commonplace name like Dick Hansen or Henry Johnson, who, with a friendly smile, said, "It's been a long time since high school." Oh, God, I thought, why can't I remember this guy? I strained to do so; then, certain he would think me a great snob and a creep into the bargain, I caved in and apologetically admitted that I wasn't sure I remembered him from high school. He allowed as how this was understandable, since we had never gone to high school together, adding that what he had just done to me he had done to scores of other strangers roughly his own age upon first being introduced to them. I chuckled insincerely, regretting one more time that I was not six-seven.

No question about it, folks do tend to get a bit touchy about being put on. My dear friend the audacious and resourceful Robert Ginsburg once demonstrated for me just how touchy they can get. He had visited me at my office at a large corporation for which I then worked. At the close of his visit, I walked him to the elevators, where I introduced him to a youngish vice president, who happened also to be awaiting an elevator, and they went down in the elevator together. The next day the vice

president greeted me by saying that he had had no idea that I
was a professional bowler. I knew immediately what had happened. In his twenty-five-second-or-so ride in the elevator, my
friend Roberto had filled this fellow with a mine of misinfor-
mation about me. I now had to explain this to the astonished
man standing before me, who was in a state of considerable
consternation. "You must understand," I said, "the joke here
is really on me. I now have to go through this elaborate explanation, telling you how I intensely dislike bowling, that my
father does not weigh more than three hundred pounds [an-
other piece of false information Roberto had filled him in on],
and God knows what else. You were the foil, yet I am the butt
of this put-on." All he could say in return was, "Boy, is that
guy sick!" And for roughly two weeks afterward, whenever I
would run into him, he would say, "You know, that friend of
yours is really sick."

The young vice president failed to understand the methods
of a true artist such as Roberto: his readiness to seize an opportunity, his not needing to be on the premises when his art
achieves its effects, his fine and even-handed disinterest. What
I suspect really puzzled him was the absence of obvious motive
in all this. But for Roberto it was motive enough that his old
friend be caught in his cunningly set trap, which I was. I could,
of course, have neglected to tell him that his trap had sprung,
catching my nose firmly within; yet artists working in such
minor genres as the put-on need all the appreciation they can
get, so I did indeed tell him, cur that he is, that his ploy had
worked exquisitely.

The famous one-upmanship, devised by Stephen Potter
and promulgated in such of his books as *One-upmanship,
Gamesmanship,* and *Lifemanship,* usually has a clearer motive
and, when working well, combines the qualities of the put-on
and the put-down. Potter's idea was to formulate those ploys

and gambits that, in everyday life, will provoke, put off, and generally get the other fellow down. The classic illustration, the paradigmatic (an O.K. word I suspect Potter would greatly approve) case, is that of the one-upman who, upon hearing someone tell a joke about a man with a wooden leg, does not laugh but instead walks stiffly away with an emphatic limp. Potter felt that there were certain situations in life that were essentially unfair—one's relation to one's physician, for example—and he set out to redress the balance. (His plan for combating "the natural one-downedness of the unclothed" in a physician's office involves having oneself telephoned in the midst of an examination by a woman with an aristocratic, confident, and obviously sexy voice, and not only taking the call but engaging the woman in a lengthy, uproarious conversation.) Through his comic methods, Potter sought to create a creeping sense of "dis-ease" in the hearts of the natural intellectual bullies, social frauds, and general hustlers one encounters in the traffic of everyday life. Quoting what he falsely claimed to be one of the unpublished notebooks of Rilke (very much an O.K. name), Potter affirmed: " '. . . if you're not one up *(Blitzleisch)* you're . . . one down *(Rotzleisch).* ' "

Laudable though Potter's ends were, and wonderfully perverse his means, I fear that his banner has been captured by his true enemies, so that today one-upmanship is rampant in such intellectual black holes as university faculty lounges and lecture halls. There it tends to be used less to redress life's natural injustice, less to come to the aid of those born unbeautiful and unlucky, than to reinforce snobbery and to puff up petty vanity. Academic put-downs do not usually excite much interest, for the reason that they tend to be rather too specialized, with the exception of those in philosophy. Among the many stories told of Morris Cohen, the philosophy teacher at CCNY, one of my favorites takes the form of a put-down. A student, in a state of considerable agitation, asks Cohen, "How can you prove to me that I exist?" In his Yiddish-accented English, Cohen shot back, "Who's esking?" The so-called ordinary-language philosopher J. L. Austin once gave a lecture in New York at which he pronounced that while in most languages two negatives in a sentence were equivalent to a positive, in no language did two positives equal a negative, whereupon a voice thick with sarcasm from the audience called out, "Yeah, yeah!"

Writers, though, remain the supreme champions of the put-down, and women writers may be best of all. I have always prized a gem of the genre provided by the novelist Josephine Herbst, who, after telling the critic Leslie Fiedler that he looked not at all as she had imagined, was supposedly asked by Fiedler what in fact he did look like. "Well, if you must know," said Miss Herbst, "you look like one of those soft people in Turgenev," which of course Fiedler precisely does. Dorothy Parker seemed to speak in put-downs almost exclusively, in-cluding, a specialty with her, self-put-downs. Coming up preg-nant as a result of an affair with a man who deserted her, she is said to have remarked, "That's what I get for putting all my eggs into one bastard." And of course there was the famous incident in which Clare Boothe Luce held open a door for Dorothy Parker, announcing, "Age before beauty," to which Dorothy Parker, blithely walking through, rejoined, "Pearls before swine."

The best example of Dorothy Parker's put-down power I know, however, I recently read in Dorothy Herrmann's biog-raphy of S. J. Perelman, who was Dorothy Parker's friend and neighbor in Bucks County, Pennsylvania. As Miss Herrmann tells the story, one day Perelman, invited to dinner at Dorothy Parker's, arrived at her home shocked to find that she and her husband had cut down three magnificent Norway maples that stood in front of their house. Perelman, a lover of nature, said

sarcastically, "You must have needed the wood awful bad."
The remark offended Dorothy Parker so much that she and
Perelman did not speak for years. Trying to make it up, Perelman invited Dorothy Parker and her husband to dinner, including among his guests a rather dull man who greatly admired her writing. After the dinner, Perelman asked her what
she thought of the man. According to Perelman, she said: "You
must have needed the wood awful bad." This strikes me as the
most brilliant, delayed, wow, hot damn, oh-vengeance-is-
mine-saith-the-Lord put-down I have ever heard.

   If one's personal style is ironic, if one uses irony to punc-
ture what one takes to be deceit, hypocrisy, and illusion, then
it is likely to be received as having an air of put-down to it, and
one is oneself likely to make everyone (or, at any rate, many
a one) a bit uneasy. I believe that I have a minor but probably
just reputation as a put-down artist, chiefly based on some
literary and political criticisms I have written. I shouldn't like
to be thought principally a put-down artist, though, and I hope
that such put-downs as I have executed, in person and in print,
have not been gratuitous but reasonably well deserved. I do not
think of myself as someone who gets excited at the prospect of
committing a resounding put-down. Frankly, I'd rather sit on
the couch, my cat on my lap, and listen to Mozart. Yet why
can't I drive from my mind this picture of myself walking into
the restaurant at the Watergate, proceeding back into the
kitchen, where I drop a twenty-five-pound bag of salt at the
feet of the chef and cry out, "Jean-Louis, baby, what's sha-
kin'?"

The Bore Wars

W<small>AS IT IN</small> a book by F. L. Lucas that I read about the eighteenth-century English duke who, with the brutality of wit not uncommon to his century, used to organize a dinner to which he would invite everyone he knew who had a stutter, stammer, or other speech impediment? At the head of his own table, the duke would casually toss out a largish general question to his guests, then sit back to enjoy the halting, dithering, sputtering, expectorating responses. An amiable fellow, the duke, you will agree, and a man who, to have invented so vicious a form of entertainment for himself, must have suffered greatly from boredom. Let us hope he is now in a place where the extreme heat takes his mind off the discomfort of his boredom.

Yet, given the duke's resources and his taste for delight at the prospect provided by his guests in pain, I wonder if he would not have done better instead to have organized a dinner for the most brilliant talkers of his time, and sat back to watch them suffer in one another's presence. Imagine them there assembled at one table—Voltaire, Samuel Johnson, Mme de Staël, Lord Chesterfield, the Duc de Saint-Simon, Edmund Burke—each utterly fluent, dazzling in his or her own line, a conversational superstar. What a melée would result: Voltaire trying to maintain a steady stream of elegant outrageousness, Johnson firing off his sonorous put-downs, Mme de Staël rattling away about Marie Antoinette, Chesterfield and the little *duc* falling all over each other in the attempt to achieve a superiority of decorum, Burke trotting out his astonishingly elaborate metaphors. With all that brilliance packed into one room, there could scarcely be sufficient mental oxygen to go round; intellectually, one would be gasping for breath. Competition would doubtless have sent the volume all the way up. Bedlamic, absolutely bedlamic would be the spectacle set out before the mischievous duke, who could not fail to delight in it hugely.

Yet even if one could be alone with any of these great talkers, how much of any one of them could one take? A weekend of Voltaire's unrelenting cleverness might just make one long for the blatant attractions of, say, Thanksgiving in Acapulco. Four hours in the company of Edmund Burke might fire up one's appetite for the laconic inarticulateness of the late Mayor Richard Daley. Every great talker carries the seeds, not of his own destruction, but of his ability to bore. Great talkers there have always been, but how many great listeners can you name? Apart from James Boswell, I can think of only one other, the Bloomsbury writer Desmond Mac-Carthy, whom Max Beerbohm once described as being a splendid conversationalist because he always used those lovely words "Please tell me."

"Please tell me" are delightful words to hear, for they are of course an invitation to speak, and one is rarely bored when allowed to do the talking. I was once invited to lunch with a very wealthy man who, after we were seated with a great flurry of attention on the part of the servants at his club, asked me my age. I was then thirty-nine and told him so. "I," he said, "am seventy-three, and therefore much older than you, and

since I have less long to live, I shall do most of the talking."
That seemed to me, if not quite reasonable, at least fair, and I
did most of the listening throughout a long and sumptuous
lunch. Not everything he said was interesting—what was it
Sydney Smith said of Macaulay, "He has occasional flashes of
silence, that make his conversation perfectly delightful"?—but
as I listened to him I thought, I have heard the phrase "money
talks" all my life, and here I am actually listening to money
talk. And money, as I say, on this occasion talked fairly interestingly.

I go to lunch at least once, sometimes twice a year with a
woman with whom the question of interest never arises—at
least for me it doesn't. How I got myself into these lunches is
too elaborate a story to go into here, but I believe I shall never
get out of them until one of us dies. She pursues me with
occasional postcards, seasonal greeting cards, and then one day
that telephone call comes inviting me to lunch. I put her off
for as long as possible ("The next month looks pretty bad for
me"), but she is patient ("How does the first week of the
following month look?"). As I recount this, you will doubtless
think me cold if not cruel. This woman longs for my company,
my conversational charms obviously please her, her great regard for me cannot imply other than a high compliment.
None, as they say on the multiple-choice tests, of the above is
true.

When we go to lunch, she does the talking—all of it. Her
subject is herself, her exploits, her gripes, her grievances, her
superior rectitude. Every fifteen minutes or so, I drop in a
question, though none is really needed. I fight to keep the glaze
from my eyes, the sag from my facial muscles, my hands from
drumming impatiently upon the table. Once, to keep consciousness, I counted the words I used while in her company
for roughly ninety minutes; the sum was three hundred and

forty-eight, including salutations and excusing myself once to go off to the men's room, where I balmed my face with cold water lest I fall asleep. I have heard most of her stories three or four times by now. I try to let my mind drift off while keeping my eyes on her. It doesn't work for long. When we finally part, she appears to have enjoyed herself greatly. "Stay in touch," she calls as I drive off, fatigued yet immensely relieved at being off the hook for six or seven months.

Am I not afraid of her reading this? I shouldn't want her to do so, but I think the chances are very slight. Although we have been going to lunch like this together for roughly seven years, she knows almost nothing about me, apart from the fact that I am married and that I do a little writing. If you asked her if I had children, if you asked her how I earn my income, if you asked her what my dreams are, she could not tell you. How could she—she has never asked. I am to her an ear with legs, a breathing microphone into which she opinionates, expiates, and divagates. I assume she must have other walking ears and breathing microphones with whom she also makes lunch and dinner dates, to whom she tells the same stories, of whom she asks no questions.

Why do I continue to go with her for these excruciatingly boring lunches? ("Hey," I hear a raucous voice call out, "you're really sick, fella, you know that?") I go in part because, short of moving to another city, I know no gentle way of putting her off; and I go in part because, knowing her to be fifteen or so years older than I and someone who lives alone, I do not want to hurt her feelings by refusing. ("You're a real sensitive guy," the same voice cries out, "sure ya are, baby.") More to the point, when I think of her I also think of a then young man, the hairdresser of a woman I know, whom I interviewed for an article I wrote years ago on the subject of homosexuality. This young man was self-advertised as wildly promiscuous. "You know," I recall him telling me, "sometimes I'll be in the baths, and for no reason I'll just give myself to some poor old queen. Do you suppose I figure that someday maybe I'll be that poor old queen and some delectable thing like myself will offer himself to me?" The analogy ought to be plain enough: I see myself as one day being an old bore who is himself sadly in need of somebody to talk at.

The signs of my encroaching boringness, I fear, are beginning to show up. Where once I used to be content to sit back and listen, I am content to do so no longer. Any occasion on which I do not get in my licks, on which I do not at some point hold forth on one of my subjects, has for me now become a dull evening. If I feel someone else is going on at too great a length, I wait for him or her to make the mistake of taking a longish breath, then cut—sometimes barge—in. I have reached the age where a man has acquired a copious supply of jokes, anecdotes, and apposite quotations. In my own case, I think of these as so many cassettes stored in a filing cabinet in my mind; I can slip one in at a quarter-second's notice. I have begun to repeat myself. Sometimes it seems to me as if a whole evening has gone by on which I have said nothing fresh; all I have done is play my cassettes through the night. My wife, who has already heard many of these cassettes of mine several times, may soon be described as "long-suffering." Perhaps that time has already arrived. Can one really describe a woman who has had to hear the same anecdotes told, in some instances, ten and fifteen times, and the same jokes told more often than that, can one really describe such a woman as "short-suffering"?

When did it first occur to me that I might have in me the stuff of which serious bores are made? I believe the moment came with the realization that I truly love to talk. I do not think I am an atrocious, or even a poor, listener; still, beginning about seven or eight years ago, I noticed myself increasingly listening for the point at which I might insert one of my cassettes into the conversation. For the true talker, there is no listening—only waiting. Like a political candidate from a hopelessly obscure right- or left-wing political party, I began to demand, psychologically at least, equal time; and on some occasions I do believe that I have availed myself of rather more than equal time. Do I so wish to talk because I am certain that what I have to say—even if I have said it before—will give pleasure? Or do I wish to talk because it is I who get such a bang out of hearing myself talk?

I do not say that it takes a bore to recognize a bore—if that were so, the punishment would fit the crime with a delightful sense of proportion rarely met with in life—but it may help. As an incipient bore (am I being much too modest here?), I was recently interested to find Edmund Wilson, in the volume of his diaries and journals entitled *The Fifties,* discovering the bore in himself while at the same time struggling in the presence of those whom he found to be boring. On the self-discovery side, Wilson first notes that his wife Elena is much more sensitive than he to other people's conditions and relationships; doubtless this is owing to his not being much of a listener. "Don't talk all the time," he instructs himself. "It is an error to assume that other people can have nothing interesting to say." A pre-cassette man, Wilson writes: "So I sometimes make speeches to people that are merely old phonograph records, with no particular relevance to the person or situation." In London he remarks that Cyril Connolly, "like many wits and raconteurs, never listens to anyone else's sallies or stories"; and he is put off by Isaiah Berlin's exhaustive loquacity: "Once started on a story, he cannot stop giving the whole of his [in this instance the historian Lewis Namier's] career from the beginning, pointed up with anecdotes." In Paris he finds himself irked by the "compulsive monologizing" of a woman named Esther Arthur. As I say, you don't have to be one to know one, but it helps.

Do people with the power to bore ever tire of hearing themselves talk? Even the indefatigable Edmund Wilson, traveling in Europe, allows: "I get rather tired of doing my stuff . . . mentioning the national authors and showing off the little I know about them." As a small bore (sounds rather like a rifle), I must confess that even though I generally find what I have to say fascinating, on occasion I wish that I would shut the hell up. I especially wish for this when, while out of town giving a talk, I appear in my unfamiliar but all-too-comfortable role as general expert. After my talk, people not infrequently come up to me to ask what I think of little things like censorship or higher education or the Middle East. They cannot, of course, know that in doing so they are in effect handing over the key to the wine cellar to the town drunk.

Your genuine bore does not mind repeating himself over and over again—and then just one more time. How many times have I, while removing the cork from a bottle of wine, announced to my company, "I think you will find this wine a bit fey yet not without seriousness, a touch promiscuous yet ultimately responsible." This joke on wine bores is, I am afraid, itself becoming rather boring. I try not to use it before the same people—though my suffering wife has had to hear it countless times—yet use it I do when presented with a fresh audience. It usually gets an appreciative (polite?) giggle, so, when my hand slips once more around the neck of yet another bottle of wine, I prepare to press it into service one more time. By now even I begin to grow weary of it; it has become, to adapt a phrase from old-time Communist Party argot, "boring from within." It reminds me of a story told by Rayner Heppenstall about Dylan Thomas, who, after having talked endlessly one evening, remarked, "Somebody's boring me. I think it's me."

But generally every bore feels he has the right to do as much talking as he does by virtue of his being more entertaining, more knowledgeable, or (somehow) more worthy than the company in which he finds himself. Bores are not noted for their insecurity or for suffering powerfully from inferiority complexes, though I suppose it is possible for someone to become boring by insisting, at tedious length, upon his own uninterestingness. Yet a crucial distinction needs to be made between being boring and being uninteresting. Some people can be militantly, profoundly, oppressively uninteresting and can lower the wattage of any room they enter with the shadow cast by their mental torpor. But it is not quite their fault, whereas the act of being truly boring implies something akin to an act of aggression. Your serious bore has no doubts about his interestingness; he badgers, bulls, bores ahead. "Every hero becomes a bore at last," wrote Emerson, but every bore remains a hero to himself.

However certain bores are of the delight and importance inherent in their conversation, even the most confident knows that what he has to say is not of equal interest to everyone. I should have been most hesitant to have trotted out my cassettes before Henry James, Marcel Proust, or George Santayana. Someone I feel confident I could not have interested even for thirty seconds would have been André Malraux. Nothing in my file of cassettes—not any of my anecdotes, jokes, bits of extraneous information—could possibly have been of the slightest interest to Malraux, whose roster of friends and acquaintances included Leon Trotsky, Albert Einstein, Chou En-lai, Nehru, and Charles de Gaulle and whose résumé might have been written in the following single sentence: "See twentieth-century history." "Say, Andy," I might open my conversation with him, "have you heard the one about the little fellow from Tel Aviv who knocks on the door of the expensive bor-

dello in Manhattan?" Or I might tell him, a man who flew
sixty-five missions in the Spanish Civil War and was decorated
by six different governments for his fighting (under the *nom
de guerre* Colonel Berger) in World War II, of my own army
days in the late 1950s as a clerk-typist in Missouri, Texas, and
Arkansas. Perhaps he would have been interested in my teaching adventures—kids, after all, do say the darnedest things.

But were such a meeting ever to have taken place, apparently, from all reports, I need not have worried, for quite likely
I should not have gotten a word in edge-, side-, or any other
wise. Malraux was a furious, a tireless, I gather a somewhat
tyrannical talker—a monologuist of the first magnitude. Janet
Flanner has described—without machinery one could not
really record—Malraux's conversation:

> Malraux paces the floor as if he were propelled by the jerking energy
> of his speech. As he walks, words and ideas rush from his brain and
> out of his mouth in extemporaneous creation, as though they were
> long quotations from books he has not yet written, and they flow at
> a rate that is almost the speed of thought, and sometimes faster than
> the ear can catch. His extravagant memory accompanies him as he
> paces back and forth, bringing reminiscences out into the air, along
> with history, art and man's dangerous destiny—whatever he needs
> at the moment. From time to time, for punctuation, he lifts his right
> hand, to warn the dazed listener about the paragraph to come, which
> passes in a revelatory gust.

Malraux's talk was not merely inexhaustible but often unintel-
ligible into the bargain—a winning combination, surely—and
not merely to non-French-speaking listeners. In his *Journal*,
André Gide noted that Malraux "talks with that extraordinary
volubility which makes him so hard for me to follow . . . in awe
before his dazzling and staggering flow of words." Whenever
he was in Paris, Edmund Wilson would call on Malraux, and,
though Wilson writes that "it is always bracing to see him,"

he also records: "After lunch, when Mme M. and Elena had withdrawn, he sat beside me on the corner of the chair or the desk, talking vehemently into my face." How would you like to be the third party here? Perhaps one could get the floor with an attack of whooping cough ending in a cerebral hemorrhage, but even this is not certain.

Can André Malraux, who lived perhaps as passionately adventurous a life as any in the twentieth century, possibly be counted a bore? Never having met him, I cannot with certainty say, but reading others' accounts of his conversational style one is reminded that somewhere within the word *dazzle* its root, *daze*, is buried. True, one does not think of the French as having a strong tradition of bores. The English and the Germans seem stronger in this line. All that is boring tends to be heavy, but German boringness tends to be served with extra scoops of pedanticism and pomposity. So much a fixture of the culture are bores in England—older clergymen, retired colonial administrators, garden-club chairwomen—that the English bore has actually become a stock comic figure. At Oxford, I have been told, there used to be an annual Bores Dinner, to which were invited the most boring men in the university, with the check having to be paid by the man whose guest proved the least boring. Bores in English novels can be delightfully funny: Dickens did fine bores and so did Evelyn Waugh; and Anthony Powell, in his character Kenneth Widmerpool, in *A Dance to the Music of Time*, created a bore of such comic richness that the novel comes most alive when he is on the page. Contemporary American novelists seem to have no interest in creating bores, but then, writing thinly disguised autobiography in their novels as so many of them do, they tend in themselves to supply their own bores.

While some countries produce a rich harvest of bores, other countries seem to have boredom, like nitrogen, in their soil.

Poor Canada, for example, is the butt of an old publishing joke about a group of editors who, meeting over drinks, tried to invent a title for the world's most boring-sounding book and came up with *Canada: Sleeping Giant to the North.* Or much of provincial South America, which, in the renderings of its novelists and poets, seems to exist under a miasma of heat, dust, and extreme boredom while awaiting either a knife fight over a woman or a full-blown revolution. Russian life has always contained heavy doses of boredom, especially as portrayed by Chekhov, who set so many of his stories in provincial Russian towns where on still evenings "even the dogs are too bored to bark" and the only notable event occurred when the deacon ate a four-pound jar of caviar. In *Fathers and Sons,* Turgenev writes of the mother of Pavel and Nikolai Kirsanov having actually died of ennui. And it was another Russian writer, Ivan Goncharov, who gave the world the character Oblomov, who suffers from that advanced state of inertia known as Oblomovitis, which is boredom in action (or is it inaction?) when raised to the highest (or is it lowest?) power. Certainly, the Soviet leadership kept the tradition of boredom alive by doing all it could to perpetuate one of the most boring societies in the history of mankind. Boring though Soviet society may have been, it nonetheless created, in my limited experience among Soviet emigrés, some of the liveliest people in the world. Conversely, perhaps it takes a lively society to create serious bores. Just as primitive societies have no knowledge of the concept of vulgarity or poor taste, neither, one gathers, do they have bores. You need to attain a certain level of civilization to develop serious bores.

Some places, I find, aren't quite boring enough, at least for my taste. I find this true of Manhattan, a city that tends to overstimulate me. While in Manhattan I often feel as if there are vibrators in my shoes, highly percussive symphonies playing in my head, something akin to a moving Hogarth, George Grosz, Reginald Marsh montage playing before my eyes at fast forward. So many people to call upon, things to do, see, eat— no, the problem with Manhattan for me is that it isn't quite boring enough. After all, though they are not manifold, neither are the virtues of boredom nonexistent. I am told that Robert Hutchins, when attempting to lure a famous scholar or scientist to the University of Chicago, used a sales pitch that ran roughly along the following lines: "In Chicago, of course, the weather is impossible—blazingly hot in summer, insultingly cold in winter. The cultural life in the city, apart from the Chicago Symphony and the Art Institute, is practically nil. Of serious society, there is little; of the beauty of nature, even less. It's all really quite excruciatingly boring. You must come— you'll find that, with so little else to do, you'll get an immense amount of work accomplished."

Are there particular conditions or occupations in life that help bring out the bore in one? Success can sometimes do it. I have been on the circumference of circles in which it was tacitly yet still perfectly plain that the men or women who had the most money were permitted—not that they ever asked permission—to do all the talking. The assumption here seems to have been that their success in their particular financial or commercial line lent them general authority on, say, the subjects of raising children, foreign policy, and Astroturf. You can't argue with success, an old saying has it, but that is probably because success, full of self-confidence, will not yield the floor. Nothing succeeds like success, another old saying has it, but, when the element of perspective is missing, nothing quite bores like success either.

My own credentials as a bore seem to me impeccable from the standpoint of occupation. I am a teacher and an intellectual, and neither is a line of work that encourages one to keep one's own counsel. "Too damn wordy," an older friend who was not a famous reader once remarked about his failed attempt to read one of my books, but the remark perhaps applies to my entire life, which is also pretty damn wordy. As a teacher, I am paid to keep the words flowing. Jorge Luis Borges once noted his genuine pleasure at being able to keep a class interested in what he had to say for a full hour—and he was Jorge Luis Borges. I am Joseph Epstein, and my classes never run fewer than ninety minutes. Highly borable myself, I do not look forward to boring my students. Yet it is difficult to believe that, over the stretch of an academic quarter, I can keep them intellectually alert for the roughly one thousand eight hundred minutes that they spend with me, during which I (having less long to live, not to speak of the power of grading) do most of the talking. Some of my fellow teachers teach with the doors to their classrooms open, and often, as I walk by, I look in, noticing the sunken cheeks, the slack jaws, the lightly glazed eyes of students in their struggle with somnolence.

It's a war out there, man, a bore war, and there's one thing you might as well face right now: you have to be either bored or boring, and you'll eventually have to choose sides. As Byron quite correctly put it: "Society is now one polish'd horde / Form'd of two mighty tribes, the *Bores* and the *Bored.*"

Herewith an axiom from the physics of pedagogy: gas expands to fill time. When I began teaching I worried gravely about being able to fill a fifty-minute class; now, a decade or so later, I have been known to run over when teaching a two-and-a-half-hour class. Whence did this extra steam and stamina derive? From my own ever-expanding wisdom and ever-increasing powers of intellectual penetration? How nice to be able to think so, which I for a moment don't. More likely a leak has been sprung in my modesty. In what kind of work other than teaching can one rattle on at such prodigious length without fear of being told, mate, to stow it? Some of the most interesting people I know are professors, but so also are some of the most profound bores. I have been in putative conversations with professors that were, essentially, lectures delivered in counterpoint. It is the pedagogic habit of being listened to, the confidence of the talker with the captive audience, that makes the gas in certain of us professor-bores flow with the surge of a freshly found offshore find. No one ever has to instruct us to go with the flow; the problem is to find a way to turn it off.

Ah, the flow, the flow, how often have I reached for the faucet to stem my own flow of talk, but in vain, in vain. Although I do have it in me to go on—and on, and on—I am not, strictly speaking, loquacious. Of the two main categories of bores, performance bores and loquacity bores, I feel that I fall into that of performance bores. I look for any opportunity to perform my repertoire of anecdotes, jokes, medium-long stories, puns, and fancy patter. Your standard performance bore operates under the quite unproven assumption that he is a delightful and generous fellow. What makes him generous is his readiness to share his endless conversational delights with you and, for that matter, nearly everyone else. Sometimes the performance bore really can be delightful; the problem is that he usually chooses to perform unbidden. And once begun, he resembles a radio without an off switch, a triple-thick issue of the Sunday *New York Times,* an endless but not finally very nutritious strand of linguine.

The distinction between the performance bore and the loquacity bore, which is also that between talkers who are show-offs and talkers who are hopelessly garrulous, is not always easily made. The performance bore is often loquacious, and the loquacity bore is in turn often performing, but I think of the garrulity of the latter as rather more compulsive. The performance bore loves to talk, but the loquacity bore really cannot bring himself to stop talking. I know a greatly garrulous couple who have been married for decades, apparently quite happily. The husband once asked me if my wife and I found it difficult to retire at night, as they evidently do, for he and his wife often find themselves continuing to talk to and at each other until three or four in the morning—in the middle of the week. This is somewhat unusual, for loquacity bores, in my experience, are often formed by being too much alone, so that when they find themselves among company they unload. I know such a woman, a loquacity bore with oak-leaf clusters, to whom you daren't ask, "Sarah, how are you?" unless you are prepared to set aside a weekend to hear out the full answer.

Which brings us to the tricky question of male and female bores, their nature, number, and the differences between them. Here I speak in my capacity as chairman of the Committee to Re-establish Stereotypes Built on Gender. Clearly, neither sex has anything to be ashamed of in the production of bores, for both have always produced stellar examples. Casting back only in recent memory, I recall the female academic ill-luck seated me next to at an official dinner, who regaled me, from soup through soufflé, with the astonishing news that Las Vegas, which she had recently visited while attending a conference, was—are you ready for this?—vulgar. As she went on and on, banging away at the gong of the obvious, I felt only two things: the leaden oppressiveness of boredom and the desire to be, specifically, in Las Vegas. "Ah, to be in Vegas," thought I, while doing a difficult impression of a man who was mildly interested, "now that you're not there." Not long after, I met a man who held a cigarette in the old Peter Lorre style, vertically and between thumb and forefinger, and who, I came too late to recognize, was reciting for me, in not very abbreviated form, his doctoral dissertation, written some twenty-five years earlier, on Karl Marx. Fortunately, I was able to extricate myself before he got to the footnotes. But to return to stereotypes based on gender, my sense is that men tend toward being performance bores while women toward being loquacity bores, though there is, as the social scientists say, a good deal of overlapping and much research yet to be done.

The taxonomy of bores is no small subject. Many are the world's bores—male and female, created He them—and just as many the subjects on which they can exercise their special talents. Barely to touch the surface, there are wine bores, sex bores, name-dropping bores, let-me-tell-you-my-dreams bores; there are politics bores, trendy bores, culture-vulture bores, health-and-diet bores. If one wishes to avoid the booby traps of boredom, which are not few, here are some subjects about which not many people are likely to be highly interested: your children, your seductions, your surgical operations, your plans for the future. As for general subjects about which nearly everyone figures to be interested, I can think of only two: scandalous behavior and the misfortunes of others.

The ultimate bore is the person who has only one subject—himself. (Whew, it's beginning to get a little warm around here.) He is followed by the person whose chief subject is not himself but some other single subject: free silver, budget deficits, national health insurance, vegetarianism. And this kind of bore is followed by the person who relates free silver, budget deficits, national health insurance, and vegetarianism to a single set of ideas, nowadays most likely Marxism or psychoanalysis or post-structuralism. We are discussing here, of course, our good friends the monomaniacs. The old pop tune used to lament for "poor Johnny One-Note," but the real sympathy ought to go to the unfortunate devils who have to listen to him.

Mustn't, in any even preliminary taxonomy of bores, neglect drinking bores. Here that one comes to the dreary cross-

roads where bore meets bore. F. Scott and Zelda Fitzgerald
lent glamour to the notion of the charming drunk. But from
all accounts, in order really to appreciate the charms of the
Fitzgeralds when drunk, it was decisive that one *not* know
them. ("If you want to get your furniture antiqued up," someone who did know them once said of Scott and Zelda, "you
want to get the Fitzgeralds in—they'll antique it up in a single
night.") I have known mean drunks and I have known jolly
drunks, but what both have had in common, along with a
powerful thirst, is an equal power to bore, for such charm as
booze confers is usually drowned after the third drink. The
odd thing is that many people drink out of fear that they are
boring when sober—and they may well be correct. In Anthony Powell's novel *Afternoon Men* (itself rather a boring
book in the understated English manner), one character says
to another, "It's awful. One has about two drinks and one
becomes a nuisance," to which the other replies, "You're dan-
gerously near being one of the people who are a nuisance
before they've had the two drinks."

The boring Andy Warhol, in what has by now become a
rather boring observation, once noted that in America everyone would one day be famous for fifteen minutes. What he
neglected to add was that to be famous for much longer than
that put one at risk of becoming a bore. In the history of
boredom, the celebrity bore is a relatively recent but fairly
pervasive phenomenon. Television has aided this phenomenon
immensely. To appear on television for any length of time and
not prove boring is given to only a few. Some celebrities are
able to bore without the aid of television—the novelist John
Irving has been able to do it through the repeated use of the
photograph of himself in wrestling togs; the singer Neil Diamond has been able to do it through the sameness of his falsely
energetic songs—but at the level of big-time boringness, noth-

ing quite works like television. Certainly when I consider
"America's really big bores"—a phrase I think of as being said
by the late television variety-show host Ed Sullivan—all have
done it through television. As for those "really big bores," here
is my top ten:

1. Walter Cronkite
2. Ed McMahon
3. All anchor men and women, in towns large and small
4. All talk-show hosts, the more serious the more boring
5. Mary Lou Retton
6. O. J. Simpson
7. Barbara Walters
8. Phil Donahue
9. Jerry Lewis
10. Bill Cosby

I am sure that other people might have other entries or
points of disagreement, but one of the things I like about my
list is that it shows that one can be man or woman, Jew or
Gentile, black or white, and still bore the pajamas off millions
of one's countrymen. "Hey," as anyone on my list might say,
"that's what makes America great."

What makes the really big bores so boring is not merely
their overexposure, which television visits upon them all, but
that they are so predictable—and hence so caricaturable. They
do themselves, over and over and over, but then so does every
bore, with his repeated jokes and his anecdotes and his confidence in his own suavity. Unlike the big celebrity bores, he
does not work before millions, but does what he can at dinner
parties, or in classrooms, or *hombre a hombre*. Many of his
sentences begin with the word "Listen" and end with the
phrase "which reminds me." He does not recognize the difference between small talk and large; the only distinction he

observes is that between his talk and the next fellow's, and, truth to tell, he finds his rather better. I could go on. Listen, I could tell you a hundred stories about the bores I have encountered in my life, which reminds me . . .

Autodidact

SOCRATES MAY HAVE HAD to take the hemlock, but at least he was spared the indignity of that relatively recent addition to the teaching transaction known as "teacher evaluation." On these evaluations, generally made during the last minutes of the final session of the college term, students, in effect, grade their teachers. Hemlock may on occasion seem preferable, for turnabout here can sometimes be cruel play, especially when students, under the veil of anonymity, take the opportunity of evaluation to comment upon their teacher's dress, or idiosyncrasies, or moral character. For the most part I have not fared too badly on these evaluations, though my clothes have been the subject of faint comedy, my habit of jiggling the change in my pockets and my wretched handwriting have been noted, and in one instance I have been accused of showing favoritism (a charge I choose to interpret as my preference, in the classroom, for calling upon the relatively intelligent over the completely obtuse). None of these student comments, as you can plainly see, affects me in the least; such personal criticisms roll right off me, like buckshot off a duck's heart.

Unless they have long since been rendered catatonic by boredom, or are people on whom everything is lost, teachers of course make similar observations about their students—certainly this teacher does—and the one subject on which all teachers ought to be connoisseurs is that of the studentry. The difference is that teachers, unlike contemporary students, must keep these observations to themselves. Yet observe one will, nothing for it, and sometimes, as I am standing before a class, the subject of observation, I am myself observing my observers observing me. In this particular zoo, it is not always clear who is the spectator and who the ape. I do know that I carry the mental equivalent of a camera with me whenever I step into a classroom, and it is always clicking away, the monster of observation in me perpetually at work. To alter Christopher Isherwood's famous title slightly, "I am a chimera."

"Ah, Miss Fogelson, you nod exuberantly, smiling in broad agreement, as if to say, 'I take your point exactly.' All quarter long you imply that you have taken my points. Your smiling nods are meant to convey that we are in some sort of intellectual complicity and are obviously on the same wavelength. But beneath that nodding, invariably agreeable smile, why do I sense that in the high noon of your soul you are tuned to a hard-rock AM station?"

"Mr. Gold, you scowl, sometimes fully glower, at what I say, which implies passion for and penetration into the subject under discussion, which your contemptuous countenance suggests I am making a terrible hash of. I would more readily believe in your perturbation had I not had the displeasure of having read your midterm examination, which reveals you to have greater control over your facial muscles than over your punctuation."

"Mr. Kantor, sitting in the back of the room, what are you whispering to and then laughing with Miss Reilly about? Have I stumbled verbally—committed a lip-o, the aural equivalent of a typo—resulting in my having mistakenly said something lewd? Is there a shred of broccoli from lunch stuck between my front teeth? Can my fly be open? Damn it, kiddo, what is so blasted amusing?"

"Miss Simpson, need you look so young and fresh and uncomplicatedly beautiful? Your earnest, not very clever presence in this hall of learning is a distraction to a dry man in a cold month, being without much joy, waiting for brains."

Thus does my mental camera click away, ever on the lookout for one or another kind of student performance. Of course, I much prefer the genuine article, bright students truly interested in learning, of whom I have had more than my fair share. But my mind is naturally attracted to falsity in student behavior, for I have in my own time been a nodder and smiler, a scowler and glowerer, a whisperer and laugher. For the better part of my sixteen years of formal schooling, I was a fake, a boy and then a young man who in the classroom aspired no higher than to mediocrity and frequently fell well short of the mark. I was precisely the kind of student whom today, as a teacher, I should view as obviously hopeless. Lest this seem false humility of a retrospective kind, an attempt to display a phony set of Before and After photographs, let me hasten to add that were I forced to return to school as a student now, I am reasonably confident that I would still be a bad student; and this for reasons I am not altogether clear about but shall nonetheless attempt to discover.

The question of what it is that makes for a good or a bad student never occurred to me quite so vividly as it did five or six years ago, when I served on a committee for student awards at the university where I teach. As a member of this committee, I read the classroom essays of an English major who was a shoo-in candidate for the best junior-year student in the department. These essays were, each one of them, impeccable. Cold *A*'s, every one—not a semicolon out of place, flawlessly typed, perfectly shaped paragraphs led off by tidy topic sentences. Here was a boy who knew his job, who could deliver the goods.

It was only taken together that I found his classroom papers despicable. For a Marxist professor, this boy produced a correctly down-the-line Marxist analysis of *Sister Carrie;* for a survey course, he wrote a tribute to Benjamin Franklin as a hero of the American way of pragmatism and capitalist good sense; for a Freudian-minded teacher of nineteenth-century fiction, he discovered unresolved complexes and sexual tensions in *David Copperfield.* (Had he taken one of my courses, doubtless he would have played for me whatever intellectual music it is I wish to hear.) To each of his teachers he gave what he or she asked for—no less and a little bit more. As I read these essays en bloc, I grew first to feel uncomfortable about, then to dislike, finally actively to despise this young man, whom I thought of as an academic stock boy happily filling orders. He went on the following year to graduate with all possible honors. I hope I may be forgiven when I say that I do not wish him any too well. Like others who have chosen early in life to go with the flow, may he one day before too long be made to taste a little lava.

I was not a bad student in the way in which I think of this young man, who combined real intellectual gifts with genuine sycophancy, as a bad student. I did not give my teachers what they wanted; and I was distinctly not a sycophant, for the sound reason that I hadn't the basic skills to mount anything like a decent campaign to please my teachers. I was a bad student in the fundamental sense of being an inept student. Although I believe I was mildly precocious as a very young child—I could print my name before I went to school and my father gave me columns of numbers that I added up with alacrity and joy—once I hit the classroom my brain all but ceased functioning. I was not a discipline problem, I had no learning disabilities, but I was absolutely, even profoundly mediocre. Almost all the things one was called upon to do in the early grades, I could not do. I could not draw, and my coloring with crayons always strayed outside the lines; I sang badly off-key; and my printing and early handwriting looked like the work of an incipient psychopath. I did not use scissors well, I could not draw a straight line, I made my inkwells look as if they were Oklahoma gushers that had just come in, and with paste I was simply out of control. In later grades I brought something like the same impressive ineptitude to making outlines, diagramming sentences, assembling one or another kind of notebook. I remember especially those notebooks in which a student pasted down and catalogued the various kinds of leaves—you're nondeciduous now, so whaddaya gonna do?— easily marking the nadir of my grade-school productions; it was at least four or five full cuts down from disgraceful.

I used to say that I had too happy a childhood ever to bother learning grammar. But it would be more accurate to say that I did not learn anything that I found uninteresting. This might put me in the same category as George Santayana, who, reflecting on his years at the Boston Latin School, remarked that "I have always been recalcitrant about studying what doesn't interest me." One of the many differences between Santayana and me, however, is that almost nothing interested me, with the possible exception of spelling. I was all right at spelling, chiefly, I believe, because it was competitive, or at any rate competitively taught through the exercises known as spell-downs, from which I, for some reason, didn't wish to be too soon eliminated. I hope no one reading this will think that, had my teachers taken more "creative" approaches to learning, I would have been a better student, for I am convinced that I would have been even worse. Thinking back on my own early days of schooling, I realize that I reacted to only two stimuli, fear and competition, and when both were absent, so, mentally, was I.

As for competition, in my case it was highly selective. I rarely competed when I didn't have a decent chance of, if not winning, at least finishing respectably. I very early knew that I could not compete with the bright kids in my class who had a special aptitude for science, so by the time I was, say, ten or eleven, all science became uninteresting to me. So it went with other subjects. A few of my classmates had only to show strong aptitudes for me to show a countervailingly strong apathy. This, combined with my ability to take my pleasure in life from being a fair playground athlete and a more than fair general screw-off, left me a perfectly mediocre student—one of those children who merely gets by. If I was in any way in doubt about my own mediocrity as a student, I had it confirmed for me when, before going off to high school, I learned that I was not recommended to take Latin, as even the minimally bright students were.

Having myself been such a poor student, I naturally adore stories about geniuses who were judged to have been either poor or indifferent students in their day—in the way, I suppose, that failed writers take special delight in learning about classic works that were sorely neglected in their day. The most famous such story is about Albert Einstein's difficulties with mathematics in secondary school, though there is reason to believe that this may be a myth. But it is not mythical that St. Thomas Aquinas when a student was known as "the dumb ox." In the classroom, Henry James was no great shakes. Theodore Dreiser made a rather poor showing in his single year at Indiana University. The physicist and philosopher Ernst Mach was deemed by his teachers to be utterly without talent, and they suggested that he be apprenticed to a cabinetmaker. (I blithely pass by all those geniuses who were splendid students right out of the starting gate.) Yet my guess is that all these men I have named probably failed to do well in school because they were dreamy, or unorthodox, or ran their trains of thought along different, wider-gauged, more far-reaching tracks than conventional teaching could accommodate.

Along with distinctly not being a genius, I was not dreamy, or unorthodox, or anything other than prodigiously uninterested. I went to a high school with lots of bright kids, but with no intellectual traditions. Anti-intellectual traditions ran much stronger. What are now called "street smarts" were greatly valued, but if there was wisdom in the world, surely no one in his right mind at my high school expected to find it in the words of teachers or in books. "In my school crowd, insofar as I had one," Mary McCarthy has recently recounted of her high school days, "nobody read." If anyone in my school crowd read, he kept it a secret. I had read the sports stories of John R. Tunis in grade school. I must have been assigned the dreary little project known as "book reports" in high school English, but I evidently gave mine from Classic Comics, the comic book versions of great works of literature. Many years later, in New York, I met a free-lance writer down on his luck who had actually written some of the scripts for Classic Comics. Acknowledging his important contribution to my education, I thanked him warmly.

Over the course of four years in high school, I have no recollection of doing any homework, with the exception of preparation for geometry. Here, I must report, fear operated. I quickly realized that I could not fake or finagle my way through this subject as I could—in fact, did—through every other. Besides, I happened to like geometry, the intellectual order and clarity of it; I also rather enjoyed manipulating theorems and axioms, and being able to close an argument with one of Euclid's rhythmic punch lines: "The angle of the dangle equals the flip of the zip," or "If the square of the hypotenuse equals the longest side, then the giraffe emits a laugh." The point I would underscore, however, is that, liking geometry and working at it, I nonetheless received for my efforts a *C*.

One of the fine shiny sociological clichés of our day is contained in the phrase "peer pressure." It might be mildly comforting to me to think that I did so poorly in school owing to peer pressure. Yet I cannot remember feeling any such pressure; it is far more likely that I was one of those peers who put the pressure on other kids. I recall the rather lighthearted contempt with which my friends and I viewed the category of students we referred to as "science bores." These were students who took an earnest interest in such subjects as math, physics, and chemistry (as opposed to my own circle's interest in gin rummy, blackjack, and poker), and who were usually identified by a uniform that consisted of thickish spectacles, rumpled cotton-flannel shirts, unmanageable curly hair, and a light coat of acne. I used to believe that there were no good teachers at my high school, but then it occurred to me that if a teacher was thought to be good—which meant serious and demanding—I steered clear of him. I remember a teacher of chemistry named Dr. Davidson, one of those gallant pedagogues with a Ph. D. who preferred to teach in the trenches of a city public high school. He was dark, with a receding hairline, a perpetually furrowed brow, and rimless glasses. He taught and walked the corridors in a white lab coat and, with every gesture, radiated an air of high intellectual purpose. I would just as soon have taken Dr. Davidson's chemistry course then as I would enter myself in a backwards naked marathon now.

I was able to get through what was then called "the general course" in high school without learning a thing—apart from the instruction available in the air provided by Dr. O. S. Mosis—and yet without ever actually failing a single subject. Lest anyone misread this as a chronicle of misgiving, let me hasten to add that during this time I enjoyed myself hugely, while devoting my days to the extracurricular and my nights to the para-curricular. I was able to achieve this through the application of mother wit and the careful selection of the weakest courses taught by the poorest teachers.

My parents had a respect for education but, not having gone to college themselves, they had very little interest in schooling. When I would bring home my invariably dismal report cards—a couple of *C*'s, a *D*, a rare *B*, a more frequent *A* in gym—my father would read it, recite a little homily to me about trying harder to do my best, sign it, and let it go at that. I gather that my parents must have concluded that their eldest son's talents, if he had any at all, lay outside the classroom. I am grateful to them for this, especially today when, as a teacher, I regularly encounter students who work under the extreme pressure of parents who have grandiose educational plans for them and who have not been able to conceal their disappointment that their child did not get admitted to Harvard or Yale, Princeton or Brown. (What, I have long wondered, was Brown's first name? Somehow I have the feeling that it wasn't Irving.) If you are looking for a big tax write-off under medical expenses (therapy chiefly), my advice is that you get behind your children and push them really hard to get into the very best universities.

Far from being pushed, I decided quite on my own to go to college. (After about the age of ten, it occurs to me, I made all the educational decisions in my life.) If I had chosen not to go to college but instead directly to work, no one would have been in the least surprised and no one certainly would have been aggrieved. To give my mediocrity a numeric character,

I graduated 152 in a class of 211. Today it would be difficult to find a respectable college for a student who had done so poorly—finishing just above the lowest quarter of his class. But in the middle fifties, if you were a resident of the state, the University of Illinois had to accept you as a student, with the single proviso that students who finished in the bottom quarter of their high school graduating classes were accepted on probation. This can be a bit tricky to explain to the young, but college then was at once more casual and more serious than it is now. Getting in was not so difficult—I never, for example, had to take the College Board Examinations, as I believe the SATs were then called—but flunking out was much easier. Nowadays the reverse seems to be the case. A friend who has taught at Harvard in recent years remarked to me that, by and large, students at Harvard did not seem to him all that interested in what goes on in classrooms there. "After all," he said, "what is likely to be the greatest achievement in most of their lives has already taken place—this is that they have been admitted to Harvard."

In England, in France, in Germany, a boy who had done as poorly as I in secondary school would have been scrubbed, washed up, finished. In education, however, America is the land of the second chance, a condition of which I, for reasons not entirely impersonal, vastly approve. My own experience has left me a half-hearted elitist—someone who feels that everything possible should be done to single out, encourage, and promote true talent, yet who also knows that talent has a way of sometimes not showing up on schedule. In *Out of Step,* his autobiography, the philosopher Sidney Hook reveals himself to have been a rebellious high school student of the wise-guy type; I recently read, in a collection of his letters, that the widely talented poet and painter Weldon Kees never received other than mediocre grades in school. Doubtless hundreds of other names of talented men and women could be adduced who performed poorly in school, and out of this list a National Dishonor Society could be formed, though where exactly the dishonor ought to fall—on the students for not working very hard, or on their teachers for not contriving to get the best out of them—is by no means clear. My own rather jaded view is that no matter how efficient and finely meshed an educational system one devises, many children will slip through it and some among them will be the (secretly) talented. A few may scarcely need any schooling at all. "The only school Beethoven attended, and then only for a short time," reports J. W. N. Sullivan in his study of the composer's spiritual development, "was a lower grade public school in Bonn called the Tirocinium."

I blush to speak of the talented, even the secretly talented, for if I had any talent at eighteen, when I went off to the state university that by law was compelled to accept me, it was certainly a secret to me. I had, however, a very keen sense of the talents that I did *not* possess. Most of the friends with whom I went off to the University of Illinois were majoring in business, a subject that I, too, should no doubt have majored in, if only because, in the context of the rather philistine middle-class culture in which I grew up, business sounded so splendidly purposeful. But to major in business meant one had to take several courses in accounting, and I knew, in the nuclei of the cells of the marrow of my smallest bones, that with my handwriting, my penchant for disorder, my unearned disdain for clerical detail, I could turn enrollment in an introductory accounting course into a Venetian tragedy. Out of fear of accounting, then, I chose to study something called "liberal arts," a phrase I heard for the first time only after I had arrived on the campus of the University of Illinois in Champaign-Urbana.

If fear of accounting sent me into the liberal arts, fear of flunking out of college kept me studying them, I will not say with intelligence but with ferocious energy. I was less than handsomely equipped for the task of staying in school: I had an unsure grasp of English grammar, knowledge of no foreign language beyond the level of *el burro es un animal importante*, a mind unclogged with even the rudiments of general science, a storehouse of historical fact learned exclusively at the movies, and no study habits whatsoever. My approach to college study was quite simple—I merely memorized everything set before me. Biological taxonomy, French verbs, seventeenth-century English sonnets—hey, as they say nowadays, no problem, I memorized them all. In a composition course then somewhat grandly entitled Rhetoric, I learned that I had a very small knack for writing, a knack I didn't overstrain by doing anything fancy; and anything fancy included using a semicolon, which looked to me like a combination of a Hebrew vowel and a Chinese ideograph and which I wouldn't have touched with a ten-foot dash. Fear of humiliation goading me on all the way, I was able to achieve something like a *B* average at the close of my first semester.

Out of the Crockpot into the Cuisinart, I transferred a year later to the University of Chicago, which must have been rather hard up for undergraduates if it accepted me, though I am very grateful that it did. Graduate students greatly outnumbered undergraduates at the University of Chicago, and the school's graduate students set the tone for the place, which was bohemian, slightly neurotic, and very serious. What made the University of Chicago seem especially impressive, at least to my untrained eyes, was the Europeans on its faculty, many of them refugees from Hitler's depredations in Europe. The undergraduates I encountered were kilometers ahead of me intellectually; the representative undergraduate struck me then as being someone from New York who had been reading the *New Republic* from the age of eleven and decided against going to an Ivy League school because they were all deemed too lightweight. Some among them possessed what seemed to me startlingly arcane information about history, early music, philosophy, politics. Once, in a poetry class taught by Elder Olson, Olson began chanting, quite beautifully and in French, a poem by Baudelaire. He was presently joined in his chant by the student sitting next to me, whose name was Martha Silverman, who also had the poem by heart and in French. Sensing more vividly than ever before how much over my head I was, I felt a strong wave of utter hopelessness wash over me. Oh, Martha, what has become of you since that brilliant performance on that dark morning in Elder Olson's classroom? Did you, I wonder, peak at that very moment, to fall thenceforth gently into decline?

I had become more earnest as a student, but I was clearly in the camp of the drones. Even among drones I was a drone. In three years at the University of Chicago I do not believe I ever said anything in a classroom that advanced the discussion in any useful way. On the rare occasions when I spoke at all, usually after being called upon to do so, no teacher ever capped my comments by saying, "A point well taken," or "That is nicely formulated," or "Good, but can you say a little more?" or even "Interesting." The only time I ever knew an answer that no one else in the room knew was when, in a course on the novel, Morton Dauwen Zabel asked if anyone knew what other famous book besides *Madame Bovary* was then—it was 1957—in its centenary year. I happened to have read somewhere, perhaps in the News Notes of *Poetry,* that 1957 was the centenary of *Les Fleurs du mal.* I raised my hand, decided not to risk the French, and when called upon said, "Charles Baudelaire's *The Flowers of Evil.*" "Correct," said Zabel. "Thank you." I felt flush, as if I had just won the lottery.

On the few occasions when I attempted to slip free of
dronedom, it proved a mistake. In a course on satire, a very
nice professor put forth his theory of satire, which I thought
half-baked, and I criticized it in a term paper in which I put
forth a completely raw theory of my own. The result was a
charitable C. In a course in Greek history, I was asked to do
an essay on why Philip of Macedon chose Aristotle for his son
Alexander's tutor. Cutting through a good deal of historico-
political claptrap, I said it was really quite simple: Philip, being
no dope, wanted the best possible teacher for his son, and there
was none better than Aristotle in the whole of the Pelopon-
nesus. Another icy C, this time accompanied by the gentle
remonstrance that I should try to control a tendency toward
glibness. The evidence was beginning to weigh in: as a drone,
I was a B student; as an original thinker, I was a C.

I should have been delighted if, when I was young, some
teacher had taken me aside and said, or in his behavior implied,
"There is something extraordinary in you, and I want to help
you develop it." None ever did. But, then, it occurs to me to
add, there wasn't anything extraordinary in me. I was a rough
without a diamond in it. It would be convenient for me now
to say of myself that I was obviously a late developer; that, at
any rate, is the conventional category in which my intellectual
autobiography would seem to fit. But I do not truly think I am
a late developer. (I began publishing in magazines, somewhat
precociously, in my early twenties.) I think instead that I am
someone who has never been able to profit much from the kind
of education that is available in classrooms and lecture halls. I
may be, in the strict schoolroom sense of the term, ineducable.

Not that I was entirely impervious to my teachers, but such
influence as they exerted upon me was, in the main, stylistic.
Watching a lecture delivered in the grand European manner,

or a social scientist unsentimentally dissecting a serious subject, or an art historian passionately conveying his love for Guido Reni—all this was very exciting to me, yet the problem may have been that I *watched* it so intently that I never quite *heard* what they were saying. Observing my professors seemed so much more interesting than actually listening to them.

Had I gone on to graduate school, which I never for a moment contemplated doing, I might have fallen under the sway of some powerful teacher and become, say, a Straussian, or Wintersian, or Leavisite. Yet I rather doubt it. I was plenty ignorant, but I wasn't gullible. I had a strong father at home and wasn't looking for one away from home. I also had a street-learned skepticism, and I believed with Santayana (whom I hadn't yet read) that "skepticism is the chastity of the intellect, and it is shameful to surrender it too soon or to the first comer. . . ." In any case, I think I should have bridled under too firm an intellectual influence. One of the things that college taught me was that I cannot be taught in the conventional manner. Autodidactically, I have to go about things in my own poky way, obliquely acquiring on my own such intellectual skills as I have, assembling such learning as I possess from my odd, unsystematic reading. Are there many such people as I? The inefficacy of teaching in his own life, if I may say so, is an unusual thing to have to admit on the part of a man who himself spends a good part of his own time teaching others. But there it is—or, rather, there I am.

As a former poor student who is now a teacher, I study good students rather as Malinowski did the Trobriand Islanders—as an outsider, someone, that is, who is distinctly not one of them. I am tempted to steal a formulation from Tolstoy and say that all good students are alike while every bad student is bad in his own way, except that I don't quite believe it is so. My quotation in the previous paragraph from Santayana re-

minds me that one of Santayana's best students was Walter
Lippmann, whom he asked to stay on to be his assistant at
Harvard, though that young man had other ideas about his
career. Traditionally, good students at Harvard have been
thought to have a certain intellectual sophistication and suavity
without being very deep, whereas good students at the University of Chicago have been thought to be deep but without
much in the way of intellectual sophistication or suavity.
Owing perhaps to such go-getter alumni as Henry Luce, William Benton, and Chester Bowles, one tends to think of good
students at Yale as training themselves for success in the world,
while at Princeton the social question—that is to say, snobbery—still seems uppermost, though this may be a hangover
from F. Scott Fitzgerald days (Fitzgerald was himself a very
poor student, and so was another famous Princetonian named
Adlai Stevenson). Good students at St. John's in Annapolis
seem almost too earnest—the good life is all very well, but
leading it surely cannot entail talking about it so much, as all
"great books" education seems to require of its students. But
good students have a way of popping up in odd places; and,
besides, it is probably more sensible today to refer not to good
schools—viewed close up, no contemporary school seems very
good—but instead to schools that are difficult to get into.

Still, I remain astonished at the sheer proficiency of certain
students. When I was myself a student, I was much impressed
with the type of good student known as "the quick study."
The girlfriend of a friend of mine at the University of Chicago,
who did not appear to be more than mildly interested in intellectual things, seemed unable to score poorly on an examination or to write an unsuccessful paper. One felt about Dottie
that she could write a $B+$ paper on John Stuart Mill while
sitting under a tree during a monsoon, or score an $A-$ on a
mathematics exam administered to her during a car crash. At

the school where I teach, I have come across a number of students with the happy knack of knocking out term papers that quite simply cannot be given less than an *A*. These students are like beautifully trained retrievers: "T. S. Eliot and Catholicism"—O.K., girl, fetch! "Dostoyevsky's Politics"— C'mon, boy, go get it! And they do: efficiently, tidily, sometimes quite brilliantly. Often behind what I have called "the happy knack"—my old tendency toward glibness is still intact, I see—is a great deal of effort; and careful writing is, after all, the best evidence going for having an orderly and lucid mind. And yet the superior writers among my students are often merely those students who best sense what is wanted of them and, through skills they have developed over the years, are able to deliver it. I am generally delighted, in the locution of the car dealers, "to take delivery." Still, in my intellectual greed, I hope that my best students will be more than merely good at school.

Everyone who teaches must at some point ask himself what he wants from his students. If one is teaching a science, or a foreign language, or the skills required for such vocations as law or journalism, the answer ought to be clear—one wants one's students to master the material in the course. But in the teaching of literature, which is what I teach, I don't believe the materials are quite masterable; I have no notion how one masters Henry James or Joseph Conrad. Far from having mastered the materials I teach, I frequently find that from semester to semester, I cannot even remember them myself, and so have to reread five- and six-hundred-page novels. It would be foolish to expect one's students to be better at this than one is oneself.

In my case the matter is complicated by the fact that, so far as I know, I teach no strict doctrine, no clear method; I have no architectonic ideas, or even any very tonic ones. I try to make sense of literary works, convey my appreciation for their

subtlety and power and beauty, and make plain their signifi-
cance. If my teaching has a central message, it is probably the
intellectual equivalent of "Don't accept any wooden nickels."
(Usually these intellectual wooden nickels have "isms" attached to them.) All this being so, my ideal student is one who
has that intolerance for nonsense otherwise known as skepticism. But his must be skepticism of a certain kind—skepticism
reinforced by seriousness. By seriousness I mean the understanding that art and ideas have real consequences—consequences over the long haul as great as and sometimes greater
than those of politics and technology—that life is at once a gift
and a puzzle, and that the attempt to make the most of this life
through coming to an understanding of the puzzle is not the
only game in town but surely the most important one. Of
course, in the young such seriousness is almost always inchoate, but it does from time to time turn up, and when it does
it is immensely impressive and makes merely being good at
school—you will pardon the expression—academic.

As a teacher who was not himself good at school, I have a
special sympathy for students who do not perform well in
class. I rather prize C students—were my younger self to walk
into one of my current courses, he would doubtless get a C,
perhaps a C+—for in the current day of grade inflation, to be
able to give a student a C helps convince a teacher that he still
has high standards. When I sense a student's nervousness, my
own nervousness as a student comes back to me. In a sense, I
still am a poor student, or at least have the psychology of a poor
student. When an undergraduate, I would occasionally have
what I think of as student nightmares: these usually involved
my having to take an exam in some branch of higher mathematics or some language, such as Persian, for which I was
wholly unprepared. Now, generally near the beginning of a
new term, I can count on a teaching nightmare: these usually

involve my having lost my notes before a lecture, or being unable to find the room in which I am to teach, or knowing nothing whatever about the subject in which I am to instruct others. Today, even awake, when giving an examination, I feel a slight shudder of terror pass over me—terror and relief at not having to take another college examination myself.

A few years after I began teaching, it occurred to me that being a teacher—not being a student—provides the best education. "To teach is to learn twice," wrote Joubert, in a simple-sounding maxim that could have several different meanings. It could mean that one first learns when getting up the material one is about to teach and then tests and relearns it in the actual teaching. It could mean that being a teacher offers one a fine chance for a second draft on one's inevitably inadequate initial education. It could mean that learning, like certain kinds of love, is better the second time around. It could mean that we are not ready for education, at any rate of the kind that leads on to anything resembling wisdom, until we are sixty, or seventy, or beyond. I favor this last interpretation, for it accounts for the strange feeling that I have had every year of my adult life, which is that only twelve months ago I was really quite stupid.

Quotatious

A REVIEWER OF A RECENT BOOK of mine accused me—I believe it was an accusation—of being an uninhibited "phrase dropper," by which he meant that I seem to go in for quotation in a big way. He is perfectly correct, of course. I do tend to quote extensively, sometimes even extravagantly. What is more, now that I think about it, I have done so for much of my life. Although I like to attend to constructive criticism, reform here is, I fear, quite hopeless. "*Vi tsu zibn,*" as the old Yiddish saying has it, "*azoy tsu zibetsik.*" ("As at seven, so at seventy.") See what I mean? I just did it again. I am not merely a habitual quoter but an incorrigible one. I am, I may as well face it, more quotatious than an old stock-market ticker-tape machine, except that you can't unplug me.

As it turns out, my first serious quotational work did come, as the Yiddish saying I just quoted has it, at roughly the age of seven. It was my father whom I first chose to quote. I happened to grow up in a neighborhood in which I was the youngest boy by some two years. This carried certain penalties. In choose-up baseball games I could count on being sent out to the Siberia known as right field; in football I was invariably assigned the position of center (as in the then-popular phrase "dunk the center"). When someone was required as the target for the kind of free-lance vicious teasing that boys on a playground tend to go in for to break the monotony, I, younger and smaller than everyone else, was always at hand. When I reported my dissatisfaction about these matters to my father, he instructed me never to back down before a bully. "Remember," he said to me, "the bigger they are, the harder they fall." I guessed that this must be true, but it seemed to me even then to elude the serious technical problem of how in the first place to make them fall, which, when one is three feet nine and weighs sixty or so pounds, can be troublesome. "Remember," my father said, "behind every bully lies a coward." I rather liked that one, and a day or two later used it on one of my chief tormentors, a muscular (for ten years old) Irish kid named Denny Price. "My father says," I reported, always careful about correct attribution, "that behind every bully, Price, lies a coward." "Aw," he replied, "ya fadda's an ————," and here he let fly a word that spun me around more than any of his rabbit punches on my arms and that not even today am I prepared to quote.

I cannot say that I did much quoting as an adolescent. This was owing to the fact that I read so little, and from little reading little quotation can flow. Instead I often quoted my friends, as they often quoted me. Comedy was a big item among us, and we always took delight in reporting the wild or witty things one or another of us had said to a substitute physics teacher, a coach, or a date. Retelling anecdotes, with a quotation as a punch line, was one of our leading forms of entertainment. I know that when anything even faintly amusing happened to me, I worked it up—editing it, embellishing it, exaggerating it slightly when necessary—for oral publication among my friends. If I then had any clear notion of what a writer was, which I didn't, I should have understood that I had the temperamental makings of a writer, insofar as no experience was ever quite complete for me until I retold it, and the retelling generally turned out to be as sweet—often sweeter—than the original experience. I also discovered, in this very small circle, that I hugely enjoyed being quoted for having said clever things when my own stories were retold by various of my friends.

"Only my tailor measures me correctly," exclaimed the young man, as he began his fall from atop the dining-room table at the fraternity-house dance. He was then heard to mutter "Samuel Johnson" from his prone position on the floor, head resting on his crooked arm, before passing out, I won't say "like a patient etherised upon a table," yet in pretty bad shape nonetheless. The young man is nineteen and undergoing a conversion, not a religious but an intellectual conversion. More precisely, he has found himself aflame with passion for things he does not half understand: the poetry of T. S. Eliot and E. E. Cummings, serious music, modern art, the idea of the avant-garde, bohemianism. He has been called a "pseudo-intellectual," a label that isn't quite accurate, for he is not even a true fake. However inchoately he may understand the world of books and art and intellectual things, he feels he genuinely loves them. While attempting to penetrate the meaning of the poetry of Hart Crane, he nevertheless reserves the right to sit in on high-stakes poker games. Owing to such behavior, that line of Samuel Johnson—"Only my tailor measures me correctly"—applies nicely to him, or so he believes, and he is thrilled enough by it to announce it just before passing out on a college boy's rowdy drunk.

Where I found that Samuel Johnson quotation I cannot now say. Certainly, at nineteen I had not read *The Life of Johnson,* or anything by Johnson himself. (I have, on subsequent searching, not been able to rediscover it, and I hope that

I have got it right.) When I think about that quotation today, however, I must say that I think Samuel Johnson, dressing as sloppily as he did, had a hell of a nerve bringing his tailor into any discussion. Nowadays, given the scruffiness of Johnson and the litigiousness of modern life, the tailor would probably sue and deserve to win his case. At the time, the appositeness of Johnson's line to my own life appeared exact; it seemed, to adapt a sartorial phrase of which Samuel Johnson apparently had no personal experience, a very snug fit. To think that another human being had thought about his life as I had about mine, and that the man was as profound as I had heard rumor Samuel Johnson was—well, it went right to my heart.

It still does. So, too, do a great many other quotations. A quotation, which I take to be something looser than a proverb or a maxim or an aphorism, all of which are themselves usually quotable, is anything well or interestingly put that bears repeating. Any statement, comment, or remark that is apt, elegantly formulated, comical, or outrageous qualifies. "Remarks are not literature," Gertrude Stein once said to Hemingway, but they can nonetheless be very interesting, as is the foregoing remark by Miss Stein. Someone—Cyril Connolly? Ezra Pound?—once said that anything that can be read twice is literature; I would say that anything that bears saying twice is quotable.

Or, as the case may be, written twice. I shall tell you how the case is with me. So enamored am I of a striking thought neatly formulated that roughly twenty years ago I began writing down in small notebooks all such thoughts I came upon in my reading. I have only recently begun my twenty-second such notebook. Never much of a collector as a child—not of comic books, tin soldiers, baseball cards—I now collect striking thoughts found in the work of other writers. I was never very good at keeping my toys in order as a child, and I am not

much better now with my quotations. "Every man of character," says Nietzsche, "repeats the same experience throughout
his life." I don't know if I have the character to qualify, but my
repeated experience has to do with file systems that break
down. I have left jobs—I won't say promising jobs—because
my files for these jobs had become hopeless. So now with my
twenty-one books of quotations. The prospect of finding anything in them is hopeless, absolutely hopeless.

Still, I persist. In me the habit of writing out quotations,
like that of quoting itself, has proceeded from a habit to a tic.
I seem to be unable to stop it. "That's marvelous," I say to
myself when reading. "Must write it down." The witty ("Stu-
pidity is always amazing, no matter how used to it you
become"—Jean Cocteau), the amusing ("A teacher is a person
who never says anything once"—Howard Nemerov), the profound ("It is only the very greatest kind of artist who presents
us with experiences that we recognize both as fundamental and
as in advance of anything we have hitherto known"—J. W. N.
Sullivan)—all get scribbled down in my perforated Mead notebooks. While reading writers of great formulatory power—
Henry James, Santayana, Proust—I find I can scarcely get
through a page without having to stop to record some lapidary
sentence. Reading Henry James, for example, I have muttered
to myself, "C'mon, Henry, turn down the brilliance a notch,
so I can get some reading done."

I may be one of a very small number of people who have
developed writer's cramp while reading. We're a compulsive
but amiable crew, those of us who feel, or have felt, the compulsion to re-record the bright thoughts of other men and
women. In recent decades our numbers have included Louis
Kronenberger, W. H. Auden, John Gross, and J. Bryan III, all
of whom have published collections of aphorisms or commonplace books. In the nineteenth century, Robert Southey pro-

duced a commonplace book, and Arthur Conan Doyle bestowed one upon Sherlock Holmes. I suppose that my twenty-one notebooks constitute something like a commonplace book, which the *Oxford English Dictionary* defines as a book "in which one records passages or matters to be especially remembered or referred to, with or without arrangement."

The oddest among us may have been an Englishman named Geoffrey Madan, who was born in 1895 and died in 1947 and whom Harold Macmillan recalls at Oxford as having "something of the look of those young men who stand about to no apparent purpose in Renaissance paintings." Madan, educated at Eton and Balliol, was handsome and learned, wonderfully well connected and full of a promise that never came to fruition. He was shaken, apparently for life, by service in Mesopotamia during World War I. After an attack of meningitis in his thirtieth year, he retired permanently on (naturally) a private income, and gave himself over to the connoisseurship of claret, beautiful books, and charming sentences, anecdotes, phrases, and jokes, which he collected in a series of notebooks. For a time, from 1929 to 1933, he annually culled fifty-two items from these notebooks and had them elegantly printed and sent to friends at Christmas. In 1981 John Sparrow and J. A. Gere brought out a selection entitled *Geoffrey Madan's Notebooks,* which contains such jollily offbeat items as the seven-year-old daughter of a friend asking why no food is blue, and two other friends remarking, respectively, that "Diana Manners has no heart, but her brains are in the right place" and "the Bible tells us to forgive our enemies; not our friends."

Although there is very little of Geoffrey Madan in *Geoffrey Madan's Notebooks,* which is composed chiefly of things he had read or heard other people say, when you have read through this slender volume you feel rather as if you have come to know Madan—and in a way that you may not feel you know the author of a book of twice the length, every word of which was written by the author. Merely by knowing what he finds amusing, and what profound, one feels one comes to know the man himself. W. H. Auden, who was nervous about being the subject of a biography, felt that he had tipped his mitt quite as much as he cared to when he published *A Certain World*, his commonplace book, a compilation that he called "a sort of autobiography." In a brief foreword to the volume, he noted: "Here, then, is a map of my planet." I believe it was Gayelord Hauser, the nutritionist, who said that "you are what you eat," but if you happen to be an intellectual, you are what you quote.

Old billiards players will have noticed that I have just used that largely irrelevant Gayelord Hauser quotation as a cushion against which to kiss off for a more relevant point. Conventional use of quotation is, of course, more straightforward, and its most common use is to supply authority. Clergymen have been known to use scripture in this way—to support, nail down, Q.E.D. an argument. In secular life, Marxists do much the same thing; in the work of a Marxist literary critic, a quotation from the Boss (and I don't mean Bruce Springsteen) carries the same authoritative weight as a passage from the Gospels at a revival meeting. But then argument by quotation is something that at one time or another most people in intellectual life have engaged in. As long as you know you are in for a fight, you may as well bring along a few heavies, tough guys with names like Al de Tocqueville, Fred Nietzsche, Slapsie Max Weber, with whose help you can wipe up the opposition.

Whom one brings along can be decisive. I have, for example, just had second thoughts about Tocqueville, who by now may well have been used in too many such scraps. How often, after all, can a man be quoted? Or how often the same quotation used? Santayana's "Those who cannot remember the past are condemned [not "to repeat it," as is often misquoted, but] to fulfil it" has by now been used so often that it has had to be brought back into the shop for retreading. As for Yeats's "the centre cannot hold," well, I am sorry to report, neither can this quotation or any part of the famous passage in the poem "The Second Coming" from which it derives. Even the most dazzling brilliance can lose its luster. As a clever high school student is once said to have asked, "If the Bible and Shakespeare are so important, how come they contain so many clichés?"

Few things are literarily drearier than indiscriminate quotation, by which I mean not quoting too much but quoting the wrong people. I know a sophisticated historical scholar who judges a book in part by the quality of its quotations—that is to say, by its index more than by its cover or table of contents. She has a point. In a work of political science, it is much more exhilarating to find the names of Niccolò Machiavelli and Alexander Herzen than those of Christopher Lasch and Michael Walzer; in a work of literary criticism, it is much more delightful to find quotations from Matthew Arnold and Paul Valéry than from Frank Kermode and Stanley Fish. In general, quoting living writers is a tricky business. I have read essays in which the authors have quoted such writers as Erik Erikson, David Reisman, and Robert Penn Warren as if they carried talismanic authority; but they don't, not to everyone they don't. That Erik Erikson, David Reisman, or Robert Penn Warren may happen to have said something that agrees with your general point may be nice, but among serious folks they don't, by the mere magic weight of their names, cut much ice, lox, or even cream cheese. A quotation, when you get right down to it, is no way to win an argument.

Quotation outside argument can be a most idiosyncratic business and, as with other departments of life, not without its little snobberies. No matter how on the money something they may have written is, writers I do not think well of I do not quote. Nor will I quote, for obvious reasons, those who write badly; here poor John Dewey, by all accounts an admirable man, gets short shrift. Since I mentioned idiosyncrasies, I may as well confess that I would rather not quote writers who have a middle initial in their names: "As Loren M. Singer put it . . ." is not likely to appear in my pages. As for snobbery, the act of quotation has its own little fashions. Just now highly quotable writers, at any rate among academics, include Wittgenstein, Foucault, Clifford Geertz. Quotation follows intellectual fashion, as form is said to follow function. Stephen Potter, in *Lifemanship,* notes that in 1937, during the Spanish Civil War, Federico García Lorca was hot on the quotation market. In the same book, Potter instructs students of lifemanship (a variation on one-upmanship) that "easily the most O.K. [names to mention or quote] for 1945–50 are Rilke and Kafka." The general gambit of mentioning and quoting O.K. authors Potter calls "Rilking." Rilke is still pretty much O.K., though, being largely ignorant of German poetry, I cannot say that, in a life filled with rilking, I have ever specifically rilked by quoting Rilke himself, though I gather that there is still plenty of time, for it was Rilke who, in *Letters to a Young Poet,* wrote: "The future enters into us, in order to transform itself in us, long before it happens."

As for my own personal taste in quotations, I tend to avoid the fashionable (perhaps out of reverse snobbery, though what is in fashion just now does not much interest me), to shun the highly abstract, and to go in for flat, commonsensical statements by writers with rock-solid reputations. My notion of a quotational good time is T. S. Eliot on the best way to become a literary critic: "There is no method but to be very intelligent." Even better is this from Chekhov: "There are a great many opinions in this world, and a good half of them are professed by people who have never been in trouble." That seems to me smart and true and wise, a sentiment taught by experience, tempered by sympathy, and triggered by impatience with foolishness. I wish I had thought to say it myself, but since I didn't, the least I can do is quote it approvingly and thus align myself with that smallest of minority groups, the party of good sense.

Quotations, especially those that come in the form of aphorisms, are wisdom inspissated. Every aphorism, it has been said, is a condensed essay, and the aphoristic writers are of course the most quotable. As a quotatious writer, I like it when into each of my own essays a little aphorism does fall. While writing this essay, for example, I have also been reading Tom Wolfe's best-selling new novel *The Bonfire of the Vanities,* about which I have been asked to write. In going through one of my old notebooks of quotations (one marked "begun 11/2/73"), I discovered that I wrote out the following sentence from Joseph Conrad's story "Prince Roman": "It is only to vain men that all is vanity; and all is deception only to those who have never been sincere with themselves." An apt quotation can light up a mind; it also inevitably finds its place in some conversation or piece of writing. Conrad's interestingly aphoristic sentence will probably serve as an epigraph to what I eventually write about Tom Wolfe's novel; and it may well contain the key to what it is about the novel that makes me uneasy. Thus, to suggestive literary minds, an apt quotation can be a powerful lubricant.

When I first acquired the habit of quotation, part of the motive behind it must have been intellectual display—or, less euphemistically, simple showing off. In quoting one is, after all, proclaiming that one reads widely; and one is also suggesting into the bargain that one reads carefully and retains much of what one has read. If I was showing off, I cannot say that it did me much good. When young I never met and swept away any beautiful women through my powers of quotation—whispering sweet Valérys in their ears. Nor, my guess is, have I won friends and influenced people through my quotations. For every person who admires the quotatious their small skill for being able to call up old reading matter, three other people are likely to find them pretentious in the extreme.

I would gladly have accepted "pretentious in the extreme" one night when I appeared on a radio talk show in Chicago, but I am fairly certain that the meter went well beyond "pompous ass." We were a small group of writers, each come to peddle his book over the air. The man whose show it was began by asking me what I thought it took to be a writer. Clearly, he had come to the right man. I got out of the blocks fast by saying that Hemingway thought the first requisite of the writer was "an unhappy childhood"; I gave him a little Henry James; I popped in a Tolstoy; at no extra charge, I added that Byron said, "Who would write, who had anything better to do?" For three or four minutes I was a Gatling gun of citation; quotation marks were flying around the studio like shrapnel. A woman named Liz Carpenter, white-haired and a Texan who had written a book about being social secretary to Lady Bird Johnson when Lyndon Johnson was president, spoke next. "Mr. Epstein is very learned and all," she said, in a cheerful Southern drawl, "and I was fascinated by everything he had to say. But I just happen to have finished a book about working with my friend Lady Bird Johnson in the White House, and I'll tell you what, you want to be a writer, honey, first thing you need is a real comfortable chair."

That happened roughly seventeen years ago. You might think it would have taught me a lesson. Let me assure you that it did not. The Gatling gun has fired away many a time since;

it has, alas, a hair trigger. Anything can set it off. The other day someone mentioned to me, with a touch of chagrin, that his work was not known outside a small academic circle. I replied that I had recently read that Virgil Thomson once said, "When I find myself among those who don't know my name, I know I'm in the real world." I could have added that Lincoln Kirstein once remarked of Virgil Thomson's profound good sense that "he undazzled me," but I thought that more than one quotation on the subject was pushing it. I mean, as Isaac Bashevis Singer has one of his characters say, "one can have too much even of *kreplach.*" As you see, once one begins all this quoting, stopping, for the truly quotatious, is a real problem. "Ah, that is no problem," an old Chinese saying has it, "that is impossible."

I suppose the argument could be made that those who quote abundantly are really living off the wisdom of others. Quoting, after all, is not the same as thinking. Once upon a time it was, however, a badge of learning. Carlo Marsuppini, a youngish humanist and friend of Cosimo de Medici, was thought tremendously learned because, in the course of a single lecture, he was apparently able to work in quotations from every known Greek and Latin writer. Pope Leo X, another of the Medicis and a most bookish man, could quote lengthy passages from his most beloved authors. In the sixteenth century the arguments of lawyers and the decisions of magistrates were often studded with classical references. (In nineteenth-century America, lawyers were expected to be handy with a quotation from Cicero, and a library of classics was part of the furniture in many a legal office.) On his deathbed, Etienne de La Boétie, the dear friend of Montaigne, quoted Catullus, though letting your last words be someone else's may be further than even the most quotatious among us is willing to go.

Montaigne, whom I myself like to quote every chance I get, himself had a hardy appetite for quotation. In the book-lined study in his famous tower, to which he retreated after his retirement from public life, he had arranged to have written out along the beams of the ceiling some fifty-odd quotations in Greek and Latin, many of them, Montaigne's fine biographer Donald M. Frame reports, emphasizing the ignorance and fragility of man. Included among them was Terence's famous remark "I am a man; I consider nothing human foreign to me." Not much was, either, and certainly not books written in foreign tongues. Montaigne, in his essays, quoted freely from Aristotle and Plato, Ovid and Horace, and anyone else whom he needed to make his point. Montaigne believed, as Professor Frame puts it, that "what we learn we must digest and make our own . . . ," and in Montaigne's case one feels that those authors he quotes are truly in his blood. Still, late in life, he regretted, as Professor Frame writes, "having been persuaded to quote as freely as he has; his own preference would have been to speak only in his own words." Yet Donald Frame closes his own book on Montaigne with a quotation from Montaigne—"A generous heart should not belie its thoughts; it wants to reveal itself even to its inmost depths. There everything is good, or at least everything is human"—and it seems perfectly appropriate that he do so.

I am rather sorry to learn that Montaigne regretted having been so quotatious in his essays. I myself love to quote Montaigne; if I were a black teenager, I might even go so far as to say, when it comes to quotation, "That Montaigne, man, he be my main man." I enjoy quoting Montaigne and the other writers I admire not because I do not think that I have anything fresh to say on my own, but because they have said so many impressive things that it would be a shame not to repeat them from time to time. Sometimes, too, it happens that someone has said something long before you have come upon the scene that so perfectly fits your own feelings that you cannot resist quoting it, even to yourself. I, for example, often have occasion to enter an office that, for complicated reasons too boring to go into here, brings out the aggressor, even the bully, in me. I know well enough what causes these feelings, but I had never quite been able to describe them until, in a not very good book about Gilbert and Sullivan, I discovered that W. S. Gilbert had a strong distaste for churchmen and particularly for curates, whom he found dreary and pusillanimous. One day Gilbert found himself in a small town where a church conference was meeting, and when asked how he felt about being among so many curates, he replied, "I feel like a lion in a den of Daniels." Well, that is precisely how I feel upon entering this office, and each time I do so, I turn the handle and mutter, "a lion entering a den of Daniels. Exactly." It is, somehow, a great comfort to me.

Yet the older, the more refined one's taste becomes, the fewer the people one takes pleasure in quoting. For one thing, prejudice sets in. I prefer not to quote any psychologist beneath the intellectual stature of Freud or Jung. I once thought it very posh to quote anyone associated with the Bloomsbury group, the more obscure the man or woman the better. Now I steer clear of those folks, though I grant you that Virginia Woolf said many penetrating things, and her husband Leonard deserved, if such an award were given, the Nobel Prize for Marriage. For another, one hesitates to quote things already too often quoted; hence my earlier (and perhaps too extreme) prohibition against Tocqueville. While a good quotation, unlike a metaphor, cannot be original, it ought, like a metaphor, to be fresh at least in the sense that one's readers are unlikely to have seen it before. In this line of work, one must never worry about being too arcane or, if the need arises, about availing oneself of foreign languages and phrases. *Et nunc erudimini.*

The possibilities for quotation are further limited by the fact that one feels one should not quote approvingly writers one believes less intelligent or amusing than oneself—and, with the usual abnormal increase in a writer's vanity as he grows older, this can narrow the field dramatically. It can result in one's being able to quote, among contemporaries, only oneself. Now everyone knows that to quote oneself is seriously to violate good taste. But, then, wasn't it Alfred Jarry who said: "Screw good taste"? (A fine instance, do you not agree, of allowing a quotation to do a writer's dirty work for him.) Matthew Arnold remarked upon "the proverbial and ferocious vanity of authors and poets." Matt, babes, you don't know the half of it. Stick around.

I find it difficult to resist quoting myself, and every so often in my notebooks I discover an observation upon humankind or what I take to be a witty comment written out with my own name or initials written under it. On a few occasions I have smuggled some of these into my published writing, assigning them to that charming rogue who goes by the name of A. Wag, as in, "The chief contributors to *The New York Review of Books*, as a wag once put it, seem to be mad dogs and Englishmen." (A further refinement in the annals of authorly vanity: here I am quoting myself quoting myself; and they say that there is nothing new in the world.) Other examples of my notebook brilliance I have thus far had to keep between spiral-bound covers. There I noted, for example, asking a young writer what his parents did, and when he reported that his mother was a housewife and a hypochondriac, I replied, "Ah, two full-time jobs." Upon finishing a novel by William Maxwell, I jotted down in my notebook, "I greatly admire William Maxwell's fiction, except that he tends to anthropomorphize children."

The other day I was talking with a friend about a slyly ambitious colleague of ours, and I found myself saying, "I fear he is not the simple two-faced young man he at first appears." My friend rejoined that he was certain one day to see that remark turn up in my writing. I hope he finds it as amusing the second time around.

A man extremely fond of quoting himself was the late Oscar Levant. Everything about Levant was extreme, apparently, including his exhibitionism about his own illnesses, which he like to chronicle in great detail in his radio and television appearances and in his books. He was a man who proved he wasn't a hypochondriac by dying in 1972 at the age of sixty-six, though to hear him tell it he was already the late Oscar Levant by 1950. Levant was a professional wit whose specialty was in giving utterance to the outrageous, and his books—*The Unimportance of Being Oscar, The Memoirs of an Amnesiac, A Smattering of Ignorance*— are sample cases of undisguised self-quotation. A characteristic instance is when a Broadway playwright named Phil Yordan appeared on Levant's television talk show and asked if Levant wanted to hear about his, the playwright's, failures. Levant replied, "No, your successes are depressing enough." Gertrude Stein, Levant notes in *The Memoirs of an Amnesiac,* once wrote the following stage instructions for one of her plays: "Witty remarks are made offstage." Of course, Levant, like many another quotatious type, can bear to leave nothing witty offstage; and he is, moreover, a great appreciator of the wit of others, even when it is at his own expense. Of the many stories he tells of which he is the butt, my own favorite is that of his meeting with Greta Garbo, whom his friend S. N. Behrman had told beforehand of his, Oscar Levant's, legendary wit. When introduced to Garbo, however, Levant was so shaken by her fame and glamour that he became shy and, as he tells it, "stammered stupidly,

'Sorry, I didn't get the name.' " Garbo, turning to S. N. Behr-man, announced, "It is better he remain a legend." I should say that a man who can tell a story like that ought to be permitted to quote himself whenever he wishes.

Along with quoting yourself, there is always the prospect of being quoted by others, which can be very nice, and even rather thrilling to someone who is himself highly quotatious. Being quoted with mischievous intent, though, can drive one bonkers and beyond. I have more than once been choked on the three dots of an enemy's ellipsis, hoisted on the petard of partial quotation, garroted by simple misquotation. Of course, it doesn't take an enemy to botch a quotation. Anyone who has ever edited a magazine or written a book with many quotations in it will be able to testify to the fact that one of the most difficult chores known to writers is to get a quotation copied out correctly. Lady Diana Cooper reports that "Lord Ribbles-dale . . . told me, when I was too young to believe him, that it was gentlemanly to get one's quotations very slightly wrong. In that way one unprigged oneself and allowed the company to correct one." Getting one's quotations very slightly wrong is not a major problem for most of us who write; to be able to get them only very slightly wrong might even be considered something of an achievement. Now that I stare at it a bit, I have suddenly become worried lest I miscopied my quotation from Lady Diana Cooper.

Accuracy in quotation is not a subject I prefer to dwell on. Not only am I one of those people who are never quite certain whether it is fences or their absence that makes good neigh-bors, but in my notebooks I frequently mark down items with-out noting whence they derive. In one of these notebooks, for example, I have written down the line "Every room has its gloom," under which I wrote, "Gertrude Stein, attributed to Shorty Lazar." But who is Shorty Lazar? And where, exactly, did Frederick Rolfe, the infamous Baron Corvo, use the phrase "infinitives split to the midriff," which appears in the same notebook? Not, I am sure, in the same place that Noël Coward remarked (I am quoting from the same notebook), "It has strengthened me in my decision not to become a nun." Although I do not like to say it, my sense is that truly first-rate minds—with such rare exceptions as Montaigne and William Hazlitt, another quotatious writer—do not go in much for quotation. Like those powerful business executives who do not have ulcers but instead give them to others, truly first-rate minds do not quote but instead furnish quotable material for others. At the end of an evening, after all, Samuel Johnson did not scurry home to copy down everything that James Boswell had said. Tolstoy, near as I can recall, quoted rarely, and then chiefly from the New Testament. Goethe did not quote abundantly; nor, to drop to a smaller but no less original figure, did Max Beerbohm. Such writers never felt the need to call on the authority of others to reinforce their own. "I may be old-fashioned," Beerbohm once said, "but I am right."

I, on the other hand, feel the need of all the help I can get. When I am attempting to make an argument, I prefer to bring along Aristotle, Cardinal Newman, Matthew Arnold, George Orwell. So you believe that income can be fairly redistributed in a few decades if people will only listen to reason. Go ahead, George, tell him what we think of that: "You have to be a member of the intelligentsia to believe things like that—no ordinary man could be such a fool." When I set out to amuse, I prefer to bring along Evelyn Waugh, H. L. Mencken, A. J. Liebling, Karl Kraus. So you would like to know what I think of much of the literature being produced today? Go ahead, Karl, tell him what we think of it: "Today's literature is prescriptions written by patients." Thanks, boys.

Yet my penchant for quotation runs deeper than the uses I find for it in supplying authority and amusement for my own conversation and prose. I spend something like a third of the hours I am awake reading, and when I read something really striking I feel the need to copy it in my own notebook: first, because I admire it; second, because I hope that copying it will help me to remember it; third, because copying it out, in some vague way that I do not wholly understand, gives me partial possession of it. When the ballet critic Edwin Denby writes that intelligence in a dancer "is shown by how interesting to look at she can make her body the whole time she is on the stage," I feel that this is a complex point so cleanly made that I must copy it down. It isn't enough that I own *Looking at the Dance,* Denby's book, in which I read it. I want it in my own notebook, too, for reasons I am not prepared to defend.

This may be quite nuts, but it is nice to know that I am not alone in my nuttiness. In E. M. Forster's *Commonplace Book,* after Forster had copied out what looks to be roughly a four-hundred-word passage from *The Decline and Fall of the Roman Empire* on the coronation of Justin, he notes: "—Copied from Gibbon's Decline and Fall, ch 45 on August 17, 1962 for various reasons: partly stylistic; partly in homage; partly because I am just back from Lombardy and wanted to read something of the people who gave it its name." A man in his eighties taking the time to write out four hundred or so words in a notebook nobody besides himself was intended to see—a little crazy, no? Not to me; I understand it completely.

Even in "the valley of the shadow of books," to quote a phrase of George Gissing, we quotatious folks are a bit odd, to put it gently. Few things delight us quite so much as to be able to insert that Plato said this, Pascal said that, Bagehot said the other. To be able to break, in Henry James's words, one's own "fruitless fidget of composition" with a fine line from, say,

Hazlitt ("It is utterly impossible to persuade an Editor that he is a nobody," for example), lightens our load. We who are quotatious are never truly alone, but always hear the cheerful flow of remarks made by dead writers so much more intelligent than we. It may well be that tuning into this flow is as close to wisdom as those of us who are quotatious are likely to get. "The wise only possess ideas," wrote Coleridge, "the greater part of mankind are possessed by them." But, I beg of you, please don't quote me quoting Coleridge on that.

Confessions of a Low Roller

Ours has long been a distinguished publishing family, if you take the adjective "distinguished" in a loose sense and if you allow a definition of "publishing" broad enough to include bookmaking. I don't mean to brag about family lineage, but I had an uncle, dead some years now, who had fully two sobriquets: in some quarters he was known as Lefty and in others as Square Sam. All gamblers, it is often enough said, die broke, but my uncle, whom I scarcely knew, is reported to have left the planet with something on the order of twenty-five Ultrasuede jackets hanging in the closet of his home in Los Angeles. Beginning life as a professional gambler, he soon went into publishing (or bookmaking) and eventually owned a small piece of a large casino-hotel in Las Vegas. To place him for you socially, he was a man at whose granddaughter's wedding a guest was Frank Sinatra. Need I say more?

Although this uncle did not carry my family name, there was a prominent gambler who did. Some years ago I read a lengthy obituary in a Chicago newspaper about a man who carried my exact name, Joseph Epstein, and who was described in the obit headline as "Gentleman Big-Time Bookie, Dies at 75." My namesake—or am I his?—turns out to have run, in the words of the obituarist, "a large betting layoff operation from offices [that covered] wagers that bookies across the nation could not handle." The obituarist continued: "Although his associates were more often coarse, devious, violent men, [he] had the reputation of a bookmaker who kept his word and was mild-mannered in the extreme. He was well-read, fancied himself as a Talmudic scholar and was clearly the intellectual bookie of his time." It gets better. It seems that this Joseph Epstein also served as a Professor Henry Higgins to a gangland moll named Virginia Hill, who came to Chicago from Alabama at seventeen, whose great and good friend, as *Time* magazine used to put it, he was, though she finally left him for Benjamin (Bugsy) Siegel. "A nonsmoker," the obituary notes, "he remained in robust health almost until his death by taking long, daily walks through the city [of Chicago] from his hotel on Ohio St."

The gentleman big-time bookie bearing my name died in Chicago in 1976, a fact that fills me with double regret, first for his death, for he appears to have been a decent sort, and second because I wish I had had the chance to meet and talk with him. It is not about the Talmud that I wish I could have talked with "the intellectual bookie of his time," but about shop—specifically, about gambling. No photograph appeared with his obituary, but I imagine him to be a smallish man, silver-haired, expensively yet not gaudily dressed, good shoes well shined, nails manicured. We might have walked along Michigan Boulevard together on a late, lightly breezy afternoon in May, past Tiffany and Cartier and Saks Fifth Avenue and Neiman Marcus, stopping off for an aperitif in the cool, wood-paneled Coq d'Or bar in the Drake Hotel. Seated at one of the small tables in the dark room where sound tends to be gently muffled, I would have encouraged him to recount anecdotes about noble behavior on the part of crooks, in exchange for which I would have supplied him with anecdotes about what crooks academics can be. We should, I do not doubt, have addressed each other as "Mister," with the charm of adding to it our selfsame last name.

If the mood were right, perhaps our talk might have ascended to philosophy, always within the confines of shop, of course. Why do men gamble? I might have asked him. Is gambling in the end always a ruinous diversion? Is there something masochistic about it? Was Malraux right when he called it, in connection with his character Clappique in *Man's Fate*, "suicide without death"? Is gambling not a metaphor but a metaphorical activity, since, as has been noted, life itself goes off at something like 6-5 against, though some think these odds unduly generous? Why does gambling excite, exhilarate, and depress some people while not arousing the least interest in others? What does gambling do for those people who go in for it in a big way? For those who enjoy it only occasionally? And, while I am at it, I might just have lowered the tone of the conversation and inquired if I was a chump to agree to an arrangement whereby I would have to pay 10 percent juice, or vigorish, on a $300 bet on this past year's World Series.

Consider, please, that figure $300, or $330 if I lost. Something rather hopeless about those numbers, if you ask me, something neither here nor there. I had originally intended to bet $1,000 ("a grand," in the grand old term), which is a good deal more than I have ever bet on anything, and then I decided that $500 was sufficient. But when I reached an old friend who has a bookie—I bet much too infrequently to have my own bookie—I heard myself say $300. I don't mean to suggest that $300 is a negligible sum; if one is down and out, it is a most impressive sum. I am sure that someone reading this is ready to inform me, in a properly moral tone, that a family of four could eat for a month on $300. Nowadays, though, there are restaurants in New York where one has to cut corners—go for the California wine instead of the French—to get a full dinner for two for less than $300. I myself consider it immoral to dine in such places. "It is all," as Albert Einstein must at some time have said to Max Planck, "relative."

If all this sounds a little goofy, it is merely because it is. No activity has been more rationalized than gambling—odds figured, probabilities worked out, point spreads meticulously established—and no activity, surely, is finally more irrational. In this essentially irrational activity, the first item that must be fixed, and with some precision, is the stake. Above all, it cannot be too little; it must be enough to stimulate whatever those spiritual glands are that gambling calls into action. The punishment must fit the crime; the agony of losing must be roughly equivalent to the ecstasy of winning. In this sense, it becomes clear that no bet can ever be too large; and herein lies the madness inherent in gambling, for the more you have, the more you need to risk.

"Important money" is what professional gamblers used to call big bets, and such fabled gamblers as Pittsburgh Phil (a horseplayer), Nick the Greek (cards and dice), and Ray Ryan (gin rummy) never played for unimportant money. Nick the Greek, whose last name was Dandolos, claimed once to have bet $280,000 on a five coming up before a seven in a crap game. The same Mr. Dandolos is said to have lost $900,000 in a single night in New York on the eve of a holiday trip to Europe, which—surprise! surprise!—had to be canceled. Winning a bet, Nick Dandolos used to say, is man's greatest pleasure; the second greatest pleasure, he held, is losing a bet. In more than fifty years of serious gambling, something on the order of $50 million is supposed to have trafficked in and out of his hands. Yet Nick the Greek was no money snob. The late Jimmy Cannon, the sportswriter, told the story of the Greek's playing twenty-four hours straight at Arnold Rothstein's crap table and, after the crap game broke up, sitting down to play casino for twenty-five cents a hand with one of Rothstein's stickmen. "Action is all he wants," Cannon concluded, "and he has lasted longer than any of them and held on to his dignity."

Some gamblers get a thrill out of the action itself, while others need to be in action at high prices. The greater the stakes, the greater the pressure, the greater the cool (or courage) required. Damon Runyon, a gambler all his life and a student of gamblers, maintained he knew "men who will beat far better card players at gin [rummy] if the stakes are high enough just on simple courage." A gambler is like an airplane in that at a certain altitude—for the gambler, at certain high sums—the controls start to shake. I earlier mentioned certain "spiritual glands" that needed to be stimulated by gambling, but anatomical ones are often also called into play, producing sweaty hands, dry mouth, inconvenient loss of control of the facial muscles. No, nothing quite relaxes a fella like an evening of gambling.

Growing up in Chicago, I had a friend whose father was reputed to have bet $100,000 on a baseball game—and lost. This was during the early 1940s, when $100,000 was extremely important money and not the annual salary of a utility infielder or a Marxist professor of English at Duke University. Inconveniently, my friend's father didn't have the money; conveniently, there was a war on. As the story goes, he showed up the next afternoon at the bookie's with a smile and in a set of U.S. Navy bell-bottoms, having enlisted that morning. The uniform, supposedly, saved his life, for no one was about to kill a man in uniform during wartime, and he was able to arrange terms to pay off his debt.

What made him bet such a sum? He was living in Los Angeles at the time—always a hot gambling town, according to Damon Runyon—and must have waked one sunny week-day morning (I always imagine it to be a Tuesday) in an impatient mood. A voice within must have whispered, "Let 'er rip!" He did, and it nearly tore him in two. Almost all baseball games were played during the day at that time, so he must have known not much later than 3:30 P.M. Los Angeles time that he had made a serious mistake. I am pleased not to have been the one to serve him that evening's dinner, or to have to ask him if the lamb was properly underdone.

He died before I knew him, whether of heart attack, cancer, or stroke I cannot recall, but he couldn't have been more than in his early fifties. His wife and only son lived on after him in what I think of not as shabby gentility but elegant shabbility. They lived in a small one-bedroom apartment in a building with a doorman on a once posh but now fading Chicago street. Wife and son spoke of him with affection and awe, and in one corner of the small apartment were framed glossy signed photographs taken of him in the company of famous Jewish comedians and Italian singers—or was it Italian comedians and Jewish singers? Not a marathon man, he lived life at a sprint, going fast and dying young. Why is it that we look with wonder upon a man who one day bets $100,000 on the outcome of a game and loses yet feel no wonder whatsoever looking upon a man who works a lifetime to stow away a few million?

My own interest in gambling—and now we return to someone never likely to have the mad courage to bet $100,000 or the powers of concentration to earn millions—initially derived from the social atmosphere in which I came of age. By this I certainly don't mean my home. My father had not the least interest in cards, sports, or gambling generally, preferring situations, such as the one he had inserted himself into as the owner of a small business, in which as far as possible he could control his own destiny. Most of the men in the rising middle-class Jewish milieu that I grew up in felt much the same. They were physicians and lawyers and businessmen and worked hard so that their children could have an easier life than they, as the sons of immigrants, had had. Some among them gambled—played a little gin rummy or in a small-stakes poker game, bet $50 on a prizefight—but clearly work was at the center of their lives. They believed in personal industry, in thrift, in saving for the future. Entrepreneurial in spirit, they also believed that only a fool works for someone else.

On the periphery, though, were a small number of men who lived and believed otherwise. Two boys among my school friends and acquaintances had fathers who were bookies, and rather big-time ones, judging by the scale on which they lived. Nothing back-of-the-candy-store or Broadway-cigar-stand about them; they were rather like the rest of our fathers, but home more often and with better tans and more telephones in the house. They lived on the edge of the criminal world. So, too, I gather did the father of a girl I knew in high school; he played golf from April until October and from October until April played high-stakes gin rummy at a place atop the Sheraton Hotel called the Town Club; the younger brother of a Capone lieutenant, he was rumored to collect a dollar a month on every jukebox installed in Chicago. The brother of a man I once worked for when I was in high school was said to be a full-time gambler, making his living (he was a bachelor) betting on sports events. In his forties then, he carried the nickname "Acey"; if he is still alive, he would now be in his seventies, which is a bit old to carry around such a nickname. I would often see him at baseball games on weekday afternoons, where, well groomed and well rested, he looked as if his personal motto, an abridged version of my father's and my friends' fathers', might read: "Only a fool works."

When young, I felt a strong attraction to such men. The

attraction was to their seemingly effortless access to what I
then took to be the higher and finer things in life. Their connection to corruption also excited me. Corruption was en-
demic to Chicago, a city that prided itself on its gangsters the
way that other cities were proud of their artists, and one had
to be brought up in a glass bubble—make that an isinglass
bubble—not to come in contact with it. Dickens, Dostoyevsky,
Dreiser, and many a novelist since knew that corruption is
more alluring, and more convincingly described, than goodness. Goodness, on first acquaintance, is a bit boring—and,
when young, the only thing duller than goodness is common
sense.

I had an acquaintance whose father became a very rich man
in a very brief time through selling very ugly aluminum aw-
nings. One Saturday afternoon I went with him to his father's
small factory, where, among his father and his father's salesman, each with a high stack of bills in front of him, a serious
poker game was in progress. My own father often used the
phrase "place of business" with something of the same reverence that some reserve for the phrase "place of worship," and
the idea of a poker game on the site of his business would have
appalled him. At the time, it rather thrilled me. But then it
would be many years until I came round to my father's view,
which was essentially the view set out by Henry James in a
youthful letter to his friend Charles Eliot Norton: "I have in
my own fashion learned the lesson that life is effort, unremit-
tingly repeated . . . I feel somehow as if the real pity was for
those who had been beguiled into the perilous delusion that it
isn't."

So beguiled, I spent much of my adolescence in imitation
of what I took to be the model of the gambler. During our last
year of grammar school, my friends and I met for penny poker
games on Saturday afternoons before ballroom dancing les-

sons. There we sat, at thirteen years old, neckties loosened, jackets draped over the backs of chairs, cigarettes depending unsteadily from the sides of our mouths, smoke causing our eyes to water and squint, playing seven-card stud, deuces usually wild. Quite a scene. Each of us must have thought himself some variant of George Raft, James Cagney, Humphrey Bogart, or John Garfield, when Leo Gorcey and the Dead End Kids gone middle-class was much more like it. "My pair of jacks see your three cents, Ronald, and I bump you a nickel."

A misspent youth? I suppose it was, though I never thought of it as such. Perhaps this was owing to its being so immensely enjoyable. In high school, gambling went from an occasional to an almost incessant activity. Although we never shot dice, my friends and I played every variation of poker, blackjack, and gin rummy. From city newsstand vendors we acquired and bet football parlay cards. Every so often, on weekend nights, we would travel out of the city to the sulky races, or "the trotters" as we called them, at Maywood Park. Some unrecognized genius invented a game called "pot-luck," a combination of blackjack and in-between, which guaranteed that no matter how minimal the stakes to begin with, one would soon be playing for more than one could afford. With its built-in escalation element, pot-luck was a game that produced high excitement, for it was not unusual for someone to walk away from these games a $200 winner. I won my share, but more vividly than any win do I remember one gray wintry afternoon when, between four and six o'clock, I lost $125—this at a time when that figure might pay a month's rent on a two-bedroom apartment in a respectable middle-class neighborhood. If the end of the world had been announced on that evening's news, I, at seventeen, shouldn't in the least have minded. In fact, as I recall, I felt it already had.

Gambling, though scarcely a valuable education in itself,

did teach a thing or two about one's own nature. I learned about the limits of my courage with money, for one thing; for another, I learned that in gambling, as in life, you could figure the odds, the probabilities, the little and large likelihoods, and still, when lightning struck in the form of ill luck, logic was no help. I learned I had to put a good, and insofar as possible stylish, face on defeat, even though losing was very far from my idea of a nice time. If you were even mildly attentive, gambling revealed your character to you, showed it in operation under pressure, often taught you the worst about yourself. Some people wanted to win too sorely; they whined and moaned, banged the table and cursed the gods when they lost and seemed smug and self-justified in victory. Others sat grim and humorless over their cards, gloomy in defeat and always ready to settle for a small win. Still others exhibited, even at sixteen or seventeen, a certain largeness of spirit; they were ready to trust their luck; they had a feeling for the game, which I took to be a feeling for life itself, and were delighted to be in action.

"In action" is an old gambler's phrase; and "the action" used to refer to gambling generally. Yet, for all its insistence on action, gambling can be excruciatingly boring. During one stretch in the army, I played poker at Fort Chaffee, in Arkansas, almost nightly for roughly six weeks; I played less for the excitement of gambling than to combat the boredom of army life when one is confined to a post. It turned out to be boredom pitted against boredom. In a rather low-stakes game over this period I emerged roughly a $400 winner. Some of this money I sent to a friend to buy me books in Chicago. The rest I spent on a steak and champagne dinner in the town of Fort Smith, Arkansas, for eight or nine barracks mates. Doing this seemed to me at the time a gesture of magnificence befitting a gambling man.

I remember this especially because it is the only use to which I can ever remember putting any money that I have won gambling. I cannot otherwise recall buying with gambling winnings a sweater, a shirt, a sock, a Q-Tip. Such money has had a way of disappearing from me. Poof: not very easily come, altogether mysteriously gone. Which reminds me that gambling has never, for me, been primarily about money. I was fortunate, of course, in never having to gamble with money intended for rent or food, thereby, as a character in Pushkin's gambling story, "Queen of Spades" puts it, risking "the necessary to win the superfluous." When the money wasn't there— when I was a young husband and father with no extra "tease," as the old horseplayers used to call money—I was easily enough able to refrain from gambling, which strengthens me in my cherished belief that as a gambler I am merely a dreamer and a fool and not an addict.

Gambling addicts are not on the whole an elegant sight. The crowds one encounters at a Nevada casino or at a sulky track on a wintry Wednesday night are quite as depressing as those at a national meeting of the Modern Language Association. Many years ago, in an effort to turn up a bit of tease without actually having to gamble for it, I wrote a piece of journalism on an outfit known as Gamblers Anonymous, which operates on the same principles—confession and comradeship in crisis—as Alcoholics Anonymous. At these meetings one hears an *Iliad* of woe, with enough material left over for an *Odyssey* of misery and an *Aeneid* of heartbreak: story after story of disappointed children, weeping wives, broken bones accompanying unpaid debts, busted-up homes destroyed by busted-out gamblers. On view here is the other side of gambling, the creepy and crummy side, where one hears a man recount how one morning, when his wife is out at the beauty shop, he sells off all the family furniture to get the money to support his hot hunches at the track that afternoon ("I figured I'd buy all new furniture with my winnings," he reports, "a nice surprise for the wife"), hunches that of course didn't work out; another man recounts how he broke into his son's silver-dollar piggy bank for action money, then says nothing when his wife accuses his young son's best friend of taking the money; a man . . . but you get the general idea.

A more particular idea that attendance at these Gamblers Anonymous meetings conveys is the power that gambling can exert over those hooked on it. In its thrall, all other appetites tend to diminish. While one is gambling, food is of no interest, nor is alcohol. Gambling can also throw off one's interior clock, and while at it one is capable of prodigious wakefulness, so that, within limits, gambling can be said to triumph over time and fatigue. When serious gambling is going on, sex seems quite beside the point. At the compulsive level, gambling is all-consuming, and while it doesn't, like drugs or alcohol, fog the mind, it generally monopolizes it. When winning at gambling, one is in the country of the blue; when losing, the world seems mean and red and utterly hopeless. Gambling, one is either flying or crawling, elated or degraded. If any gambler was ever able to find the golden mean, he would probably bet it on the six horse in the fourth race at Pimlico.

As an activity that issues only in extreme states, gambling is of course a great Russian subject. Russians have gone in for gambling in a big way, both actually and literarily. Pushkin turned a card or two in his time, and his story "Queen of Spades" gives ample evidence of his knowing at first hand the desolation of a resounding defeat at the tables. The dissipated young Count Leo Tolstoy was passionate about cards, and not very good at them, even though he devised a system that he set down on paper under the title "Rules for Card-Playing"; like many another such system, it plunged its creator into great debt. A 3,000-ruble loss forced Tolstoy to put himself on a 10-ruble-a-month budget. After suffering gambling losses, the young count would proceed to flog himself—in his diary, of course. When his debts grew too great, he could always sell off a meadow or forest or horses from his estate. This is the stuff out of which nineteenth-century Russian novels are made. Tolstoy didn't simply make it all up.

Nor did Dostoyevsky, whose gambling problem ran deeper than Tolstoy's if only because he, not being an aristocrat, had no estate to sell off to clear his debts. Unlike Tolstoy, too, Dostoyevsky's gambling was not a form of dissipation. He gambled for the most commonsensical of reasons: he needed the money. The problem is that gambling—especially roulette, which was Dostoyevsky's game—may be the quickest but is clearly not the most efficient way of obtaining it. According to Joseph Frank, in his splendid biography of Dostoyevsky, the novelist was unfortunate in winning 11,000 francs in his first attempt at gambling. The hook was in. Yet Dostoyevsky, again according to Professor Frank, was not a pathological gambler but a fitful and sporadic one. He did suffer the inability that gamblers share with gluttons—that of not knowing when to leave the table. After each of his inevitably disastrous gambling episodes, Joseph Frank reports, "Dostoyevsky always returned to his writing desk with renewed vigor and a strong sense of deliverance." Dostoyevsky's losses, then, turned out to be world literature's gain. Fate sometimes uses a strange accounting system.

A highly superstitious man, ever on the lookout for omens and portents, Dostoyevsky had a theory about how to win at gambling that was utterly opposed to his own nature. Dostoyevsky's theory, or system, or secret called for mastery of the emotions while in action. "This secret," Dostoyevsky writes in a letter, "I really know it; it's terribly stupid and simple and consists in holding oneself in at every moment and not to get excited, no matter what the play. And that's all; it's then absolutely impossible to lose, and one is sure of winning." Tolstoy's system, too, called for control of the emotions and moderation—precisely the two things Tolstoy himself was incapable of achieving. "Those who are indifferent are those who are rewarded," wrote Jack Richardson, formulating this view in a single, short, well-made sentence in *Memoir of a Gambler,* his elegant, amusing, and profound book that itself sadly came up snake-eyes, double-zero, and busto in the casino of American publishing when it first appeared in 1979. Richardson's view, like those of Dostoyevsky and Tolstoy, assumes that the gods who watch over gambling are themselves not indifferent or are likely to be fooled by men pretending to a coolness it is not theirs to control. That either assumption is correct is, at best, 9-2 against.

If gambling seems an activity well suited to the Russian temperament with its taste for provoking fate, it is, even though illegal in forty-eight of America's fifty states, very far from un-American. To have come to America in the first place was to take a serious gamble. To advance with the country's frontier was another gamble. When one says that Americans like to gamble, one is of course really saying that the people who have come to America like to gamble. Whenever I have been in a casino, I have noted what seemed to me a high percentage of Asians, most of them Chinese. Jimmy Cannon recalls the older Irishmen in Greenwich Village, where he grew up, disapproving of gambling unless a man was single. Blacks were big for the numbers game and are now, I observe, heavy players in state lotteries. Jews and Italians grew up in gambling cultures—or at least they did when I was a boy—and some among them cross to the other side of the table, becoming bookies or casino owners, donning the expressionless face and

the Ultrasuede jacket, like my deceased uncle, most righteous
of Leftys, squarest of Sams. Texans, to touch on what is almost
another ethnic group, have been known to be most earnest
about poker played for heart-attack stakes. All of these are what
are known as risky generalizations, subject to vehement exceptions: a friend who grew up in a Jewish working-class neighborhood, for example, informs me that in his youth a gambler
was considered lower even than a Rumanian. Various anti-
defamation leagues—Chinese, Black, Jewish, Italian, Irish,
Texan, Rumanian—wishing to protest this paragraph may
reach me at my office, care of the director, Center for Advanced Ethnic Insensitivity.

Men seem to go in for gambling more than women because,
as boys, they often play games and thus early acquire the habits
of competition. (Competition among women, even as young
girls, is subtler, having to do with refinement, sophistication,
beauty, and generally less blatant things than strength, agility,
and speed.) Games that absorb one's energies in the playing of
them do not require gambling for enjoyment. This is true of
football, basketball, and baseball—on which men do often bet
to get their competitive juices flowing after they are no longer
able to play the games themselves—as well as tennis, running,
and gymnastics. It isn't true of golf, which needs the stimulus
of little side bets to get one round the course, or billiards, every
shot of which seems to cry out for a bet. Chess and bridge are
games of sufficient intellectual intricacy to be played without
gambling, even though I realize many people—Somerset
Maugham among them—have played bridge for high stakes.
Poker, blackjack, and gin rummy without money riding on the
outcome are games suitable only for some knotty-pined recreation room in hell.

In bringing up boyhood with regard to gambling, I am, I
fear, playing into the strong hand of the Freudians. This is a

dangerous thing to do, for those guys will sandbag you and whipsaw you. They endlessly raise the stakes. If you open by allowing that gambling is connected with youth, they will call and raise you by saying that it is a neurosis. Bid that gambling can give pleasure, they return by saying—I quote Dr. Otto Fenichel in *The Psychoanalytic Theory of Neurosis*—that the passion for gambling "is a displaced expression of conflicts around infantile sexuality, aroused by the fear of losing necessary reassurance regarding anxiety or guilt feelings." Aver that gambling issues in excitement, they—I quote Dr. Fenichel again—will counter by asserting that "the unconscious 'masturbatory fantasies' of gambling often center around patricide." I realize that W. H. Auden once remarked that "the attitude of psychology should always be, 'Have you heard this one?'" but "masturbatory fantasies" and "patricide"? Is this what is truly going on when one gambles? I wouldn't bet on it.

Freud claimed that much of what he knew he learned from the poets, and I, for one, would rather consult the poets than the Freudians on the subject of gambling. Unfortunately, the poets—and writers generally—do not seem to have had all that much to say about it. Pushkin's story "Queen of Spades" is about a young officer who commits murder in the attempt to obtain a secret system for winning at cards, a murder that is revenged when the system betrays him and causes him to live out his days in madness. Pushkin's is a morality tale and is not quite up to the mark either in explaining or depicting the passion for gambling. Dostoyevsky's *The Gambler* is much more like it. The novella's scenes set in the casino are absolutely convincing, not only in detail but in the understanding behind them of the wild roller coaster the gambler travels from exhilaration ("I was only aware of an immense enjoyment—success, victory, power—I don't know how to describe it") to damnable despair expressed in "calm fury" at realizing that one is not "above all these stupid ups and downs of fate" but finally, like everyone else, their victim. *The Gambler* is not among Dostoyevsky's great works; with its characters' propensity for bizarre behavior and the many loose ends that never quite get tied up at the story's conclusion, it is perhaps rather too Dostoyevskian, but it does have the immense authority of a work written by a man who knew his subject from the inside.

For my money, though, the best literary work on the subject of gambling was written by an outsider. That story is "James Pethel" in the collection *Seven Men* by Max Beerbohm, who, so far as I know, had no interest whatsoever in gambling. The James Pethel of Beerbohm's story is known as an active taker of big risks and one who has had tremendous good luck: in stock market speculation, at the baccarat tables at the casino at Dieppe, on wildly venturesome foreign investments. Beerbohm makes plain that the mere sight of habitual gamblers "always filled me with a depression bordering on disgust." Pethel, however, is no ordinary gambler. On the night that he and Beerbohm meet, after Beerbohm warns him that the water isn't safe to drink, Pethel is encouraged to order not one but two glasses of it, the risk of typhoid only making it more enticing. Casino gambling, one learns, is really only Pethel's way of keeping in trim for such ventures as swimming in dangerous water, driving at maniacal speed (with his wife and daughter, whom he dearly loves, and Beerbohm in the car), and stunt flying. Pethel is, in short, a risk freak, the ultimate gambler who can finally be stimulated only by the ultimate gambles—those in which his own life and the lives of those he loves are on the line. The story is made all the more chilling when at the end we learn that Pethel has died of a heart attack after a flying session, with his daughter and her infant son aboard, and that he had been suffering from a bad heart condition for many years. Beerbohm, with consummate artistry, concludes: "Let not our hearts be vexed that his great luck was with him to the end."

Max Beerbohm despises James Pethel; adore Max Beerbohm though I do, I cannot come down so strongly on his creation, even though I recognize him for the monster he is. The reason I cannot is that through my veins run a few stray particles of the virulent virus that has him firmly in its grip. To the vast majority of people it never occurs to gamble—on anything. To others the possibility of gambling is scratched at the painful prospect of losing; Montaigne, interestingly, was among this group, for, though a cardplayer and crapshooter in his youth, he gave up gambling for the reason that "however good a face I put upon my losses, I did not fail to feel stung by them within." A small group of us feel the same sting Montaigne did—with, I suspect, quite the same intensity—but persist. Why?

Why, I ask myself, do I, who am surely among the world's luckiest men (I touch wood as I write out that last clause), need to risk $330 on a series of baseball games, the outcome of which is otherwise of less than negligible interest to me? I think it has to do with the need I from time to time feel for venturing forth, for striking out against what has become the general quietude and orderliness of my life. As a boy, I never expected to live so calmly as I now do, with the risk of sending up my cholesterol count from eating an occasional steak being perhaps the biggest chance I take. I live, by a choice I do not quite recall having made, a quiet life, for the most part contemplating the world's foolishness instead of partaking in it directly. But when the quiet life grows too quiet, when it threatens to lapse into the most dread disease I know, which is fear of living, then I call on the antidote of gambling.

Perhaps there are quicker antidotes than a World Series bet

on which the tension can be drawn out over more than a week's time. But this was the medicine nearest to hand, and I availed myself of it. Observing myself in action over the course of what turned out to be an extended gamble provided its own slightly tortured amusement. As the Series unfolded, I went from mild depression to measured hopefulness to dignified optimism to serene confidence. I passed a local jeweler's window and noted that he was running a sale of 40 percent off on Movado wristwatches. I already own a Movado watch, but I thought I might use my winnings to buy another. Then it occurred to me to begin a small gambling account, out of which I would begin betting more regularly than I do now. Grand plans were abuilding when—*wham!*— the team I had bet on lost the last two games of the World Series, and I was seated at my desk writing out a check for $330.

The gods, it is pleasing to learn, are still watching over me.

Calm and Uncollected

A s PART OF an unending quest for ever more frivolous closings to letters, I have of late, in writing to people who know me fairly well, taken to signing myself "Yours in Scouting." I may have picked this up from the young H. L. Mencken, who used to sign some of his letters "Yrs. in Xt.," the "Xt." being an abbreviation for Christ. Mencken's relation to Christianity was not so different from mine to scouting. Mastery of the map and the trail, the lanyard and the camp fire, even minimal competence in the arts of self-sufficiency, let us not even speak of survival—no, decidedly, these have never been my long suit. I may not have reached the stage of the late Whitey Bimstein, who, when asked how he enjoyed the country while training a fighter outside New York, replied, "It's a pretty nice place." But when lost in a strange environment, I call a cab; alone and hungry, I dial room service. I can make two knots: one for my shoes, the other for my necktie—but that's it. Put an X-acto blade in my hand and I am likely to show you an all-too-lifelike imitation of the great pitcher Three-Fingered Mordecai Brown. It is, then, every bit as appropriate for me to sign my letters "Yours in Scouting" as it might have been for Marcel Proust to have signed his "Power to the People" or Thomas Mann his "Rock 'n' Roll Forever."

Unlike Mencken in his relationship with Christianity, I actually was a scout, a Cub Scout to be precise, but not for very long nor very happily. I think I joined for the uniform. As a kid, I was daffy about uniforms. The one existing photograph that shows me in a state of uncomplicated contentment was taken when I was four years old and wearing the uniform of the Royal Mounted Police. The Cub Scout uniform, which I donned at nine, was nowhere near so elegant, but it did have a yellow-and-blue scarf, a blue shirt of military cut with yellow trim, and a blue belt with a brass buckle. (I took a pass on the blue beanie with yellow stripes, which seemed to me hopelessly unheroic.) But for the uniform to become at all interesting it wanted covering with patches, cloth arrows, and various insignia of achievement. I was for sewing them on straightaway. Unfortunately, one had to earn them, and here my problems began.

I found no difficulty in learning the Cub Scout motto and salute, in honoring the flag, in finding an old lady—from the perspective of a nine-year-old, any woman past thirty would qualify—to help across the street. Where things became the least bit technical, however, I was in trouble. When I say "the least bit," I really do mean "the least bit." On the way to earning a Wolf badge, for example, one was supposed to be able to identify tools and to know how to use them. But, living in an apartment in a large city, we had no tools in our family, so there was no way I could, to quote the *Wolf Cub Scout Book*, "use a pattern or a plan to make a birdhouse, a set of bookends, or something else useful." Many of the scouting projects required to earn badges seemed to assume suburban or country living. One was asked to grow something, or know boating safety rules, or name five fish. I could only think of four: 1. White, 2. Smoked, 3. Herring in cream sauce, and 4. Gefilte.

What was a bit more disconcerting to me was the item that

appears in the current *Wolf Cub Scout Book* as "Achievement 6. Start a Collection." Instructions for this begin: "You can collect almost anything. Put the things together so that you can show them to your family, den, and pack." This is followed by illustrations of collections of stones, shells, butterflies, stamps, coins, leaves, and patches. I not only collected none of these items, but I saw no reason to do so. Such things as I collected— odd bits of knowledge, baseball statistics, many prohibitions from my parents—were all stored in my head. I could not have been more different from the young Vladimir Nabokov, who, when eight or nine, roamed the woods on his father's estate chasing butterflies and fantasizing that "the only specimen of *Eupithecia petropolitana* was taken by a Russian schoolboy. . . ." At roughly the same age, I, without a net, sat at the counter of West's Pharmacy, a cherry Coke before me, catching if not quite capturing among Mr. West's customers some fairly exotic though wingless specimens of my own.

With so little interest in collecting, I was unlikely to collect any of the badges that I yearned to have for my Cub Scout uniform, and so before long I quit and left the scouting life behind. Yet many a boy I knew in those years didn't require the reward of a badge to keep a collection on his own. It was the day of the cigar box—Perfecto Garcia, Optimo Palmas, King Edward Imperials: names redolent of an adult masculinity that has now gone up in smoke—and boys filled these boxes with such treasures as marbles, lead soldiers, bubble-gum baseball cards, matchbooks, cigar bands. Girls tended to use their mothers' shoe boxes in which they kept collections of playing cards with lovely patterns, doll clothes, pictures of movie stars, sometimes beautiful seashells. After World War II, when metal was again available in greater supply, some boys with a bit of money in the family assembled elaborate electric train layouts, collecting on birthdays or at Christmas additional cars, buildings made to scale, billboards, shrubbery, and other bits of scenery. Middle-class girls had impressive doll collections; there were storybook dolls and a line of dolls from all nations that came in native costumes. This was before the odious doll known as "Barbie" came on the market, which, with a wardrobe suitable to a divorcée looking for a loose man during a Labor Day weekend at Vegas, swept away the competition.

I don't wish to make myself out the bedraggled urchin with his nose pressed against the window of the pastry shop, but I collected nothing. I shot marbles, traded baseball cards, owned a small electric train (an American Flyer), but none of these activities really lit my fire, let alone inflamed me with the kind of passion that is required to organize a systematic collection. Why? Like Virginia Woolf in this if in no other wise, I had no room of my own, but grew up sharing a bedroom with my younger brother, and so I suppose there was not a great deal of extra room to store large collections. Yet had I the interest in collecting something, I am sure that my parents would have found the space for it, even though neither of them felt the collecting impulse in his or her own life. My mother brought back elegant china cups from trips to Canada, but she scarcely pursued this ardently enough for it to constitute a collection; my father, to hear him talk about some of the people with whom he did business, collected only bad debts.

Although there was plenty of good feeling to go round, ours was not a family much interested in things. We had no camera, therefore took no pictures, therefore kept no albums. Photographs, the majority from the 1920s and '30s, that were given to my parents were stored in a shoe box. Along with being collectionless, no one among us had that curious thing that would later turn up on job application forms with a question mark after it and that I never quite knew how to fill in—I refer to hobbies. (Perhaps this is why I have always liked the joke about the recently retired man whose new hobby is bee-keeping and who keeps five thousand bees in a box in a closet in his small Manhattan apartment. When he shows the box to a friend, the friend tells him, with some alarm, that there are no air holes in the box and that the bees, without getting any oxygen, are certain to die. "Oh, well," says the man, with a shrug, "it's only a hobby.") Probably because my parents were the children of immigrants, who perforce traveled light, we had in our home no heavy nineteenth-century furniture, no portraits of ancestors—nothing, in short, in the way of family heirlooms. As a family, we lived with an extraordinary light-ness of being, but—apologies to Mr. Kundera—it was far from unbearable.

Not that I didn't feel a tinge of admiration for boys my age who could form and sustain a collection. At age ten or eleven, I knew a boy who had an impressive collection of miniature cars. This same boy had a large collection of comic books, all neatly arranged. His room was nicely organized: a place for everything and everything in its place. He was an only child. Only children, unless I am mistaken, seemed to be more drawn to collecting than children from larger families. Perhaps this was owing to their having more time to themselves; not having a younger brother or sister to mess about with one's belongings may also have helped. I don't know if this boy had a stamp collection, but two dear friends of mine started to collect stamps, though they soon dropped their collections. Philately, as the Chinese say, got them nowhere.

Had I attempted such a collection, I am confident that I would have got no further. Was there, I sometimes wondered, something in my temperament that made the enterprise of collecting impossible for me? Was I perhaps deficient in an important element of character? Had I insufficient patience, ambition, imagination, in much the same way that Evelyn

Waugh once described cowards in World War II as having an insufficient death wish? I was, God knows, keen enough on possessions: I loved good food, liked nice clothes, wished for the best bicycle and sports equipment. No one could accuse me of being above desire. But everything I desired was intensely and immensely practical. An Abyssinian commemorative stamp in mint condition, a Carthaginian coin, a sixty-three-pound ball of tinfoil, none of these things worked any magic on me. Was I missing something essential in life?

People who were excited by their collections seemed to find nothing else quite so exciting. In childhood collections, I knew, many people had early discovered clues to their adult vocations: the girl interested in doll clothes became a fashion designer, the boy with the rock collection grew up to become a geological engineer. Others, once grown up, never ceased the collecting that in childhood gave them such delight. Recall the young Vladimir Nabokov, dreaming of discovering the rare specimen that will introduce his name into the lepidopteran equivalent of *Who's Who*. In *Speak, Memory*, his autobiography, Nabokov writes: "I have hunted butterflies in various climes and disguises: as a pretty boy in knickerbockers and a sailor cap; as a lanky cosmopolitan expatriate in flannel bags and beret; as a fat hatless old man in shorts." In a letter to Edmund Wilson, written when Nabokov was forty-three, he describes his excitement at catching moths in traps set along tree trunks in Vermont, and closes by imploring Wilson: "Try, Bunny, it is the noblest sport in the world."

Bunny—"the Bunny," as Karl Shapiro refers to Wilson— never did, but then it is unlikely that he ever would have, for obsessions, which collections often tend to become, cannot easily be encouraged or passed along to the next fellow. I have never read a comprehensive definition of the word *collection*, but one might set out a working definition as "an obsession organized." One of the distinctions between possessing and collecting is that the latter implies order, system, perhaps completion. The pure collector's interest is not bounded by the intrinsic worth of the objects of his desire; whatever they cost, he must have them. Except in the case of the rare and exciting find that turns out to be a bargain, he generally knows that he is paying more than he probably ought to for the items in his collection, but he cannot help himself. If he has any introspection, he begins at some point to sense that his collection possesses him.

I knew a man who owned a Dunhill pipe. The pipe was expensive, as he readily allowed, but it was a superior piece of goods, and he enjoyed smoking, and therefore the pipe was judged worthy of the expense. In time he bought another. He alternated between the two pipes, which in the arcana of pipe smoking is said to be good for pipes as well as for smoker, and this made very good sense, too. Then he bought a third Dunhill pipe, whose elegant shape and lovely rosewood lured him into further and now no longer quite justifiable expense, and then a fourth. Unlike a plumber, I shall not lay this out pipe by pipe. Suffice it to say that in the fullness—the emptiness?—of time he acquired some twenty-odd Dunhill pipes. He continued to take pleasure in smoking them, or at least his favorites among them, but his pleasure in contemplating them, arrayed in their shapeliness and their rich woody luster in racks upon his desk, seemed even greater.

A bachelor, he lived on the twenty-ninth floor of a Mies van der Rohe building, where one night, well past midnight, a fire alarm sounded. When he stepped out of his apartment into the hallway, he, along with his neighbors, was instructed to avoid the elevators and to proceed quietly down the stairs. He had only time to return to his apartment for his bathrobe and—ah, you are a clever reader—his pipes. The fire turned out to be a minor one, the alarm a mere precaution, but that night, as he afterward related the story to me, he received another alarm, for standing there in the hallway in pajamas and robe, his arms filled with his pipes in their racks, he discovered what was really important to him. A man of learning and with a philosophical temperament to go with it, he was astonished at his own behavior.

A true collection ought to have—and a true collector is usually aroused by—an element of the hunt. In this sense, a collection of Dunhill pipes is not, technically, a true (or, better, pure) collection. One could, after all, with enough money, simply walk into Dunhill's, order the full line of the company's pipes, write a check, and be done with it. A true collector is excited by the rarity, above all by the apparent inaccessibility, of the objects of his desire. Money alone, to the exclusion of cunning and connoisseurship, oughtn't to be decisive. I not long ago heard a story about a Texan—such stories always seem to have Texans in them—who, wishing to become an art collector, made a beginning by buying, sight unseen, all the works presented in a fashionable contemporary show in New York. That, somehow, doesn't seem in the spirit of the thing.

Not that money doesn't generally lurk about the activity of collecting. Certain collections—gems, visual art, rare books—assume big money. But even collections of originally inexpensive items have a way of quickly getting expensive. Rare bubble-gum baseball cards can sell, among collectors, for thousands. At conventions of baseball-card collectors, ballplayers occasionally turn up to sign autographs for six and nine bucks a whack—and a pretty dreary whack it seems, at least to me. As eating is to touch, so miserliness is to collecting—the ultimate expression of the activity. The great misers of literature—Molière's M. Harpagon, George Eliot's Silas Marner, Balzac's M. Grandet—are essentially collectors who have cut out the middleman, the objects that make up a collection, and gone straight for the money.

Balzac describes M. Grandet as combining "the characteristics of the tiger and the boa constrictor"; such characteristics have not been unknown among collectors. The *New York Times* not long ago carried a story about a man, a collector of historical papers, maps, and books about Massachusetts, who in a New Hampshire bookstore discovered a rare first edition of Edgar Allan Poe's *Tamerlane* that he bought for $15 and that Sotheby's is expected to knock down for between $200,000 and $300,000. Describing his find, the man is quoted as saying, "I got very excited." "Very excited," though, is not likely to describe adequately the feelings of another man, a dealer in antique Judaica, also reported in the *New York Times,* who, along with a partner, was taken for $60,000 when he bought a counterfeit version of a twelve-page Passover Haggadah supposedly printed in 1482. The first is a case of a boa enjoying his engorgement; the latter, a case of having been engorged. Let in the dollar and you welcome the squalor.

Yet it will not do to think of collectors chiefly as greedy, or fixated, or snobbish, although these have doubtless been among the private pleasures felt by some collectors. To collectors generally a great debt is owed. Consider, to take a stellar case, the Medicis. They were not, as they say, a fun family, the Medicis, even though compared to the Borgias their family history reads like three centuries of "The Adventures of Ozzie and Harriet." Yet for all the family's faults—and toward the end of the line, in the late seventeenth and first half of the eighteenth century, these were not minor—its place on the honor roll of history is secured by its generous patronage to artists and its collecting activities. This place was permanently secured when the last of the Medici line, Anna Maria, before her death in 1743 at the age of seventy-five, in her will be-

queathed all the property of the Medicis, paintings and statu-
ary, books and manuscripts, furniture and jewels, to the suc-
ceeding grand duke, with one unalterable condition: that
"nothing," as Christopher Hibbert puts it in *The Rise and Fall
of The House of Medici,* "should ever be removed from Florence
where the treasures of the Medici should always be available for
the pleasure and benefit of the people of the whole world."

Collectors can be as different as Khalil Bey, a nineteenth-
century Turk who assembled one of the finest private collections of art in the Paris of his day, and Benjamin Altman, the
New York department store owner whose bequest of his art
collection to the Metropolitan Museum at his death in 1913 was
the greatest the Met had received up to that time. Khalil Bey
was a woman-chaser and a fabled gambler and a man who used
his art collection to elevate his position in Parisian society;
Benjamin Altman was deeply reticent and despised the notion
of using his art collection to advertise his business and kept his
treasures to himself and a close circle of friends in a gallery he
built especially for his collection in his Fifth Avenue home.

No less remarkable in his way was the Fra Carlo Lodoli,
who in eighteenth-century Venice began collecting Cimabue,
Giotto, and other fourteenth- and fifteenth-century Italian
masters at a time when these painters were altogether ig-
nored—Lodoli found their work among dealers in old clothes
and near junk—in favor of such High Renaissance painters as
Titian, Raphael, Correggio, and Veronese. In telling the story
of Fra Lodoli, Joseph Alsop, in his book on art collecting, *The
Rare Art Traditions,* at one point quotes Lodoli's pupil Andrea
Memmi on the clutter, common to the surroundings of all
collectors out of control, of the padre's quarters:

To make his finds, he searched the stocks of "ragpickers and Jews
who dealt in anything which had been discarded by others." Eventu-

ally, the finds became so numerous that the collection took over his whole life. The pictures were stacked, many deep, along the walls of his humble rooms. "There was nowhere to sit," except on "a pile of books or on his narrow cot, which had become his best sofa."

The tableau of Fra Carlo marooned among his masterpieces reminded me of a trip I made more than twenty-five years ago in New York to the apartment of a Russian emigré, a Kremlinologist, to pick up a manuscript he had written for a magazine on which I was a sub-editor. Any conversation that may have taken place during that brief visit has long since been washed away by the memory of the flood of paper that greeted me upon entering. Bundle upon bundle of pamphlets, pile upon pile of yellowing newspapers, column upon column of books, almost all of this material in Russian and in German, not so much dominated as inhabited the rooms I passed through. Amidst the intense disorder of this collection, this archive really, of material having to do with the Russian Revolution and its aftermath, the owner of the collection, a white-haired man of formidable physique, seemed diminished; so, too, did his companion, a Hungarian woman of Wagnerian proportions. Not since the paper drives of World War II had I seen so much paper in one place, such clutter raised to so high a power. I tried to imagine living amidst it; a son of the American middle class, with its regard for tidiness, I could not. Five or six years later, I read that the contents of that apartment had been bought by Stanford University for somewhere around $250,000.

Is there a moral to this story? Never throw anything away, I fear, is the way many might read it. Good advice this, so long as you have a house with eight or so bedrooms, a large basement, a three-car garage, and an outbuilding or two. For those of us who don't, the moral is not one we can easily live with. Yet I am nonetheless surprised by how often I meet people who have vast collections of one kind or another. A few years ago a man who wanted me to write a script for a one-man show about H. L. Mencken began our first meeting by handing me a newspaper clipping about his having recently sold a collection of Chicagoiana for more than $600,000. More recently, I met a man who has a collection of books published in the year 1902 and another collection of books that have "Jane" (his wife's name) in the title. This is, I suppose, more commodious than having a collection of Hudson automobiles, with extra parts stored in the attic (a collection of the kind owned by a man in Ypsilanti, Michigan, named Jack C. Miller), but I would just as soon stop with a collection of books published in the year 2102 and another collection with the name Shlomo in the title, and let it go at that. But I see that I have tipped my mitt, blown the gaff, let the cat escape the silken bag. Collecting, in three words, ain't for me.

Of course, I recognize the importance of the serious collector. Hilton Kramer, recalling the donations and bequests art collectors have made to museums, has remarked that "we are all, in a way, beneficiaries of the collecting enterprise." Scholars are, similarly, the beneficiaries of collectors of rare books and manuscripts. However mixed may be the motives behind such collecting, however mad may be the prices asked for art and rare books, if in the end the public benefits and learning progresses, then I say, "Croupier, spin the wheel!" I shall never in any case have the chips to play in these games, and so my choosing to stand back from them has something of the same moral authority as my decision not to attempt to qualify for the Olympics in the hammer throw.

It is at the level of what have come to be called—rather too cheerfully, in my view—"collectibles" that I have chosen to exclude myself. By now the word *collectible* has probably made its way into the most recent dictionaries; I take collectibles to be among those items that, though they might otherwise be considered useless, through their relative scarcity or rarity or novelty have become not necessarily intrinsically valuable but nonetheless deemed worthy of collecting. Stores catering to the collectibles crowd, selling old toys, railroad lanterns, framed advertisements, things well beneath the level of antiques but above that of garbage, are now dotting the modern cityscape. They tend to have such names as Eureka!, Fibber's Closet, Recollections. All very cute—assuming you like cute. I have heard of people who collect snow-showering paperweights, political campaign buttons, sheet music for once-popular songs, chewing gum from foreign countries. People take pleasure from these collections; they do not hurt anyone along their mildly acquisitive way. As the man in the joke says, "It's only a hobby."

Far from wanting a collection, I find that it takes concentration, care, and restraint *not* to collect. My wife and I currently have in our apartment perhaps fifteen hundred or so books; in my office at the university where I teach, I have perhaps another thousand. With little effort, I could double or even triple this number. I have striven not to do so: I do not look into book catalogues; I stay out of used-book stores, which I consider, for the bookish, the intellectual equivalent of pool halls; when I require a book for something on which I am working, I prefer in most cases to use library books. I give books away, I sell books, I try to be unsentimental in my decisions about keeping books, not permitting myself to believe that because I happen to have read a book I am justified in keeping it. And still the books roll in; and still the books pile up. They multiply like rabbits, descend like locusts, covering everything.

We do not have nearly so many records as books—perhaps, in all, two hundred or so albums. Nothing very exotic here, mostly recordings of the music of the great composers—no one

beneath Telemann or Saint-Saëns—played by the famous performers; some Cole Porter, Gershwin, Rogers and Hart, and
Noël Coward; some splendid jazz chosen by a friend with
flawless taste in this line. The more I learn about music, the
more music I want to acquire, and the temptation to buy more
records is always present, even though I find it difficult to clear
time for listening to the records we now own. Although I
suspect that I have the aural sensitivity of a rhinoceros, I am
also tempted to buy compact discs, which are supposed to
provide both better sound and greater convenience. We now
have a cassette player in our car, and I have begun—slowly,
cautiously—to assemble a small collection of tapes, for when
driving on moderately lengthy trips it is delightful to listen to
Bach, or Vivaldi, or Beethoven, or Mozart without the inter-
ruptions of commercials or the sometimes pretentious classical-
music-station announcers. A friend has offered to set up an
arrangement whereby I can record all our albums on tape.
Records and discs and tapes, and I don't even want to discuss
videocassettes, which, I gather, some people are now beginning to collect in a big way. To save space to accommodate all
this, perhaps my wife and I would do best to have ourselves
put on microfiche and turn the joint over to our possessions.
"Things are in the saddle," wrote Emerson, "and ride mankind." Waldo, baby, you don't know the half of it.

"Why didn't she try collecting something?—it didn't matter what," thinks the father of Fleda Vetch, the heroine of
Henry James's novel *The Spoils of Poynton.* "She would find
it gave an interest to life, and there was no end of little curiosi-
ties one could easily pick up." More than a soupçon, there is
a fully gravy boat of Jamesian irony in this passage, for Fleda
finds herself in the middle of the attempt of another woman,
one Mrs. Gereth, to save a house filled with antiques that she
has gathered over a lifetime and that are about to fall into the

hands of a future daughter-in-law whom she, Mrs. Gereth, despises. James never describes these antiques—"the *morceaux de musée,* the individual gems," as he calls them—for, being Henry James, he works by suggestion and indirection, but he is altogether clear on the hold they have over the characters in his novel. " 'Things' were of course the sum of the world: only, for Mrs. Gereth, the sum of the world was rare French furniture and Oriental china." And later he writes: "Yes,' cried Mrs. Gereth, with a fine freedom of fancy, 'there are things in the house that we almost starved for! They were our religion, they were our life, they were *us.* ' " Henry James well knew the power that mere things can take on if enough desire has been invested in them.

James himself seems to have had a proper appreciation for things without being bound to them. I have never been to Lamb House, the house James bought in Rye, Sussex, in his middle fifties and which he would later refer to as "my celibatorium," but I gather from photographs I have seen and accounts I have read that it was laid out and set up with an eye for comfort and quiet bachelor elegance. Having signed a long-term lease, James wrote to his brother William's wife Alice: "In the meantime one must 'pick up' a sufficient quantity of ancient mahogany-and-brass odds and ends—a task really the more amusing here, where the resources are great, for having to be thriftily and cannily performed." Thriftily, cannily, James must have performed, for all who visited him at Lamb House thought well of the place, including Edith Wharton, who knew a thing or two about houses and their decoration and who wasn't the least shy about being censorious in this or any other line.

So far as I know, though he appreciated beautiful things, Henry James consciously collected nothing. He did keep signed copies of books other writers presented to him. He had some two thousand books in his personal library, which was richest, according to H. Montgomery Hyde in *Henry James at Home*, in modern first editions, many of them of authors— Matthew Arnold, Walter Pater, Tennyson—published during James's own lifetime. About 250 to 300 of James's books were spoiled in an air raid of 1940 that destroyed the Garden Room at Lamb House, Montgomery Hyde reports, and many others were dispersed after his death. Some have been recovered, but, since James did not annotate the books in his personal library, the loss is less than tragic. Besides, as some people are meant to be distinguished ancestors rather than to have them, so Henry James was meant not to be a collector but to be collected.

On the back of the dust jacket of his book sits Mr. H. Montgomery Hyde, one stout Englishman, above a caption that reads, "H. Montgomery Hyde at Henry James's desk at Lamb House." I shall not describe the desk, other than to say that it is of the kind known as a secretary, with a front that drops down to provide a platform on which to write, and it appears to be in the style known as Empire. Whether it has any serious standing as an antique, I do not know; I do know that even if it doesn't, I should stand ready to pay $10,000 for it. There is not a single piece of furniture in our apartment that is worth anywhere near $10,000 but then neither has any of our furniture been owned by Henry James, Jane Austen, or John Dillinger. Ten thousand is a significant sum to me, yet I would pay it, without hesitation, for Henry James's desk. I want it because it belonged to James; I want it because it may well be talismanic. The more I think about it, the more I want it. I want it, as James himself might adverbially have put it, immensely and immitigably. I would be willing to go $12,000 for it, but not a penny more. (Letters from people offering to sell me socks, pen wipers, or baseball spikes allegedly once owned by Henry James will not be acknowledged.)

I not long ago noted with lofty contempt an auction that fetched some fancy prices for some of the belongings of Liberace. Cufflinks worth at most $500 went for $2,750; a grand piano festooned with small mirrored tiles and covered with a clear lucite top brought $42,500. But these at least are objects. The prices that autographs can bring seem to me astonishing, not to say a bit mystifying. An outfit in Chicago called Signature Gallery, advertising itself as a place "where you can buy your piece of history," refers to its "investment quality autographs" and offers for sale autographs by Napoleon, Churchill, Ty Cobb, and Elvis Presley. An acquaintance recently told me that he had sold a small packet of letters written by the poet Delmore Schwartz for $1,800. Hearing that, I thought how pleasing it would be to be sufficiently famous to take this a step further and write and sell the originals of one's own letters, sending the carbons or Xerox copies to one's correspondents, thus earning a handsome, immediate reward for keeping up with one's correspondence.

Had I Henry James's desk, you may be sure that I would not fill its drawers with stamps or coins, or line up along its writing platform demitasse cups or enameled eggs or various *tsatskes* from the Franklin Mint. Not that mine is a full-blown distaste for collecting such as is displayed by the young woman who is kidnapped by a butterfly collector in John Fowles's novel *The Collector*. She notes of collectors of all kinds, "They're anti-life, anti-art, anti-everything." No, my antipathy for collecting proceeds from what may be a deficiency in the single-minded organizational power required to mount a serious collection. Six or seven years ago, I thought about collecting fountain pens, and from time to time would stop in at second-hand shops to see if any old pens were for sale. I found an interesting pen or two, but soon grew bored by the whole thing. Another merit badge lost.

More important than my deficiency in organizational powers of the kind required for serious collecting may be an admiration I have always had for the ideal of traveling light. The first lesson a novitiate intellectual used to learn was a contempt for what was known as "materialism." This was not the same materialism that professional philosophers concern themselves with, but instead was a shorthand phrase for an interest in material comforts. The embarrassment at displaying too keen an interest in material comforts lingers today among academics, many of whom remain fearful of seeming to put things of the earth over things of the mind, so that the phrase "rarer than an English professor driving a Cadillac" is an altogether accurate figure of speech. But my anti-materialism predated by several years my first having heard the word *materialism,* and went beyond material comfort into the realm of sentiment. As a boy, I threw away the autograph book signed by my grammar school classmates and never for a moment considered buying my high school yearbooks. What did I need such stuff for? Encumbrances, extra poundage, sheer surplus. Better to slim down, move fast, travel light.

Few things are more productive of comedy than having an ideal that in one's life one hasn't lived up to for more than twenty minutes. Such, alas, has been my relationship to the ideal of traveling light. By the time I was twenty-six years old I had four children under my charge. How is that for traveling light? I have since my early twenties owned houses and apartments and thousands of books and pieces of furniture and appliances and much livestock (in the form of dogs and cats)—more, as you can see, traveling light. One of my fantasies is to fly to Europe with only the clothes on my back and a credit card in my wallet. In fact, I am fortunate if I can get away for a weekend to South Bend, Indiana, without having to hire gun bearers. Travel lightly, I always say, and carry a three-suiter.

Otherwise weighted down by life though I may be, at least, I have been telling myself, I do not have a collection. I do not harbor anywhere in our apartment a mini-museum: an assemblage of lead soldiers in Crimean War uniforms lined up in battle array, glass bells laid out in a large plush-lined case, a knotty-pine recreation room filled with bazooka shells, Japanese flags, and other World War II mementos, a closet full of music boxes. I have, thank you very much, been spared all that.

Or so I thought, when it occurred to me that in a locker in our basement there is a cedar chest filled with old magazine pieces I have written. A drawer under a bookcase in my office contains a number of my old manuscripts. In two different closets there are large storage boxes of my correspondence; one drawer in my desk holds little notebooks in which I have copied down quotations (the same drawer in which I keep folders with notes I have made for speeches and talks); another drawer has several notebooks filled with my journals. On two shelves in the closet in the room where I work rest extra copies of my own books. In that same basement locker there is a box of remaindered copies of my first book. At my office at the university there are more of my own books and copies of more of my magazine pieces.

No doubt I have left out a good deal, but I have mentioned enough, I believe, to make plain what ought to have been plain to me long before now—which is that I am far and away the greatest collector in North America, and hence certainly in the world, of the works of Joseph Epstein. To have struggled so long to avoid having a collection and to end up collecting oneself—ah, the bitter irony, the ironic bitterness, of it all. Meanwhile, if anyone out there happens to have a copy of a review I wrote about fifteen years ago of a biography of Aldous Huxley, I am prepared to trade for it a Xerox copy, with heavy editorial emendations, of an essay on collecting. What the hell, I'll even throw in two carbon copies of letters to our plumber and a receipt for a bill for a Cub Scout manual.

Short Subject

S HOULD YOU URGENTLY NEED to reach me, here, to
save time, are a few places you are almost certain
not to find me: browsing happily in the grain section of a health
food store, sitting under a dryer reading *Popular Mechanics*
during the final stages of a male permanent at Vidal Sassoon,
pasting up Thank You for Not Smoking signs on firing-squad
walls, shopping for a cabana suit at the M. Hyman and Son Big
& Tall Men Store. Unless you happen to live in Chicago, there
is every likelihood that you have never heard of M. Hyman and
Son, where they claim to "suit the big guy at discount prices."
I have no doubt that they do just that, but, reading the store's
advertising copy, it occurred to me that no one has ever called
me "big guy." Nor has anyone ever referred to me, as I seem
to recall their female co-stars in the movies used regularly to
refer to Clark Gable and John Wayne, as "you big galoot." Not
even the very plainest woman, let alone Marlene Dietrich, has
ever slung an arm around my neck, drawn me closer to her,
and exclaimed, "Kiss me, big boy."

If you begin to gain the impression that I am not one of M.
Hyman and Son's ideal customers, you are onto something.
Although I have been called many things, I have never been
in the least danger of being called Moose, Big Daddy, or

Bubba. Quite the reverse; I have always considered myself fortunate to have evaded being called Pee-Wee, or Half-Pint, or Shorty. In a grammar school skit for an assembly on Lincoln's birthday, I, at age eleven or twelve, as the shortest boy in the class, played Stephen Douglas, the Little Giant, opposite the Abe Lincoln of Jack Sheasby, the tallest boy in the class, in a sensibly abridged version of the Lincoln-Douglas debates. This feels like the place in the paragraph where I should insert something like the following sentence: "However, in the summer between my junior and senior years of high school I grew eleven inches to my present height of 6'2"." That summer I may in fact have grown three-quarters of an inch. I kept waiting to "shoot up," in the phrase popular at the time, but never did. Today, in my early fifties, I am beginning to believe it may never happen.

Just how small is this guy anyhow? you may by now be asking. Have I all these years, you are perhaps wondering, been reading a dwarf? I shall set out some figures presently, but first I think it mildly interesting that most curiosity about male height seems to be not about how tall but about how short certain men are—and by certain men, I chiefly mean certain movie actors. When I was a boy there was much guessing about the exact height of Alan Ladd. Figures as low as 5'2" were bruited about. It was said that Ladd had to stand on a box to kiss his leading ladies. Edward G. Robinson, James Cagney, John Garfield, George Raft, Spencer Tracy were scarcely suited to be power forwards in the National Basketball Association; Humphrey bloody Bogart is said to have been no more than 5'5 ½ " or 5'6", sweetheart.

Now it is the height of Robert Redford and Paul Newman that is in the flux of controversy. Evidently neither man will divulge his exact height. One would think that the science of investigative reporting could find a solution to this problem—

have Bob Woodward or Carl Bernstein stand next to them and make some elementary deductions. Thus far neither Butch nor Sundance will apparently measure up. Estimates on their respective heights run from 5'5" to a respectable 5'10". Both actors are said to be rather touchy on the subject. Upon meeting either of them, it is probably wise not to begin your conversation by saying, "Loved your last flick, little guy."

I am nowhere near so touchy about my own height, though it, too, is in that same controversial flux. Nothing pleases a fat man more, said A. J. Liebling (himself a very fat man), than to be called muscular. What, similarly, pleases a short man is to be asked, "What're you, about 5'10"?" I was once asked, "What're you, about 5'9"?" and I glowed for a full week. I think of myself as 5'7", but I can't seem to get a clear consensus on it. I not long ago wrote an essay about living in Little Rock, Arkansas, where I have lived at two different times in my life, and in the course of the essay mentioned getting a letter from a Southern journalist who remarked that I was a small legend in Little Rock. In the essay, I noted this and my answer, which was to say that I didn't know about the legend but, being 5'7", I would accept the small part. The editor of the magazine in which the essay appeared, a friend of many years, changed my copy to read "but being *under* 5'7"" (italics mine, vicious tactlessness his), which is what I would call heavy editing.

Unfortunately, he turns out to have been factually correct. A few months later, I had a physical examination, during which I weighed in at 135 pounds and measured 66 ½ inches. When the physician wrote these figures down, he asked, rather perfunctorily, "What did I say, 67 ½ inches?" I nodded, lying, and added, "I believe so." I am now down in my own medical records at 5'7 ½ ". But what will happen when I next go in for a physical and it is discovered that I am in fact only 5'6 ½ "? Will my physician feel that I am too young to be losing height so rapidly? Will he order various CAT scans and other tests to be run in search of the cause of my lost inch? Will I be sent off to the Mayo Clinic? Or perhaps to Zurich, where there is doubtless a lost-height specialist, a man I imagine to be 4'11" with thick glasses and an impenetrable German accent? Complicated stuff, height, and not merely, as the sports announcers are wont to say about baseball, football, golf, and other sports, a game of inches.

Somerset Maugham, who was 5'7" and none too pleased about it, says somewhere that the world is an entirely different place to a man of 5'7" from what it is to a man of 6'2". Maugham's is a telling and true point, so long as one does not push it over into the chief psychological cliché about shortness. I refer to the notion that short people, in particular short men, tend to overcompensate for their size through outsized aggression and ambition. In this reading, T. E. Lawrence, had he been five or six inches taller than his 5'4", could have devoted all his time to his wretched translation of Homer and let the Turks and the Arabs fight it out on their own. Ambition, ample and aggressive ambition, turns up in every shoe size. In literature, for example, Ivan Turgenev and George Orwell were nice-sized boys; so, in politics, were Franklin Delano Roosevelt and Charles de Gaulle. The theory of compensation, as an explanation for the behavior of small men, comes up way short. (Good old language, it never lets you down.) One of the nice things about having been Napoleon (at 5'2") is that at least no one could ever accuse you of having a Napoleonic complex.

Not that size doesn't have multitudinous influences on one's life. Although there have been witty big men—Oscar Wilde comes first to mind—wit and humor seem more in the province of the smaller man. Chaplin, Keaton, the Marx Brothers were all small men. We expect a comedian to be small. He may also be fat. W. C. Fields was fat; so was Oliver Hardy. Fat is funny, small is funny. Lou Costello, of Abbott & Costello, was small and fat—a winning comic combination. Tall isn't funny, perhaps owing to its being too imposing, even slightly menacing. Tall and handsome conjoined are, with rare exceptions, especially unfunny. One can always fall back on being the tall and silent type, of whom, in the movies, Gary Cooper was the apotheosis. But if one is small and silent, one is likely merely to be counted shy. Small men are under an obligation to do more talking; perhaps this is why so many among them are always joking.

We all have certain expectations about the physical size of the writers we read—expectations that are often wildly mistaken. One of the nicest compliments I ever received came from a man who, upon meeting me after having read my work for many years, remarked that he expected a fatter man. "You are too slender to be so funny," he said. So delighted was I by the remark that at my next meal I had two desserts. Along the same line, I always thought Chekhov short, possibly for so doltish a reason as his mastery of the short story. (He turns out to have been a bit taller than average and, when young, movie-star handsome.) Tolstoy, whom I should have thought tall, was smallish though sinewy; I have seen him described as a giant dwarf. William James had the elongated head of a tall man but was rather short; his body, after that fine head, rather disappoints. I tend on the other hand to think of Shakespeare, about whose height I know nothing, as having the large head of a short man. I recently read that Freud was 5'8", though he looks smaller, as do all his early followers. No one who has ever seen a photograph of Freud and his circle would mistake it for a photograph of the Los Angeles Lakers.

I should have guessed that Jane Austen was small, chiefly because of the delicacy of her charmingly oblique observations. Wrong again. According to J. E. Austen-Leigh's memoir of his Aunt Jane, "in person she was very attractive; her figure was rather tall and slender, her step light and firm, and her whole appearance expressive of health and animation." In her novels Jane Austen frequently describes the figure and carriage of her characters, and it will scarcely come as a surprise that she held some extremely interesting views about size. Reading along in her novel *Persuasion,* I discovered Miss Austen writing of a tertiary character that her amplitude made the expression of sorrow appear unseemly: "Mrs. Musgrove was of a comfortable substantial size, infinitely more fitted by nature to express good cheer and good humour, than tenderness and sentiment. . . ." Then, to reinforce her point, Miss Austen adds:

Personal size and mental sorrow have certainly no necessary proportions. A large bulky figure has as good a right to be in deep affliction, as the most graceful set of limbs in the world. But, fair or not fair, there are unbecoming conjunctions, which reason will patronize in vain—which taste cannot tolerate—which ridicule will seize.

The point is quite indefensible, even a little crazy, yet absolutely true: there is something slightly appalling about the spectacle of a large person expressing sorrow. When a small woman cries, she weeps; a large woman, doing the same thing, is more likely to be described as blubbering.

Dorothy Parker, herself a small woman, caught the same point in "Big Blonde," her best story. Her heroine, a former model named Hazel Morse, is a large sensual woman prevented by her nature from introspection and by her many men friends from giving vent to the sadness that so often swamps her. Big babes are not permitted to give way to depression, and Dorothy Parker emphasizes that women of Hazel's kind, who don't mind having a fellow who buys them clothes and maybe pays the rent, all tend to be large:

They were all big women and stout, broad of shoulder and abundantly breasted, with faces thickly clothed in soft, high-colored flesh. They laughed loud and often, showing opaque and lustreless teeth like squares of crockery. There was about them the health of the big, yet a slight, unwholesome suggestion of stubborn preservation. They might have been thirty-six or forty-five or anywhere between.

The largeness of such women as Hazel Morse seems only to add to their vulnerability. When Hazel fails at an attempt at suicide through an overdose of Veronal tablets, a physician, looking down upon her large rumpled body, pronounces, "You couldn't kill her with an ax." There is a line whose jolt could drop a rhino.

If large men and women are nearly condemned to being robust, sporty, and full of high spirits, small men and women, however naturally full of bonhomie they may be, are often thought devious. In literature, treachery is frequently assigned to small people. Many of Robert Louis Stevenson's villainous characters turn out to be small; when Dr. Jekyll transmogrifies into Mr. Hyde, for example, he becomes shorter. I don't recall if Shakespeare ever refers to Iago's size, but no one, surely, would put him above 5'8". Cassius, of course, is "lean and hungry," but was he also short? An economist with whom I discussed this felt that Cassius is best thought of as having the head of John Kenneth Galbraith, though not quite his 6'8" frame.

"It's not what you have here," my father used to say, pointing to his flexed biceps, "it's what you have here," he added, pointing now to the right temple of his forehead. At 5'4" no Kareem Abdul-Jabbar himself, my father was fond of telling me the story of David and Goliath, with its salutary reminder of what a good little man can do. I have just reread the David and Goliath story, and, in retrospect, I'm not at all certain that it offers much in the way of consolation. To be sure, it took real courage to go up against this champion of Gath, "whose height was six cubits and a span"—by my reckoning 9'9", which makes him likely to have gone early in the NBA draft. David, a youngest son, is described as a "stripling"; he refuses armor, saying he hasn't earned the right to it. All very impressive. But the fact is that David got in the first and only shot— "And David put his hands in his bag, and took thence a stone, and slang *it,* and smote the Philistine in his forehead, that the stone sunk into his forehead; and he fell upon his face to the earth"—and scored something of a lucky punch; some might even compare it to a quick kick in the groin. I never raised this objection to my father. Nor, when he pointed to his biceps and then to his forehead, announcing that it was better to have it in the latter location than in the former, did I suggest, as it occurred to me often to do, that it might be best of all to have it in both places.

By the time I was seven or eight, I suspect I must have known that I was destined to be small and that, consequently, certain adjustments had to be made. Although I was a fairly good grammar school athlete, being small, I knew I was precluded from playing certain positions—first base in baseball, fullback in football—that called for being tall or powerful; I knew that it made no sense to swing for home runs or to attempt to knock the next guy off his feet through clean brutality. Violence as a mode of settling boyhood arguments was closed off to me, except with boys roughly my own size; in argument I would have to rely on cleverness and cunning. No point, either, in developing crushes on the taller girls in the class, no matter how pretty or sweet-natured they might be. By the time I was twelve, it was perfectly evident to me that central casting had not sent me to earth to be a tough guy, or the sort of boy girls would swoon over, or a hero generally. Central casting was a bit unclear about what role I was to play; I would have, over time, to develop my own.

I hope I have not given the impression that being smallish

was painful. It wasn't. I had enough up here—see figure 1, not shown, short man pointing to right temple—to avoid ever being tormented or even teased about being small. Besides, I wasn't as small as all that; I was even rather tall for a short fellow. Yet, given a choice, I should much have preferred to have been the toughest kid in the class and the boy all the girls were daffy about. Being small did, however, teach early the lesson that life has its unalterable conditions and limitations. Size, or more precisely height, could not be changed through diet or calisthenics, pills or surgery, or psychological self-improvement programs. Your height is the one card you cannot toss in in exchange for another.

The genius of Sir Laurence Olivier, I have heard it said, included his ability to act much taller than he was, and to do so absolutely convincingly. I find this most impressive. I do not think myself an altogether unimaginative person; I can imagine myself a woman, a member of other races, all ethnic groups, tremendously rich, completely broke, a Medal of Honor winner, on the run from the police. But what I cannot successfully imagine myself is a foot taller than my actual height. On many occasions I have attempted to do so. The most recent of these was on a sunny afternoon while watching a baseball game at Wrigley Field in Chicago.

Four empty seats to my right sat a man, in his early forties I should guess, shirtless, in cut-off jeans, gym shoes, a dark beard, aviator sunglasses; well soaked with beer, he was regaling four youngish women, who looked to be office workers out for an afternoon in the sun, with loud accounts of his sexual daring and astonishing virility. Had I been a foot taller—6'7", let us say, if you will permit me to round off that odd half inch in my favor—I do believe I should have spoken to the fellow. Standing well above him, I might have said:

"Sir, I won't trouble you more than a moment. Your

charm, I am sorry to report, has worn a little thin, and I must ask you to remain silent for the remainder of the game, with the exception of cheering for the team of your choice and singing "Take Me Out to the Ball Game" during the seventh-inning stretch. If these conditions seem to you too stringent, don't hesitate to say so, for I am sure another seat elsewhere in the ballpark can be found for you—and one I shall be delighted to carry you to, in a state of consciousness or unconsciousness, as you prefer. Do think about it."

A foot taller, might I not develop into a quiet, somewhat well-spoken, bully? Would I not suddenly find myself acting to rectify the many little rudenesses in life I find so wearying? I see myself, in a traffic jam, uncoiling my considerable length from behind the wheel of my car, stepping out into the street, my head high above the ruck, the calm enforcer, the man who straightens things out by speaking in the voice of true reason with just a hint in it of real menace. No, the more I think of it, the more I am inclined to believe my physique is nicely mated to my temperament, given my many passions, impatience, and strong opinions. It is probably best that I am not in a position to do much about these things except express them through talk and writing.

This same physique also neatly fits me for intellectual work. Not many university teachers, editorial workers, artists, my guess is, are on the select mailing list of M. Hyman and Son. Only among artists and journalists could Ernest Hemingway have got away with his bogus tough-guy act; the same act, attempted at the construction site or on the assembly line, would have had the old boy in the dentist's chair before lunch break. At most universities, however, it would have gone over beautifully. Outside the physical education department, faculties are not notable for their Olympic muscularity. If a university teacher is not short, there is every chance that he is underweight, overweight, has a slouch, is hiding a weak chin behind an unkempt beard, or is otherwise misfitted or mildly deformed. To walk around a university is to realize that natural selection never takes a day off.

Along with being a university teacher, an editorial worker, a bit of an artist—in sum, a member in good standing of the shorter classes—I am also Jewish. The notion of Jews as puny has been put to rout and final rest by the efficient ferocity of the Israeli army, or at least ought to have been. (Whenever he sees soldiers of the Israeli army on television, the comedian Jackie Mason reports, his first reaction is to think they are Puerto Ricans.) Yet I continue to think of Jews as characteristically short. Despite the notable Jewish boxers, power hitters, football and basketball players, I still think of a good-sized Jewish man as about 5'9". ("I'm a Jewish six-footer," someone once told me, "you know, about 5'10 ½".") A Jew much above six feet tall has always seemed to me overdoing it; he looks out of character, more than a touch odd, somehow slightly out of proper proportion. I think of such people falling into a category I call "Too Tall Jews," which has the same cheerful rhythm as the name of the 6'9" Dallas Cowboy defensive lineman Ed "Too Tall" Jones. If the late Harold Rosenberg, the art critic of *The New Yorker*, had not been 6'5" or so, would his criticism perhaps have seemed less cloudy? If Arthur Miller were not 6'2" or 6'3", would his plays have been more grounded in reality? Maybe so.

Forgive me for having dwelt so long on Jews and height, but being both Jewish and short I feel as if I belong to two ethnic groups simultaneously. When I learn, say, that Nijinsky was short, I feel an emotion akin to learning that Walter Lippmann was Jewish: "Ah," I say to myself in both cases, "one of our boys." Is there something similar to ethnic pride that might be called short pride? Not that I am about to begin wearing T-shirts that carry the message Short Is Beautiful, or When

You're in Love, the Whole World's Smallish. Yet I am not, apparently, alone in feeling short pride. A friend, who is also short and a baseball fan, recently revealed to me that he has assembled an All-Time All-Star Short Players team, composed of players all of whom are under 5′8″. Some of his selections are not surprising: "Wee Willie" Keeler at 5′4″ was a cinch to make the team. But I didn't know that the great Cub slugger Hack Wilson was only 5′6″. Sure'n' it's a great day for the Shortish.

The short have not exactly got long shrift in literature. There is the pathetic Tiny Tim, of course, and Walter de la Mare wrote a novel about a young girl's growing up—or, more precisely, not having grown up—titled *Memoirs of a Midget.* But most writers do not bother to describe their characters' height, unless it is extraordinary. Nor do most autobiographers mention how tall they are. How tall was Rousseau? He tells us everything else about himself, but not, to the best of my memory, his height. I have always imagined Ben Franklin short and John Stuart Mill tall, but I don't think either refers to his height in his classic autobiography. Nor do I remember Henry Adams anywhere remarking that he is quite short—no more than 5′4″ or 5′5″, I'd say, judging from photographs. Would he have been less sour, I wonder, at 5′11″? Would the country have looked different to him at 6′1″?

Montaigne informs us that "I am a little below medium height" and that, frankly, it bugs him. It is not only a serious defect, he says, but a "disadvantage, especially for men in command or office; for the authority given by a fine presence and bodily majesty is lacking." He quotes Aristotle saying that little men may be pretty but not handsome. Warming to his subject, Montaigne adds:

Where smallness dwells, neither breadth and roundness of forehead, nor clarity and softness of eyes, nor the moderate form of the nose, nor small size of ears and mouth, nor regularity and whiteness of teeth, nor the smooth thickness of a beard brown as the husk of a chestnut, nor curly hair [Montaigne was bald], nor proper roundness of head, nor freshness of color, nor a pleasant facial expression, nor an odorless body, nor just proportion of limbs, can make a handsome man.

It's almost enough to cause a man under six feet to send off for elevator shoes.

Henry James, whom no one is likely to have described as rangy, occasionally mentions the height of his characters, but chiefly, in my recollection, when they are especially small. A secondary character in *The Ambassadors* named John Little Bilham is referred to everywhere in the book as "little Bilham" because of his diminutive size. In *The Princess Casamassima*, the novel's tragic hero Hyacinth Robinson is time and again described as "little Hyacinth," even when he grows to adulthood. I once asked a class to whom I was teaching the novel why James seemed continually to emphasize Hyacinth's smallness. I was able to convince them, through the usual strong-arm tactics, that the answer might be because, given Hyacinth's relation to two women in the novel, James, by stressing his character's littleness, wished to take him out of sexual contention. One of the two women, the working-class Millicent Henning, for example, is always described as large and robust, and therefore any notion of Hyacinth being her lover is disqualified. "How small, exactly, do you think Hyacinth is?" I asked, hoping someone would answer five feet, perhaps 5'2" at the maximum. "Well, how small is he, Miss Palmer?" I asked, when no one cared to hazard a guess. "I don't know," she said. "I suppose about your size." Ah, another magical moment in teaching.

"Stand tall, soldier," I can recall our elegant, whippet-lean 6'2" training sergeant Andrew Atherton bellowing, generally as a prelude to chewing out a recruit. Tall, for him as for most people, clearly was an approbative. In bygone movie days, tall was linked up with dark and handsome to describe, say, Cary Grant. Short, dark, and handsome somehow isn't the same. Splendid to be big-hearted, but you don't want to be thought small-minded. You want to be careful, too, about coming up short. *Petty* derives from *petite*, which is of course French for *small*. Small-fry, small change, small beer—all convey the notion of triviality. The word *little* has become an intensifier, applied to people who are not themselves necessarily small, chiefly to add a dollop of contempt or to suggest insignificance, as in "that little fool," or even "what a little monster he has turned out to be." In short (so to speak), the language is loaded against us.

Still, I can recall a time when being tall seemed to have its own drawbacks. A tall young girl was usually a shy young girl, and often today, most touchingly, still is. Tall boys came in two varieties: thin and gangly or thick and oafish. To have been more than, say, 6′3″ in high school and even college was an almost certain guarantee of being ill-coordinated. With occasional exceptions, in sports the very tall seemed to convey an aura of hopelessness. (To be very tall and not compete in sports was, worse, to convey an aura of freakishness.) In basketball, where great height was an obvious advantage, the very tall were instructed to hang around near the baskets in the hope that the ball would fall into their hands, whereupon they could pass it along to someone shorter who would know what to do with it. At a side gym at the University of Illinois sometime in the middle 1950s, I recall watching no fewer than three coaches attempt to teach a 6′7″, rather thickset freshman basketball player how to jump. I felt as if I were watching three trainers working with a bear.

As if to underscore the fundamental difference between the

tall and the small, in the Chicago high school system of my boyhood two basketball divisions were created: junior basketball was for boys 5'8" and under; senior basketball for boys 5'8" and above. Connoisseurs tended to feel that junior basketball was superior; the players were better coordinated, size couldn't replace skill, the game was quicker and more sophisticatedly played. Junior basketball in Chicago may have been one of the few occasions in all Western history when a substantial number of young males lied about their height—lied, that is, downwardly. Each year there was an official measuring-in for junior basketball, and many boys who were 5'9" or 5'10", preferring to play junior ball, slumped and slouched up to the measuring standard, trying to lose an inch or two through poor posture. Many were the stories about boys staying up all through the night before in the hope that lack of sleep would diminish their already modest size. Of an older kid in our school named Harry Shadian, who was very kind to me when I was a freshman, it was said that, in the attempt to "measure in" for juniors, he stayed up for two full nights drinking coffee and smoking cigarettes while carrying another boy named Dick Burkholder on his shoulders. The picture of the two of them continues to exert its fascination. While Harry Shadian was smoking and drinking coffee, what, I have wondered, was Dick Burkholder, perched upon his shoulders, doing? Not, I suspect, eating watercress sandwiches and reading La Bruyère.

Not only was junior basketball abolished in Chicago in my sophomore year in high school—providing one of the few serious disappointments in my otherwise agreeable youth—but then, ten or so years later, as if the needle of evolution had jumped eight or ten grooves, suddenly large boys and men became normally, in fact beautifully, coordinated. Earlier such extraordinary professional basketball players as Bob Pettit and Dolph Schayes, both well above 6'5", had moved with splendid fluidity, and one was occasionally treated to the spectacle of a quick and graceful fatboy on the football field, but all at once it seemed as if there were hundreds and hundreds of such athletes. Now one regularly saw men of 6'6", 6'9", 7', 7'2", who with an antelope-like bound could spear a fly ball just as it was about to leave a ballpark, or catch up with a man a foot or so shorter who had a twenty-yard lead, or pop into the air with the clarity and tautness of Massine, except that Massine, at the end of such an effort, never bothered to finish off with a three-sixty, double-pump, in-your-face, slam diddle-do dunk. Such men had names like Winfield, Bird, Strawberry, Magic, and Julius Erving (a name at whose close I always await either the name Horowitz or Shapiro, though it never arrives). These are men who regularly manage feats of coordination that men more than a foot shorter never even thought to attempt. In sports, it has made the old concept of "the good little man" rather obsolete. If one can't at least be more graceful than larger people, what, one has to ask, is the point of being small?

Or, to put it even more blatantly, who needs small men? Certainly one doesn't find much call for them in the classified section. When once briefly unemployed and hence a powerfully close reader of all employment ads, I do recall reading an ad asking specifically for small men—to clean out heating ducts in large office buildings in Manhattan. I regret having failed to apply; it could have been my one chance to have been turned away for being too tall. To return to sports, horse racing requires that jockeys be small, or at least light in weight, and diving, gymnastics, and figure skating favor smaller competitors, who have less body to control in the difficult physical configurations these sports all require. I tend to think of great mathematicians—Einstein and Ramanujan are two examples—as smallish men, and so, too, musicians: Beethoven, though stocky, cannot have been tall; Toscanini was distinctly short, and the contemporary composer and conductor Nicolas Slo-nimsky, in his recent autobiography, gives his height as 5′5 ¾ ″ (only a short man will take every quarter inch he can get). Psychoanalysts I have met tend to be short, and so, too, violinists. The shortest audiences I know are those that attend chamber-music concerts. Pope, Keats, and Swinburne were all exceedingly short, and so was Dylan Thomas, though, when fully sauced, his height was not the first thing most folks generally noticed about him. Disraeli and Churchill, the greatest English politicians, of the nineteenth and twentieth centuries, were both fairly short. . . . But surely you can feel me struggling here, thrashing around, seeking a pattern.

Character, Heraclitus famously says, is fate, but how does one's size affect both character and fate? Had Pushkin been taller—and he was quite small—might he not more easily have walked away from the foolish duel over his honor as a husband that ended his life when he was only thirty-eight? Taller, would Evelyn Waugh still have been, as Cecil Beaton recalls him from school days, "a tiny but fierce ringleader of bullies"—for in some sense Waugh remained a small bully all his days. Not all the short tough guys were in the movies. Edmund Wilson, another short man on the stocky model, despite his deceptively friendly and furry nickname of Bunny, often played the intellectual bully. At 5′4″ or so, Milton Friedman quickly makes it plain that he is not a man to be fooled with, at least in economic argument, where he could take your scalp off quicker than you can say Joan Robinson.

Height, if I may go off on a gender bender, is no very big deal for women. To be a woman above six feet carries, I am sure, its complications, but small women don't seem to operate under some of the same constraints, compulsions, pressures that small men sometimes do. The petite, moreover, is a category of feminine refinement. Women don't, when young, have to worry about being called Pip-Squeak, Twerp, or Half-Pint. ("Lay off the 'Shorty,' " says a petulant Spencer Tracy to Clark Gable at one point in the movie *Boom Town*.) Outside the duct-cleaning business, short men have never constituted an ideal type, but for a time in American life short women did. In the late 1940s and through the 1950s, the female type of the cheerleader—short, bosomy, full-calved, energetic—was much admired. Debbie Reynolds and, at a steamier level, Elizabeth Taylor represent the type in its Hollywood version. At my high school, they abounded; a few were named Mary Lou, but more than half seemed to be named Bobbie. "They may not be all that elegant," a wag with whom I went to school once remarked, "but they sure hold the road."

For a long while now the day of the Mary Lous and Bobbies has been over. Clothes have long since ceased to be designed with such women in mind, and they have no current representative in the movies. Tall and slender is nowadays the winning ticket, for both women and men. One sees this everywhere, and not least prominently in the elaborately mounted fantasies that are the magazine advertisements of the 5′6″ clothing designer Ralph Lauren (né Lifschitz), which are populated exclusively with lithe and lanky WASPs lounging about in cowboy, tennis, or boating duds. Any man even roughly Ralph Lauren's own size showing up in any one of these fantastical ads is as unlikely as the appearance of the Modern Jazz Quartet at a Hasidic picnic.

Height may be one of the few departments in life where the best break comes with being average. Extremes to either side can be a serious nuisance: to be either 4′10″ or 6′10″ carries its own bedeviling inconveniences—from finding shoes small enough to finding beds big enough. What today is average height is not altogether clear. Like the poverty line, the average height line, one assumes, is going up all the time. When I was a kid, 5'8" or 5'9" seemed average height for a man; now 5'10" appears closer to the average. The higher the average rises, the lower I fall beneath it. It could get worse. As some people grow elderly, their faces become blurry, as if someone had fooled with their contrast button; while others, usually those who are small to begin with, tend to shrink in size. I believe I am going to be one of the shrinkers. I could one day look back at 5'6 ½ " as my dinosaur age.

Although I have said that I cannot imagine myself truly tall, and although I have gone on about height at such (oops, sorry) length, neither do I tend to think of myself as small, at least not most of the time. Usually I think of myself as I appear to myself in my dreams: a man of average height, neutral looks, and medium build. And so in my workaday life do I think of myself until I stand next to someone quite large—as when I discovered myself, in the Los Angeles airport, standing alongside the 7'2" Wilt Chamberlain, into whose belt atop immense chocolate-colored velour trousers I found myself staring. At such moments I am brought up (sorry again) short. Yet otherwise I do not think overlong *(oy!)* about my physique and go about heightless and fancy-free.

Despite these disclaimers, I do feel there was something strongly formative about growing up on the short side. I cannot say why, exactly, but I sense that, had I been four or five inches taller, I should have been a radically different person than I am now. Discussing an acquaintance at lunch one day, a friend said to me, "He's the most underconfident tall man I know"—and then he paused, and added—"just as you are the most confident short man I know." That is an interesting distinction, and a compliment with lots of slack in it for interpretation. Does it mean that I am extraordinarily confident *for* a short man? Or does it mean that, given my shortness, it is remarkable that I am so confident. Life, like me, is too short to worry about such ambiguities—and besides, with my confidence, who cares? Yet I do have the distinct sense that my confidence and size, too, are somehow linked. As Emile Zola, Teddy Roosevelt, Lenin, Lord Beaverbrook, Fiorello La Guardia, Picasso, and a few other shortish fellows would be pleased to testify, there has never been a big demand for small underconfident men. Besides, as a man once told me, it isn't what you have here but what you have someplace else that counts. And that, Bubba, is about the size of it.

Smoke Gets in Your Eyes

JUST NOW the five most menacing words in the English language may well be: Thank You for Not Smoking. One feels about these five words that a sixth word is missing but strongly implied, and it could be any of the following: chump, creep, pig, scum, leper. The war on smoking, in other words, appears to be going extremely well. Smokers are being nicely segregated in the vast number of restaurants that provide smoking and nonsmoking sections. Smokers can no longer indulge in their pleasure during flights in the United States. Smoking is being increasingly restricted in public places, and in many offices and factories it is altogether outlawed. A European couple of my acquaintance, smokers both of Gauloises, *sans filtres,* report that in a Colorado hotel they were asked if they wanted a smoking or nonsmoking room. "Towards a Smoke-Free New York" runs the title of a *New York Times* editorial, urging state legislators to turn up the screws on tougher restrictions against smoking. No Smoking Except in Designated Areas is a sign one is likely to see more and more in the years ahead, and those designated areas figure to become more and more out of the way. Perhaps one day there will be a sign that reads, No Smoking Except in the Andes.

I am myself a former smoker. As J. Alfred Prufrock measured out his life in coffee spoons, I measured out mine in Kools, filtered and mentholated, generally not many fewer than forty a day. Like Mark Twain, I found quitting smoking easy—I had done it hundreds of times. But the last time I quit was on a cruise ship in the Mediterranean under a cloudless, sublimely blue Greek sky, and that was more than a decade ago. Still, I must confess that every so often a cigarette looks good to me, though a cigar, which I smoked only infrequently even during my smoking days, can look even better. Temptation is stayed, however, because I have come to believe almost every terrible thing that is said about smoking—that it causes cancer, heart attacks, emphysema, and just about everything else except bad citizenship. And now, of course, to smoke qualifies one for being a bad citizen, too, at least to hear some people tell it.

I quit smoking for the same reasons that many people turn to religion: out of fear and hope. I fear leaving the earth any earlier than need be, for I greatly like it here; and I hope to outlive my enemies, which forces me to stay in excellent physical shape. I cannot say that I felt all that poorly when I smoked, but then, as someone who has been blessed with almost continuous good health his life long, I haven't a clear comparison to go by. As the hypochondriacal Oscar Levant might have put it, after quitting cigarettes I suppose I felt a little less lousy. I coughed less, I ate more heartily, I breathed more easily at the top of the stairs. Where I really felt fine, though, was spiritually. Stopping smoking filled me with what I can only call fatness of soul. I thought myself in control of my own life, no longer hostage to a strong habit, now calm and in command, a beautiful human being—in all, rather a superior mother-grabber. I retained this belief for longer than was seemly. Nowadays, when I see someone obviously as addicted to cigarettes as I was, something of this feeling of superiority returns, at any rate until I remember to despise myself for harboring it.

Yet most smokers I know have a conscience in worse shape than mine. Many among them are smoking scared, and I note that even the most case-hardened smokers among my acquaintances have reverted to the more sissified brands of cigarettes: Merit, True, Carlton. When death doesn't worry them, social ostracism does. They light up guiltily, and puff away apologetically. They have come to be thought, and now think themselves, walking engines of pollution. A dear friend of mine used to turn her head so abruptly to the side when exhaling smoke, lest any float under the nostrils from her companions, that I worried she would sooner die of a broken neck than from lung cancer. "Nelly," I once said to her, "why don't you simply slip under the table and finish your cigarette in peace?" One of the saddest questions one can hear these days is "Do you mind if I smoke?" for it is at once an admission of weakness and a request for what has come to be taken as a grave imposition. I should not be surprised to learn that the question "Do you mind if I smoke?" is today fairly often answered, "Yes, actually, I do mind—very much."

Yet for decades we all lived comfortably enough with smokers and smoking and the smell of smoke. Now, suddenly—presto chango!—smokers have become the most hounded and perhaps detested minority group in America. Because of this, when I do not feel superior to them I feel sorry for them. People complain peevishly about the smell of smoke. They tend to cough around smokers, making plain their protest against smokers ruining not only their own health but the health of everyone around them. Smokers nowadays tend to be treated generally as if they have a distinctly anti-social affliction, like continuous belching, except that, unlike the belchers, they have brought it upon themselves, filthy weaklings. No single bit of etiquette in my lifetime has changed so radically and so rapidly as that connected with smoking.

Except for the odd case of the asthmatic or those specifically allergic to smoke, nonsmokers in the past rarely seemed to complain about smoking, or if it disturbed them they kept it to themselves. Of course, today some of those who are most puritanically unpleasant about smoking are ex-smokers. Beware of converts; they carry stakes and fagots and matches. But the real turning point for the weakening of the social position of smokers has been the increasing evidence that smoking is bad for one's health—downright dangerous, in fact. Where smoking was once a convivial part of social life, it has now become an edgy if not slightly closeted activity. I should not be surprised to learn that many candidates for public office find it politic to conceal their smoking from the voters. Smoking, in the current health-minded atmosphere, may even be thought to show bad character.

"Midnight Run," writes Stanley Kauffmann in the *New Republic,* "has more cigarette smoking in it than any American film I can remember since the era of cigarette-danger consciousness began." Before this time the movies provided some interesting smokers. Humphrey Bogart was an almost perpetual cigarette smoker in the movies in which he appeared, and very much an unfiltered type generally. Edward G. Robinson smoked cigars in his movies, as did Sidney Greenstreet. Peter Lorre smoked in the Continental style, the cigarette perched perpendicularly upward between his thumb and index finger. Among women, Lizabeth Scott and Marlene Dietrich had rich, raspy cigarette voices, thought by some—myself among them—to be very sexy. Miss Dietrich wielding a cigarette holder could make an adolescent boy quickly forget any baton twirler he might ever have admired. But easily the most im-

pressive female smoker was Bette Davis; she could make the simple act of smoking a cigarette into a high dramatic gesture, like falling off a cliff.

Miss Davis has the female lead in what must be the smokiest movie ever produced, *Now Voyager* (1942). The male lead is Paul Henreid, who is perhaps best remembered for playing Victor Lazslo, the French freedom fighter who is Ingrid Bergman's husband in *Casablanca*. Although I don't know Paul Henreid's nationality, in his movies he seemed to represent gentle European masculine elegance to the highest possible power. The plot of *Now Voyager* is too sentimental to bear recapitulation. The movie deserves to be seen, however, purely for its smoking, which is nothing short of *exquisito*. *Now Voyager* is the movie in which Henreid regularly places two cigarettes in his mouth, lights both, and deftly hands one to Miss Davis, who inhales from it dramatically. Through the better part of the movie Miss Davis and M. Henreid speak to each other through cumulus clouds of smoke. The movie ends not on a passionate kiss but on a languid smoke, and a fine sexy smoke it is. Miss Davis and M. Henreid smoking in evening clothes over the rail of an ocean liner are, somehow, sexier than any two contemporary actors I can think of who, clean lungs and all, are going at it on screen hammer and tongs in the buff.

When actors now smoke in movies it is generally to underscore that they are villainous or weaklings or death-defying. Smokers in the movies are no longer elegant, in the style of Louis Hayward or George Sanders, who seemed not so much to smoke as to wear their cigarettes. Nor do they avail themselves of such dashing appurtenances as slender silver cigarette cases, of the kind Fred Astaire was wont to slide out from the inner breast pocket of his dinner jackets, or initialed gold cigarette lighters, of the kind that Adolphe Menjou or Noël Coward used blithely to flick under their own cigarettes. So common was smoking in the movies of the thirties, forties, and fifties that, my guess is, an actor, even if he didn't smoke, even if smoking made him ill, probably had to learn to handle a cigarette, the way he might have had to learn to handle a horse, because a great many roles required it. Today such an actor could protest having to smoke in a movie and in a trice have the Surgeon General, the PTA, the EPA, the environmentalists, and the full forces of (to adopt a phrase used in the Spartacist League journal *Workers Vanguard*) "health fascism" on his side.

Novels of the same vintage tended to be heavily nicotinified. In them, characters were often "inhaling deeply," or "exhaling the smoke slowly," or "flipping away the butt disgustedly." It gave a character something to do at the close of a line of dialogue. Most writers of that day—the twenties through the fifties—seemed themselves to be smokers, at least if one goes by dust-jacket photographs, and a lot of smoke seems to have seeped into their books. "Slowly, without turning his head," writes John O'Hara in *Appointment in Samarra*, "he pulled himself up to a half sitting position and reached out for the package of Lucky Strikes on the table between his bed and Caroline's bed." Later: "He turned. It was Father Creedon. 'Oh, Father. Good evening. Cigarette?' 'No, thank you. Cigar for me.' The priest took a cigar from a worn black leather case." And later still: "There was no newspaper on the table, but he did not want to speak to Mrs. Grady, so he sat there without it, not knowing whether the damn paper had come, with nothing to read, no one to talk to, nothing to do but smoke a cigarette." I didn't make a count, but *Appointment in Samarra* may well be a sixty-cigarette novel.

In those days a cigarette, plainly, was a novelist's friend. When nothing was happening, he could let his characters knock off for a smoke. In the current day, if a character in a novel smokes, it is likely to be merely another of his or her problems. "She takes a drag on her cigarette," a line in a contemporary story reads, "and inspects her varicose veins. . . ." In a novel by a young writer named Michael Chabon entitled *The Mysteries of Pittsburgh* rather more marijuana than tobacco is inhaled, but when a cigarette is smoked it is not identified by brand. (In O'Hara, whether a man smokes Lucky Strikes or Camels tells an informed reader a little something about the man.) And sometimes the facts of smoking are got wrong. "I smoked a cigarette in the rain," writes Michael Chabon, "which is the best way to smoke a cigarette." This, in my experience, is not true.

My first cigarette was smoked in the rain; make that my first five or six cigarettes. The brand was Herbert Tareyton, cork-tipped but unfiltered, rather loosely packed, so that filaments of tobacco stuck to one's tongue. I and my friend Norm Brodsky, who was puffing away along with me, were twelve. Tareytons were Norman's father's brand of cigarettes; my father smoked cigars, though on the rare occasion when he bought a pack of cigarettes it was usually Tareytons, too. We bought the cigarettes at Simon's Drugstore one rainy school-day afternoon. Lighting them in the rain wasn't easy, and smoking them, when raindrops first blotched, then dampened the paper was no cinch either. My recollection is that we each smoked five or six cigarettes, and then, lest it provide incriminating evidence, tossed the rest of the pack in the bushes. We can scarcely be said to have enjoyed the cigarettes we did smoke, though neither of us became the least bit sick, as young boys, toward the end of being taught a lesson, are supposed to become the first time they smoke. Norman and I both went on, as it turned out, to distinguished smoking careers.

I cannot recall the exact moment when I decided to become a regular smoker. Doubtless it was linked to the realization that

I was not destined to win glory as a high school athlete. The seal was set on this realization late one afternoon deep in the autumn of my fifteenth year. A fairly lowly sub on our school's frosh-soph basketball team, I was seated at my accustomed place toward the end of the bench next to a boy named Les Handler in the drafty gym of Kelvyn Park High School on the west side of Chicago. Les and I only rarely got into games, a situation to which I had become sadly resigned but to which Les could not quite reconcile himself. Sitting there on the bench, he had become a gonfalonier of grievance, of a not highly witty order I am bound to report, and as each game progressed he provided me with a running commentary in which he didn't mind remarking that many of the boys who played ahead of us on our own team were really quite (I euphemize) excrementitious.

Les was going on in this vein at Kelvyn Park that dark autumn afternoon when, with four and a half minutes left to play and our team well ahead, Coach Eugene Fricker called out, "Epstein, Handler." We left our places on the end of the bench to take up a position of readiness, on one knee, awaiting a time-out or a foul so that we could go into the game. Four and a half minutes, for us, was a substantial block of time—substantial and potentially delightful; it stretched out before us luxuriously, like the promise of a weekend with, say, Rita Hayworth. Except that no time-out was called nor any foul committed, and as the buzzer sounded for the end of the game, Les Handler and I were still in empty readiness on one knee alongside Coach Fricker.

Dressing in the dank Kelvyn Park locker room, neither of us spoke. I, sunk in despondency, had nothing to say. Les had already used up all his profanity in his game-time commentary; besides, the English language was deficient in that it failed to provide words adequate to his anger. Now dressed, we went off together, not wishing to ride home with the other team members. All that was left to us by way of giving vent to our extreme frustration was to break training. Not that anyone cared if we did, you understand, but it seemed the least we could do. We were too youthful to buy liquor; drugs had not yet come on the scene. Instead, wearing leather jackets and carrying our gym bags, we walked into a corner mom-and-pop grocery store and emerged with two Pepsi-Colas, a box of Dolly Madison chocolate-covered doughnuts, and a pack of Lucky Strikes. It would not be the last time that a cigarette would present itself as a consolation.

Ours was a high school in which, I would guess, roughly half the kids smoked, with boys, I would guess again, more active in this line than girls. Smoking was an emblem of adulthood, the most readily and cheapest available (cigarettes were then twenty-five cents a pack), and the ideal had not yet become to remain youthful into old age but to act as grown-up as possible when one was young. Many of my classmates—not all of whom would go on to college—appeared to have attained a quite astonishing simulacrum of maturity; they dressed, looked, and took themselves for adults. So it seemed the most natural thing in the world, when they briefly interrupted a heavy conversation about cars, pro football, or the mysteries of sex, to slide a pack of Chesterfields or Old Golds out of their shirt pocket, tamp down a butt, light it with a Zippo or Ronson, and release a thin but authoritative stream of smoke.

Many though by no means all of my closest friends smoked. I cannot make out a clear pattern among those who did and those who didn't. Odd, is it not, the way some people are never in the least tempted by those habits that keep life jumpy if not always jumping for others of us: smoking, drinking, gambling, promiscuity. In the case of "the tenacious weed," as I have recently seen tobacco described, some people were instantly repulsed by it; some others failed to see the point of it; and a fortunate few could take it or leave it. I took to it straightaway, and by the age of sixteen was a full-time and altogether serious smoker. By a serious smoker I mean someone who begins and closes and otherwise punctuates his day with cigarettes.

Although my parents knew I smoked, I did not, in high school, like to smoke my first cigarette of the day at home, lest they think their charming boy already addicted to cigarettes, which of course I was. I waited instead until I was picked up for school by Ronald Harris in his 1949 blue four-door Plymouth. I was one of five passengers in that Plymouth, along with Ronnie Harris, who made six, all of us smokers. On wintry mornings, the Plymouth's windows shut against the cold, however sunny it may have been outside, inside that car it was like London on a particularly foggy night. Hams and loxes, I suspect, have been smoked in clearer air. I remember once, just after the Plymouth had been parked and we departed from it, looking back to note smoke curling out of it as if it had earlier been on fire. That I survived more than a year of morning rides in Ronnie Harris's mobile smokehouse leads me to doubt the claims of the anti-smoking campaigners about the dangers of what they call "secondhand smoke." Were these claims true, I should be writing this essay in a room in a Swiss sanatorium.

Emerging from Ronnie Harris's Plymouth, we all strode into a cavern with a long marble-topped bar known as Harry's School Store. It was at Harry's that I ate my first bacon-lettuce-tomato sandwich, which, with baseball and the light bulb, I number among the three greatest American inventions. Along with excellent BLTs, Harry's, at all hours, provided a heavy haze of smoke, which I added to before class, at lunch, and then again after school. I could apparently still go three- or four-hour stretches without requiring a cigarette, for, though I cut more than my share of classes, I cannot recall ever doing so because I was desperately in need of a cigarette. Instead I smoked when I could, in a jolly and by my lights sporty way, drawing smoke deep down, belching it out in perfect smoke rings, French inhaling, learning to light a matchbook match with one hand, exhaling smoke through my nose like an angry bull in a comic book.

Although it was not the chief reason I went to school there, the University of Chicago permitted smoking in classrooms, which I thought a fine thing. Students and professors both smoked away—so much so that, in the context of the serious-ness of the university, smoking almost came to seem an intel-lectual gesture. (French intellectuals were evidently also heavy smokers; Camus and Malraux, both of whom I then took for culture heroes, seem invariably to be photographed with ciga-rettes pendant from their lips.) Some of my instructors at the university were nervous smokers; several unattractively so, with nicotine-stained fingers and ashes dribbling down their rumpled lapels; a few, though, could make smoking seem an elegant tic and were able to use their cigarettes to underscore points the way other people used italics. Cigarette smoke itself came to seem part of the atmosphere of intellectual discourse.

My own smoking must have increased in intensity during these years. I chose not to study in beautiful old William Rainey Harper Library because I couldn't smoke there, and smoking concentrated my intellectual powers, or so I told myself. Hyde Park, the neighborhood in which the University of Chicago is located, is an enclave, then as now locked be-tween two tough slum neighborhoods, but I found that if I ran out of cigarettes after, say, nine or ten at night, I was still ready, after much hesitation and more trepidation, to run (I use the word here in its literal meaning) out for more. I was not yet ready to kill for a smoke but evidently quite prepared to be mugged for one.

An army is said to march on its stomach, but when it isn't marching, it is, at least in my peacetime experience of the military, smoking on its duff. The army hour, like the psychotherapeutic hour and the academic hour, is composed of fifty minutes, with the last ten minutes given over to smoking a cigarette. Cigarettes were cheap—fifteen cents a pack at the PX—and therefore plentiful. Every barracks, orderly room, latrine was decorated with red cans (known as butt cans) filled with sand for cigarette ashes and stubs. No reading matter was permitted the first eight weeks in the army, not even a newspaper, but the men who designed the extremely effective exercise in the breakdown in civilian personality known as basic training were not so crazy as to try to stop young troopers from smoking. "O.K., men, the smoking lamp is lit," one or another sergeant was regularly barking out during basic training. "Light 'em if you got 'em." I had 'em, I lit 'em.

Of the time I spent in the army, I should have to say that I liked the time spent smoking best, which was roughly a sixth. As a serious smoker, I tried in civilian life to keep to a military budget of one cigarette for every waking hour. This, though, proved difficult to keep, for so many of life's activities seemed to call for accompaniment by a cigarette. Coffee without a cigarette seemed unnatural; booze without a cigarette, impossible. A meal required capping off with a smoke, a fine meal with two or three. Emerging from the subway or completing any little trip or errand called for a nicotine reward. Picking up a cigarette while on the telephone came especially easy. In a minor crisis—a deadline looming up, an argument, tension of one kind or another—all cigarette budgetary bets were off, and I smoked whenever the nicotine twitch beckoned. I began to do things like drink more coffee to heighten the pleasure of smoking. ("It was never the sex, my dear, it was the cigarettes afterward" would make a good crack in a comic novel of the kind no one writes anymore.) King-size cigarettes had long since been on the market, but the genius had not yet arisen to invent what many a serious smoker among us really required: the all-day cigarette.

During this period, I became greatly enamored of the accouterments of smoking. Had I been a cigar smoker, I should no doubt have carried around a little gold cutter and kept a humidor box on my desk. Had I been a pipe smoker, the possibilities would have been endless; from pouches to racks to tampers to humidor jars to special lighters to little holsters— one could almost build a life around smoking a pipe. For a cigarette smoker the possibilities were much narrower. A cigarette holder seemed to work well for Franklin Delano Roosevelt, but if one wasn't actually president of the United States it seemed, for a man, a mite pretentious. Cigarette cases, very slender ones, monogrammed, of gold for women and of silver for men, best received as a gift from someone of the opposite sex, always struck me as a handsome touch. Offering a cigarette to a companion from one's cigarette case, then taking one out for oneself, tamping it down a time or two atop the closed case—here was a gesture fit for white tie, tails, and Fred Astaire. (Whether Fred Astaire really smoked I do not know, but in movies he handled a cigarette wonderfully well; no one was better at flipping a cigarette away.) By the time I could afford a silver cigarette case, cigarettes of differing lengths were being produced—one cigarette, it will be recalled, claimed to be "a silly millimeter longer"—which made it difficult to purchase a case, for one didn't know what length cigarette one might next be smoking. Somehow the cigarette case had already seemed a part of a permanently bygone era, an accessory fit only for drawing-room comedies, Somerset Maugham stories set in the Malay states, and smart New York supper clubs.

Which left cigarette lighters. At one time or another, I must have owned nearly every kind made. I have owned cigarette lighters that, in retrospect, have given more pleasure than the cigarettes they lit. I once owned a gold-filled Dunhill—purchased for forty-five dollars in 1965, a great extravagance—that increased my smoking by the simple delight that feeling its heft in my hand and lighting it gave; I was always playing with it, and as long as I had it out, I would, before putting it back in my pocket, use it to light a cigarette. As a wayward youth on a visit to New Orleans, I once watched the performance of a red-headed striptease artist named Reddi Flame, and of course it is precisely a ready flame that an efficient cigarette lighter confers. To reach over to light a woman's cigarette with an elegant lighter seemed a grand thing—still does. In *Lifemanship*, Stephen Potter mentions a man he names William Staines, who won the devotion of women sheerly through the perfection with which he wielded a cigarette lighter:

He had a rack of a dozen lighters, which he cleaned and put in order once a week. Before making for his girl, he would select one, fuel it, put in a new flint, taking care to choose a large and manly one for the tiny, frightened girl, or one, for instance, with cigarette case and pencil attached for the slightly oopsy girl. At precisely the right moment in the cigarette manoeuvre, fire would dart from his hand. He had trained himself to see a pretty girl feel for a cigarette across three platforms of Waterloo Station, as it were, and to be behind her, flame ready, before the cigarette was at her lips.

Potter claims that Staines's real genius was that "by concentrating on *one part*, he was able to suggest *the whole.*" Staines was so elegant with his lighter that most women went on to believe that everything he did must be an expression of beautiful manners—"even," Potter writes, "if she found herself left with the two heaviest bags to carry, and was asked to stand over them while Staines himself went into the refreshment room for a cup of tea."

I should not like to go on the road now selling cigarette

lighters, especially table lighters, which used to adorn the coffee table in most middle-class homes but which have now all been removed. Owning a tobacco shop also strikes me as a difficult way to become wealthy, though I can remember when tobacco shops were almost as common as gas stations. The ultimate tobacco shop was Dunhill's; today, alas, it is more and more given over to selling clothes and costly kitsch. I used to go into Dunhill's near an office I once worked in, usually to buy a pack of their cigarettes or a cigar. The chief clerk in the tobacco section was a lower-middle-class Englishman who was immensely knowledgeable and not in the least snobbish. He was able to discuss the arcana of pipe tobacco mixtures in a manner that excited the interest of connoisseurs; he could tell you about the exact quality of the most recent shipment of cigars, which had such promising names as Dunhill Monte Cristo Colorado Maduro No. 1. In the humidor room, where boxes of cigars were kept in vast quantities, powerful men rented small lockers in which they stored their own expensive cigars (including occasional importations from Cuba that came by way of Canada) under ideal conditions. The names on these lockers—those of the mayor, a gossip columnist, judges, wealthy merchants, the conductor of the symphony orchestra, a cardinal—represented a healthy chunk of what once used to be called "the power structure." Cigars and power seemed to go together.

Cigar smokers were a different breed from cigarette smokers; they appeared more substantial, less nervous. While cigarettes seemed a habit, cigars seemed part of a man's character. One thinks of Winston Churchill, characteristically, with a tumbler of scotch in one hand, a good-sized cigar in the other. A photograph of H. L. Mencken on the wall above my desk shows him in a silk striped shirt, typing away, a cigar jammed into the corner of his mouth—and the cigar looks right. Groucho Marx used his cigar the way Charlie Chaplin used his cane: as a baton with which to conduct his madcap comedy. Although political cartoonists are fond of using the cigar as a symbol of the big-time capitalist, Bertolt Brecht, both an anti-capitalist and an anti-American, adored Virginia cigars. A cigar suggests prosperity, and, sometimes, corruption. The smoke in the infamous smoke-filled rooms in which political deals were made was, presumably, cigar smoke. Fight managers smoked cigars (usually chewing on the stubs); so, too, did gangsters who arrived at the upper echelons of their trade. Carmine Galante, an alleged Mafia guy, was killed in Brooklyn with a cigar actually in his mouth.

But the gentlemanly tradition in cigar smoking is richer than that of the thug and plug-ugly tradition. This tradition, largely though not wholly English, is one in which cigars were smoked in clubs and at table with port after the ladies had left the room. In this tradition a cigar becomes a gentleman's accessory, an appurtenance, like a walking stick or a fine pocket watch. Unlike these items, a cigar gave delight beyond that of mere possession. Arthur Rubinstein, who lived to the age of ninety-four, was turned on to cigars at thirty and claimed they gave him "untiring pleasure." Untiring pleasure is what Ernest Newman (1868–1959), the splendid music critic of the *Times* (of London), appears to be taking from the cigar he is smoking on the cover of the first volume of his *Essays from the World of Music*. A bald man in thick spectacles, sitting in a deep, heavily stuffed armchair, wearing a loose-fitting lounge suit, listening, one gathers, to music being played upon a phonograph, Newman holds a cigar, smoked about halfway down, in his right hand, a cigar that seems almost animate, rather like a pet, an object in any case most companionable. This, you feel looking at the photograph, is cigar smoking at a high level.

There is something not merely masculine about cigars, but

something that seems positively to exclude women. Cigarettes are androgynous, and can be shared between men and women. They have often been construed as an accessory to romance: "Here we are," runs a line from a love song from my youth, "out of cigarettes / see how late it gets . . . ," and so forth. None of this is true about cigars. Cigars are emblems of male celebration, used to mark the closing of a deal or the birth of a child. Lighting up a Macanudo, a Royal Jamaica, a Thompson Tampa, one feels a bit of a man of the world; and two men lighting up cigars together often feel a wholly masculine sense of intimacy. Unless they happen to be George Sand, women do not smoke cigars; most women, in fact, detest and protest against them, claiming it is their stench they abhor. The number of women who have made romance with a man conditional on his giving up cigars cannot be known. Kipling, in a poem of twenty-five rhyming couplets entitled "The Betrothed," wrote about a man whose fiancée asks him to choose between her and his cigar smoking. The poem's famous penultimate couplet runs:

> A million surplus Maggies are willing to bear the yoke;
> And a woman is only a woman, but a good Cigar is a Smoke.

My father smoked cigars, not very costly ones, at the rate of six or seven a day. Cigar smoke was one of the smells, a halfway-smoked cigar in an ashtray one of the sights, of my youth. I used to smoke an occasional cigar, but their chief effect upon me was to quicken my hunger for cigarettes. Pipes, which I also tried, were worse. I always liked the smell of burning pipe tobacco, unless I was the man burning it, in which case I scarcely smelled it, but had to concentrate my full attention on keeping the pipe from going out, my tongue from swelling, my clothes from being set aflame by errant ash, and my face from looking hopelessly smug and perhaps eminently punchable. Pipes were permanently out, but roughly a year ago I smoked a cigar, a cheapy Antonio y Cleopatra Grenadier (light wrapper), which I nursed through a nine-inning baseball game and which I enjoyed immensely, though I worried a bit about whether it would help put me back on the road to that dread Irish seducer, Nick O'Teen. My father, on the other hand, after smoking for more than half a century, one day in his seventy-fifth year stopped cold, without fuss or bother, and never looked back.

"Life is a sum of habits disturbed by a few thoughts," wrote Valéry, and of these few thoughts perhaps none is more disturbing than that having to do with giving up one of those habits. I don't remember exactly when it first occurred to me to stop smoking—I may have had a bad cold, or a case of flu—but, even though I did not succeed in quitting, life was never quite the same afterward. I now inhaled smoke and exhaled guilt. I could no longer enjoy smoking nor, since I found it very difficult to quit, could I enjoy not smoking.

Few things can more quickly reduce one's generous estimate of one's own character than attempting to quit smoking cigarettes. To know oneself thoroughly hostage to those little white tubes of tobacco damages one's sense of self-grandeur, not to speak of putting a frightful crimp into one's utopian politics. (In *Darkness at Noon*, Arthur Koestler is very good at showing how important cigarettes are to Rubashov, his defeated revolutionary hero.) During lost bouts with quitting smoking, I was not above going up to friendly-looking strangers who were smoking to ask, in a parody of Bogart in *The Treasure of the Sierra Madre*, "Excuse me, but do you happen to have a cigarette for an ex-serviceman?" Late in the afternoon of a day on which I had not smoked, my mind might vaguely drift off to imagining a personal tragedy of a kind that would permit me to return to cigarettes: "Oh, yes, his entire family has been wiped out in a flood. It's no wonder he's returned to cigarettes, poor man." Even now, a decade after no longer smoking regularly, I appear in one of my own dreams with a cigarette in my hand, disappointed with myself for having gone back to smoking.

When I failed at quitting smoking, I thought it certain proof of my weakness of character. Now that I have quit smoking, am I entitled to think myself a man of strong character? Life offers its tests of character, but I strenuously doubt that quitting cigarettes is among them. Besides, I didn't quit smoking to improve my character, or to help clean up the environment, or to close in on physical perfection. I quit smoking because I was afraid of dying, or at least of dying any sooner than is absolutely necessary. I have no wish to give up my room in this comfortable and amusing resort even a minute before actual checkout time.

What I think quitting smoking may be about is the comedy of human resolution. The Virgil of this subject is the Triestine novelist Ettore Schmitz (1861–1928), who wrote fiction under the name Italo Svevo. The first chapter of Svevo's novel *Confessions of Zeno* is entitled "The Last Cigarette." In it Zeno Cosini, a Trieste businessman, undergoes medical and electrical treatments and finally psychoanalysis in the effort to give up cigarettes. All are abortive, despite his endless resolutions to quit smoking. No cigarette, after all, tastes quite so good as the last cigarette. What better, then, than to make every cigarette one's last? Or, when one has resisted smoking for several hours, the clean feeling in one's mouth, as every smoker and former smoker will verify, only makes one long all the more for another cigarette. "Directly I had smoked it," Zeno notes, "I felt remorse and again began making the very resolution I had tried to repress." With the making of fresh resolutions, the remorse felt at breaking them, and the remaking of renewed resolutions, the days pass agreeably enough for Zeno. So seem they to have done in Svevo's own life, for he was fairly clearly writing out of personal experience in *Confessions of Zeno.* Most photographs of Svevo show him cigarette in hand, and P. N. Furbank, one of his biographers, tells that, on his deathbed, Svevo, seeing his physician-nephew light up a smoke, asked for a truly last cigarette. Sad to have to report, he was denied it.

Do they, I sometimes wonder, order these things better in Europe? When I was last there, no maître d' asked me if I wished to sit in the smoking or nonsmoking section of his restaurant. People in the streets of Florence and Ravenna smoked away, near as I could make out, quite guiltlessly. A friend, a physician who is not himself a smoker, reports that on a TWA flight to Stockholm he and his fellow passengers were treated to a quite menacing lecturette about not smoking on the plane, except in designated areas, and especially about not smoking in the lavatories, where there were smoke detectors—and fooling with them, everyone aboard should know, was a federal crime. "Returning on SAS we found the Scandinavians much more humane," he writes. "They didn't mention any of this." On a flight I took from San Francisco to Chicago, before smoking was banned on most domestic flights, the chief stewardess announced that, owing to the crowdedness of the flight, there would be no smoking section at all on the plane, and hence no smoking, except in the first two rows of first class. A large number of people applauded, as if to say, "Good, let those smoking dogs suffer." When the writer Raymond Carver recently died, at the age of fifty, of lung cancer, the *New York Times,* in its obituary, saw fit to note that Carver was "a heavy cigarette smoker until he became ill," thus using the occasion of a man's death to deliver a little health sermon.

The time has long passed when Americans have looked to Europe as the font of all wisdom on living the good life; if anything, the traffic here appears to be running the other way, especially among the young in Europe, who glom on to almost all things American with real excitement. But Europeans have been sensible in thus far taking a pass on the new American health fascism, in which everything is subservient—not to the state, as under political fascism—but to the ideal of extending sheer biological life. I am myself someone who is not only immensely greedy for life but who, if the truth be known, lives pretty much according to most of the tenets of health fascism: pledged to the shining if utterly unheroic goals of clean lungs, clear arteries, tidy intestines, and a glowing carcass generally.

Although I appear to live with equanimity under this regime of health fascism, within me, still very much underground, a timid resistance fighter lurks. This is the fellow who, when he learns that a middle-aged man has bitten the dust while jogging, smiles inwardly and knowingly at the futility of efforts at human perfection; who is secretly pleased to hear that an obviously alcoholic woman has died, peacefully in her sleep, at the age of ninety-six; who is always delighted to know about any man or woman who beats the health odds by simply ignoring them. This same fellow is always advising me, when confronted by a temptation that might be hazardous to my health, to let 'er rip. Sometimes I listen to him; more often I do not. On smoking we have reached a compromise, which is that, if I make it to eighty, I shall begin smoking again. It's fewer than thirty years away. If you are around then, too, try not to act surprised if I ask for a light.

"And That's What I Like About the South"

I

A BRIEF CAUTIONARY TALE for those who do not believe in fate. In my twenty-second year, in the middle of a two-year hitch as a draftee in the peacetime U.S. Army, I was informed by a lean and gruff staff sergeant at Fort Hood, Texas, that I had qualified to work as a clerk-typist at a recruiting station in either Little Rock, Arkansas, or Shreveport, Louisiana, and was asked which of the two towns I preferred. I reckoned I had roughly ten seconds to make up my mind. I recall thinking that Shreveport, being in Louisiana, probably had the better food, and I knew that it had something of a reputation for being a wide-open town; yet Little Rock was a few hundred miles closer to Chicago, where I was from.

"Little Rock, Sergeant," I said, permitting propinquity to win out over profligacy. Before the next year was out I had met and married the woman who is the mother of my two sons; and I had published my first piece of writing, which settled me in my determination to become a writer. From those three words—"Little Rock, Sergeant"—marriage, family, and vocation followed. I have no complaints about any of this, but even today I cannot keep from wondering what my life would have been like if I had said, "Shreveport, Sergeant."

On the south side of Chicago there is a restaurant named Febo's over whose bar is the slogan "Febo's, Famous for Nothing." Three years before I arrived there—the year of my arrival was 1959—one might have said the same about Little Rock. The only fact I could have cited about the city, apart from its being the state capital, was that it was the birthplace of Brooks Robinson, the great third baseman of the Baltimore Orioles. But by 1959 the city had already become famous—infamous, to be more precise—for the forced integration of its Central High School, which was accomplished in 1957 only with the aid of federal troops called in by President Eisenhower.

In the autumn of 1957, in fact, as a senior in college, I along with a friend had driven through Little Rock on a trip around the South. I remember the city as being hilly; I also remembered a rather overweight young National Guardsman leaning on his rifle and dozing off while standing guard on the lawn of Central High. From that perspective the crisis did not seem much of a crisis. But the integration of Central High School in Little Rock, considerable though its consequences were for the nation at large, was easily the most decisive event in the history of the city—and, as I discovered on a brief recent trip to Little Rock, made after an absence of roughly twenty years, it remains the decisive event.

Although I had stayed awake the better part of the night during the Trailways bus ride from Killeen, Texas, outside Fort Hood, crowded in my seat near the window next to a heavyset woman smelling of talcum powder and sachet who was reading Christian Science literature, I nevertheless arrived in Little Rock feeling exhilarated. After the sere flatness of central Texas, the green undulating landscape of Arkansas raised the spirits. There was the additional inspiriting fact that, owing to there being no army base near Little Rock, I would be able to live in an apartment by myself. This was no small luxury after spending the past eight months sleeping in the same room with some two hundred men, listening to them snoring, belching, sneezing, wheezing, flatulating, occasionally crying out in their sleep for mother, and otherwise producing a cacophony that might have been as music to the ears of John Cage but was distinctly not my notion of ideally restful conditions. The army is a total environment, from which, morning to night, one never escapes, except in sleep or in the recesses of the imagination. In coming to Little Rock, where I would presumably work only a regular day, but no more, with my evenings and weekends free, I was escaping this total environment. Arriving in Little Rock, I felt the exquisite delight of someone who senses he has really gotten away with something.

I checked my duffel bag at the bus station, bought a newspaper, and two hours later had my apartment. It was a studio with a minuscule kitchen and a private bathroom (a private bathroom—"Aladdinish!" as Theodore Dreiser might have put it). Containing a double bed that rolled out of a closet, two pieces of a battered gray sectional couch, two wooden chairs and a small table at which to eat, and another table that I could use as a desk, it was a simple enough dwelling but, hallelujah, mine own.

My apartment was at the south end of Louisiana Street, fourteen blocks from the recruiting station in downtown Little Rock where I was to work, and across the street from the eastern end of the governor's mansion, whose current occupant was the redneck populist Orval Faubus. A block away was a Safeway supermarket, where I bought a few dishes, a single service of aluminum flatware, glasses, a coffee cup, a kitchen knife, a pot, a frying pan, a kettle for boiling water, a can opener, four cans of Campbell's Soup, some packaged cold

cuts, white bread, a dozen eggs, a jar of instant coffee, a carton
of orange juice, and a $3.98 West Bend alarm clock. Apart from
the alarm clock, the only appliance in the apartment was a
small Olivetti portable typewriter that I had bought for $35
from a sergeant at Fort Hood who needed the money to pay
for a ring job on his car. The apartment had no television set,
no radio, no phonograph, no air conditioner, no fan, nothing
on the walls; it did have venetian blinds. I never had enough
extra money to install a telephone, but there was a pay phone
half a block away on the corner of Main and 17th Street. Simple
Southern living; I, at least, would never live so simply again.
After living on army bases, I felt I had it knocked—absolutely
made in the shade.

Little Rock was a city of fewer than 200,000 people, and the
U.S. Army recruiting station occupied a three-story fake-Ro-
manesque former bank building on Main Street near the center
of downtown. I worked on the mezzanine, with three other
enlisted men and a spinster civil servant who wore her gray
hair in braids pinned atop her head and who regularly invited
me, a heathen Israelite, to join her for services at her fundamentalist church. The first floor was given over to administrative
functions; on the third floor, physical examinations were done.
I typed the results of the physicals. These results could sometimes be rather startling. Boys who had been recruited from
towns in the fastnesses of the Ozarks, or in the back country,
where there were no medical services, would, on being exam-
ined, be revealed to have punctured eardrums, or hopelessly
rotted teeth, or venereal disease, or incipient tuberculosis. The
minimal weight limit for getting into service was then, I believe, 106 pounds, and some couldn't make it, so that the sergeants who recruited them would take them out and fill them
with ice cream, bananas, and beer and bring them back to have

them re-weighed. Recruiting sergeants working out in the field had strict quotas; if they did not fill them they lost their jobs, which they did not want to do, since recruiting was regarded as light duty.

But it could not have been any lighter duty than mine. I worked for a gentle and good-natured sergeant named Wilson Duncan, who was a drinking man of the kind known as a bibbler. He would duck out from time to time during the day for a few belts, returning with his spirits and good humor refreshed. We were overstaffed. We reported for work at eight o'clock and rarely had any typing to do after three. Fairly often, after spending an entire weekend alone in my apartment without speaking to anyone, on a Monday morning at ten, Sergeant Duncan would say, "We got things pretty much under control here, kid. Why don't you knock off for the day?" We typists all did a lot of knocking off.

I had enormous amounts of time to myself, more than I have ever had in my life. I filled it, insofar as possible, with reading. I was a big customer at the Little Rock Public Library, which was on Louisiana Street between the recruiting station and my apartment. A magazine and tobacco store downtown carried such magazines as the *New Statesman,* the *Spectator, Encounter,* the *New Leader,* and the *Economist,* and I was a regular there, too. (I was already a subscriber to *Commentary, Partisan Review,* and *Dissent.*) On steamy Southern days I would sit in my apartment, with no shirt on, reading away for three- and four-hour stretches—four hours was about my limit. I would punctuate these reading sessions with walks. At one point I bought a basketball, which I would dribble over to a schoolyard three blocks away, there to shoot a hundred free throws, then return to read Sidney Hook's *The Hero in History,* F. R. Leavis's *The Great Tradition,* or a Balzac novel. Days would go by in which I spoke to no one.

Nights, when there was no movie in town I cared to see, I would walk down to the empty lot on 17th and Main Street where, most weeks, traveling revivalists and faith healers set up their tents. The evangelist would usually arrive on Monday, often driving a Cadillac with the extravagant tail fins of the late 1950s and followed by a huge truck which contained the large tent, the folding chairs, the organ, and the sound system that were the tools of his trade. By Tuesday he would be in business. I could hear the music from my apartment. It would begin with gentle hymns, such as "By and By We're Going Up to See the King," and build to the driving rhythms of "We're Tentin' Tonight." The audience for these shows were usually poor and rural folk: the women often swollen by a starch-laden diet, the men often missing a few fingers, many teeth, and wearing farm overalls. A segregated section was set off to the side for Negroes. There was never a shortage of crippled and elderly. An atmosphere of the carnival freak show suffused everything, at least for me, who stood on the edge of the tent, taking it in.

These performances built to a crescendo. Much chatter about the wonder-working power of Jesus Christ was interspersed with hymns blasted out on high-powered organs. The evangelist would wing it, his accounts of heaven and hell being interspersed with cries to the Lord—"Can you hear me, Jesus?" "Do you know we love you, Jesus?" "Oh, blood of the lamb!"—followed by enthusiastic amens. After an hour or so of this foreplay, the screws were applied. The evangelist knew, oh yes he knew, there were people here tonight who needed to be saved, who had not yet come to Jesus, but would do so tonight, amen. "Won't you come forth, won't you meet with Jesus now?" he would whisper into the public-address system. Sometimes parents would bring their children forward to the stage, or wives their husbands. "I love you, Jesus," some among them would call out. Some would writhe with ecstasy, or faint dead away. Those who were saved were led off to a smaller tent toward the side of the lot, there to fill out a card giving evidence of their salvation on that night and to be assigned to one or another of Little Rock's many fundamentalist churches; there, too, I do not doubt, they were hit up for money.

The wildest of these shows were of course those put on by the faith healers, who would tell people that if they came to Jesus they could throw away their crutches, slip off their braces, shake free of their arthritis; their boils, tumors, and cancers would fall away. "Oh, thank you, Jesus, thank you, Jesus," the evangelist would yawp, not wishing to take for himself the credit for miraculous cures. "Do you love Him? Can you feel Him here with us tonight?" Organ music full blast: "Oh, we're tentin' tonight, oh, we're tentin' tonight, tentin' on the old camp grounds." "My assistants will pass among you. Give what you can to continue the work of the Lord, the Father and the Son. Give all that you can."

It was the purest Elmer Gantry. I had read the novel, seen the movie, and now night after night watched the real thing from which both were drawn—and somehow never grew tired of it. Watching it I felt a combination of pity, revulsion, and sheer admiration of craft. I became a connoisseur of these performances, a student of the methods of the laying on of hands, of the babbling in strange tongues, of the hitting up for cash at the precise right moment. Once, as I stood at my usual place outside the open tent, a fleshy woman in a house dress, pale and with thinning hair, emerged from the tent to address me. "Won't you join us?" she asked, in a treacly voice. "You know He died for you." Speechless, I turned away, a shiver running through my body, and did not return for the remainder of that week.

I yearned for company, but the kind of company I required was not available. Somehow, during the last four or five years, I had crossed the line and become a member of what I think of as the "bookish class." This had both its advantages and its disadvantages. Among its advantages, it meant that I could defy Pascal, who said that man's problems began with his inability to sit quietly by himself in a room, by being able, in fact, to sit very quietly in a room, with time out every so often for a hundred free throws, at least so long as I had a book or magazine to read. Among its disadvantages was that I now found myself a little bored after a few hours in the company of people who were not interested in the rather specialized things that I was interested in: books, ideas, writing, art.

During the week I went to lunch with the young men I worked with at the recruiting station: an airman from Alabama who was recently married; a Marine sergeant named Jackie Taylor the story of whose life was the alimony and child-support payments he had to send monthly to his former wife back in Texas; a landscape architect from Cleveland who sent out signals to me that he was secretly a homosexual; two fellows who helped administer physicals, one from Baltimore and another from Columbus, Ohio, both of whom had battled their way through college without, I think it fair to say, education ever having laid a glove on them. This sounds suspiciously like intellectual snobbery, though I prefer to think it factual reporting. We all got on well enough; it was merely that I sensed, and sensed that they sensed, that there was no place for our friendships to go—except, every so often, for a couple of beers after work.

I must have seemed, to put it very gently, more than a little strange to them: a lone Jew, a young man who brought books to read during coffee breaks, someone who had strong opinions on integration (very much for it), and who in winter took to wearing a dark gray Brooks Brothers tweed overcoat over his uniform until told, gently, by Sergeant Duncan that in wearing that coat he was out of uniform. I must also have seemed a bit dreamy, which I began to be, for all the reading I had been doing led me to believe that I could write. It was in the army in Little Rock that, for the first time, I felt the palpable excitement of writing—the sensuousness of it, the feeling of power and control that came with knowing how sentences worked. Before, I had felt vaguely, inchoately, that I might someday like to write; now I felt the day had come in earnest.

My reading, now that it had a specific motive, became all the more passionate. Whereas before I asked about everything I read, "What does the author mean?" I now asked as well, "How does he do it?" Words inflamed me. "Eschew," "deliquescent," "amanuensis"—I wished to compose sentences into which such words could be fitted. I would study sentences in writers I admired to understand their architecture. Elegance for me was available only within the frame of prose. I discovered the use of the dash—a banner day. The subtlety of the semicolon was at last revealed to me; I was delighted by its magical power of demonstrating connectedness. I lived in a state of nearly perpetual interior excitation, which could be shared with no one. I was in verbal heat.

I began working off some of this heat by writing letters to the editor of the *Arkansas Gazette,* a newspaper which, the year before, had won a Pulitzer Prize for its editorial coverage of the crisis over the integration of Central High School. These letters, moralistic and no doubt very pompous, were duly printed and went duly unnoticed. I have to strain to remember what they were about: no doubt they pointed up contradictions in *Gazette* editorials, or satirized the statements of segregationist politicians, or remarked upon the behavior of foreign regimes (about which everything I knew I had myself read in the

Economist). When I took to dropping off these letters in person at the newspaper, I was instructed to take them up to Mr. Neil, who worked on the editorial page and was responsible for the correspondence column.

A few years later Jerry Neil, who had become my friend, told me how he viewed his work as the lead editorial writer on the *Arkansas Gazette.* "I drop off my wife at her job," he said, "and get into the office by eight. I spend the first part of the morning telling General de Gaulle or Harold Macmillan or some other European head of state to get his act together. I next accuse Lyndon Johnson of chicanery, or remind Faubus what a blockhead he is. Then I break for lunch, at which I manage to stay just sober enough to be able to return to the office to paste up letters before knocking off for the day. It's a pretty good racket."

Jerry Neil was one of those superior Southerners—not a fake Southern aristocrat, or the son of a wealthy family who went off to Princeton or Yale and remained an Ivy Leaguer for life, but a bright young man who, after going to the state university, marched off to Europe for World War II and returned able to participate in the wider culture of the world while never forgetting his origins. He had read widely in European history and English literature. He admired Max Beerbohm, H. L. Mencken, and A. J. Liebling. He had the old-fashioned journalist's love of oddity of character and appetite for a comic anecdote. His laugh, which it was always such a pleasure to be able to evoke, resembled the exhale of a healthy snore. He dressed with refinement and thought the same way.

Why the heavy drinking? I do not know for certain, but I suspect that Jerry Neil was a disappointed man. As an editorialist on the *Arkansas Gazette,* he had done a good deal of the work for which the paper's editor, Harry Ashmore, had been given all the credit. He had been offered other jobs on other papers—the *New York Herald Tribune,* I seem to recall, and also the *Wall Street Journal*—but for his own private reasons turned them down. Perhaps he regretted this; perhaps he felt he lacked the nerve to try himself in the larger world. Harry Ashmore had left the *Arkansas Gazette* to join Robert Hutchins at the Center for the Study of Democratic Institutions, there to get somehow lost in the great dialogue. Another bright young writer named William Whitworth left the *Arkansas Gazette* to go to work for *The New Yorker* and eventually to wind up as editor of the *Atlantic.* But Jerry stayed on, pasting up those letters through an alcoholic haze until his death, at age fifty-eight, in the late 1970s. I do not know what he saw in me, but even now I am glad that he saw something.

It was to Jerry Neil that I ran with one of my two contributor's copies of my first published magazine article, a report on Little Rock that appeared in the *New Leader.* "Nice piece," he said, looking up as he finished reading it. He was no doubt being charitable. It was a composition modeled on those travel pieces that James (not yet Jan) Morris used to write for *Encounter,* anecdotal and heavy on impressions. I cannot locate a copy of it today, but my recollection is that it was vastly overwritten. I seem to recall a number of its sentences beginning with the phrase "In any event"; "at any rate" also got a pretty good workout. I had no illusions that the *New Leader* was a great magazine, but I was nonetheless thrilled to be published in the same journal that also published Sidney Hook, Reinhold Niebuhr, Bertrand Russell, Lionel Trilling, and a number of other writers whom I then read with nearly complete reverence.

For a young writer there is no duplicating the excitement of first publication. In *A Backward Glance,* Edith Wharton tells of the day she opened her mail to discover that three different magazines had accepted poems of hers. Such was the fever of her excitement that, long skirt lifted, she ran up and down the staircase in her house, over and over again. I carried my letter of acceptance from the assistant managing editor of the *New Leader* in the pocket of my uniform shirt for days. At work at the recruiting station, I would sneak off to the john to read it again, for the twenty-eighth or twenty-ninth time. I am now of the company of Hook and Niebuhr and Trilling, I would say to myself. Hot damn!

Had I not published that rather fragile magazine piece—"in any event" and "at any rate"—I should probably not have married as young as I did, which was at twenty-three. I recall that in one of his books, Edmund Wilson, not known for delicacy in these matters, remarks that young men seek out the company of women owing to "the accumulated brimming over of spermatozoa." Not unbrimful myself, I had carried on with such young women as life in Little Rock had set in my path. At one point, I had known (as the Bible has it) a woman who, I later learned from Sergeant Jackie Taylor, was under surveillance by the FBI for associating with potentially violent segregationists. If she was under surveillance, then so, presumably, might I have been—not too close, I hoped. But when the young woman—bright and good-hearted with a lovely sense of humor—came along whom I was to marry, I plunged ahead, in good part because I already knew what I wanted to do with my life: make more sentences, paragraphs, pieces, books, an activity to which marriage then seemed no obstacle but instead a convenience. (It is, of course, neither.) So one sunny afternoon I informed Sergeant Duncan that I needed an hour or so off, and slipped out to the office of a justice of the peace across from the courthouse and married. Two months later, on my way to being discharged at Fort Sill, Oklahoma, I left Little Rock with a Southern wife, a portable Olivetti, and a $200 dark green Ford sedan, a combination out of which someone with a proper knack would have been able to write a corking good country-and-western song.

II

Four years later, in 1964, I returned to Little Rock, now with children and furniture, after working at editorial jobs on magazines in Chicago and New York. New York on a small salary with children seemed a punishing place; it was also a city in which I was not getting much writing of my own done. A move seemed in order. Now that I had something resembling a trade—that of magazine editor—what could be cleverer than to light out for a place, Little Rock, Arkansas, where it wasn't practiced, for so far as I knew Little Rock had no magazines? But then it seemed to be my fate not so much to move to a place as to flee another place.

The last time I had landed in Little Rock I had come on a Trailways bus from the southwest; now I would be arriving on a Greyhound bus from the northeast. Not much in the way of progress, I fear. My wife had preceded me with our children, also by bus, and had rented a house before I arrived. I had stayed behind to see our furniture put on the moving van and to sell my small library to a man from a used-book store near Union Square, who carried it out in three trips with a shopping cart. I retained only my copies of Max Beerbohm's slender volumes, a beautiful green-covered Bodley Head edition of *Ulysses*, and a set of Macaulay's *History of England*, which I still haven't read.

My wife had rented a house on Cumberland Street, only a few blocks away from my Louisiana Street apartment, for the price—wondrous, after New York—of $100 a month. It had three bedrooms, a large living room and dining room, and a glass-enclosed study that led onto a porch large enough to be

called a veranda. (One morning a few months after we moved
in, my wife, in a parody of Tennessee Williams, swept onto
the veranda in her nightgown and asked, "Are the boys from
the university here yet?" "Why Blanche darling," I replied,
"you know the university moved away thirty years ago.") The
house was originally built for the daughter and son-in-law of
the woman who owned the large white house next door. That
woman had died, and the daughter, now herself a widow, had
moved into the larger house. She was of the old school, and the
last person in Little Rock, man or woman, whom I was to hear
refer to Negroes as "darkies." On the same block, to the south
of the house we lived in, in what once must have been the
stable, lived a family who had originally come from a small
town in southeastern Arkansas; the man was one of those
Southerners who, though without much conversation, could
repair anything from a toaster to a DC-10.

Throughout my time in the South I was always running
into men who could make and fix things. I met men whose
advice on how to repair my used cars involved my removing
the engine, or installing a new clutch, or putting in something
they called a "throw-out bearing"—advice I was perfectly unprepared to take. I met men who knew how to breed animals,
lay out driveways, do elaborate wiring, remove tree stumps
with dynamite. On my first job I worked with a man who, on
weekends, was building his own house—from scratch. I, on the
other hand, could make one thing: sentences. But then on a
desert island, whom would you prefer to be with, a man who
knows how to purify water or a man who can spot a dangling
modifier?

Since there was no staggering need in Little Rock for a man
who could make or fix sentences, I felt lucky to get the job I
did, which was as something called "administrative officer" of
the North Little Rock Urban Renewal Agency. During the

time I worked there—roughly seven months—I administered nothing. North Little Rock was a town of forty or so thousand people located across the Arkansas River from Little Rock. It was for the most part less prosperous, less interesting, more ragged and redneck—*mutatis mutandis,* it might be considered a Jackson Heights or Astoria to Little Rock's Manhattan. The idea behind the urban-renewal program was to give the town something like a *raison d'être* by clearing land for a sleek new produce market center and rehabilitating some of the more dismal Negro neighborhoods with the aid of injections of federal housing funds.

My job at the North Little Rock Urban Renewal Agency turned out to be, precisely, making and fixing sentences. I wrote publicity releases and edited correspondence written by other staff members that went off to Washington or to regional offices in Dallas. At one point I published a two-thousand-word profile of the town's mayor in the now defunct magazine *Pageant;* the mayor was a suave version of the good-ole-boy type who, in his late forties, was still getting into bar brawls while attending mayors' conferences in Northern cities. I omitted the brawls from my profile and featured instead the hundreds of new mercury-vapor lamps he had put up in North Little Rock. Around the office I spoke almost exclusively that lingua franca of the American male, sports, with a special emphasis on Southwest Conference football. The work was dull but the pay was low.

To supplement it I had begun to review books fairly regularly for the *New Republic;* I had, as always in the South, a good deal of time on my hands. I felt myself gradually becoming something of a Southerner. I drove a series of hopeless used cars, including a Corvair (the car, unsafe at any speed, on which Ralph Nader made his reputation) and a twelve-year-old Cadillac—a real cream puff, as they say out on the lot—the maintenance of whose shaky transmission was paid for by reviews of the works of John Updike, Norman Mailer, and George P. Elliott. At home we acquired a dog and two cats. My three-year-old son had taken to calling his infant brother "honey-chile baby." I awoke at 3:00 A.M. to go fishing in the White River with my father-in-law. I never hunted, but I did on occasion belt down moonshine. I danced to shit-kicking country bands at highway honky-tonks in whose parking lots one could always depend on finding some youthful good ole boy vomiting his guts out. Once, after someone tried to break into our house at night, I borrowed a revolver from a co-worker, which I kept in the drawer of my night table in the event the burglar returned. (Thank God, he never did.) On that same night table lay the bound galley proofs of Arthur Koestler's *The Act of Creation*. Anybody around here want to talk about two cultures?

In between discussing the relative merits of Frank Broyles and Darrell Royal, the coaches, respectively, of the Arkansas Razorbacks and the Texas Longhorns; writing letters to the director of the regional office of the Housing and Home Finance Agency; and listening to endless friendly assurances from my co-workers about how most Negroes down South liked things just as they were, I somehow managed, while on the job, to find time to write an article entitled "The Row over Urban Renewal" that was accepted by *Harper's*. Publication of this article marked a turning point. As a result of it, I became, for a period of about four months, one of this country's leading housing experts (of whom there were not too many). As for my expertise, my article ran to some five thousand words; on the entire subject of urban renewal I should say that my complete knowledge ran to something like seven thousand words. But let that pass: the country needs experts, and for the moment, however fraudulently, I was one of those in housing. I appeared on a panel about the subject along with Edward Banfield and others at the University of Chicago Law School; I was offered a job as director of public relations for the planning commission of the City of Baltimore; I was approached for the job of speech writer in Washington for Robert Weaver, then secretary of housing.

But the most interesting offer I had was to become the first director of the antipoverty program of Pulaski County (which encompassed Little Rock, North Little Rock, and the surrounding area). One afternoon I was called into the offices of the United Fund to speak to a man named Cal Ledbetter, who was from an old Little Rock family, had a Ph.D. in political science from Princeton, and nourished political ambitions as a middle-of-the-road progressive in state politics, to ask if the job would be one I would care to try. After thinking about it for a day or two, I said that I would indeed. The year was 1965, and Lyndon Johnson's War on Poverty, from all reports, had begun in seriousness. I was twenty-eight years old, and this job gave me my first opportunity—no small incentive—to be a boss. The salary was $9,600. The pay was still low, but the work suddenly seemed a lot more interesting.

Ours was not to be a large program, at least not at the outset. I had a budget that allowed me to hire four people with the job title of field workers, and a secretary. As field workers I hired two young men, recent graduates of Southern black colleges; a very savvy white woman named Ruth Arnold, who had been around in the days of the Central High School integration crisis and who had worked for the Arkansas Council of Human Relations and knew an enormous amount about the personal lives and politics of the leading figures in Little Rock; and an acquaintance who had been working as a teacher at the Arkansas School for the Blind, where some years before the

Indian Writer Ved Mehta had been a student.

Our offices were two rooms above the United Fund head-quarters. The first day on the job, a man who worked for the United Fund entered my office to inform me he had alerted the other occupants of the building that we would have Negroes—pronounced, in that day, "Nigras"—working for us who would be using the same upstairs men's room. ("Here we go," I thought, the line from Phil Harris's old song, ". . . and that's what I like about the South," playing in my head.) Our task was to define the extent and locations of poverty in Pulaski County and, after having done so, to determine which of the various antipoverty program grants we wished to apply for. We were also—and this was chiefly to be my job—to explain the purposes of the antipoverty program to the community at large and to those poor sections of the community that were to be its beneficiaries.

My preparation for this job—apart from my role as one of the country's leading housing experts, which still had another month or so to run—was that I was a liberal, and hence could be expected to care about the poor, and that I had read Michael Harrington's book *The Other America.* The rumor had it that someone had put Dwight Macdonald's lengthy *New Yorker* review of Harrington's book under the nose of John F. Kennedy, and from it the president derived the notion of someday mounting a war on poverty. I recall having been impressed by the book the first time I read it, but I can testify that it is not a book that richly repays rereading. Its definition of poverty, and especially its statistics, are wobbly in the extreme; at one point Harrington seems to have (if I remember rightly) something like between a fourth and a third of the nation as poor. Even I, who then wished to believe the worst about the United States, could not quite buy that one. But if Harrington's statistics were somewhat cooked to begin with, in the months ahead I nevertheless served them up reheated in what were to be my many local appearances as Little Rock's poverty guy.

As the poverty guy, I became a minor media figure in a small city—the adjectives are important here. I was often interviewed by the local press; I appeared frequently on the five and ten o'clock news. At 6:00 A.M. once I was on a television show called *Eye on Arkansas,* delivering my Harringtonian statistics sandwiched in between a black quartet that sang "Mack the Knife" and a woman who ran the local gourmet food shop demonstrating how to make crêpes. I spoke before Rotary and Kiwanis Club luncheon meetings. I drew misty eyes from the pretty and well-heeled young Southern ladies of the Junior League when I told them that there were children in Harlem who had never seen an orange. (How the hell did I know that? I must have read it in Harrington; but how the hell did he know?) But my most surprising speaking engagements were in Negro churches. In these churches the most humdrum things I would say would be greeted by amens, hosannas, and choruses of "Say it out, man," "Oh, yeah," and "We hear you talkin'!" Had I not had a fairly accurate sense of my intrinsic dullness as a speaker, I might have been encouraged by this response to try my hand at a little faith healing.

What did Little Rock's blacks think of me? Insofar as they thought of me at all, it was probably as another white man passing through town. I tried to deal as evenhandedly as I could with the two young blacks who worked for the antipoverty program, going to lunch with them when we were all in the office, making certain that they were invited to all parties and social functions. But they had been brought up to handle themselves with extreme circumspection around whites, and it was not always easy to break through. One of the two took to calling me "Boss," inserting the word into nearly every sentence he addressed to me, until one day, when he said "What's happening, Boss?" I replied—humor not always being a clear advantage in race relations—"Nothing much, Rochester," which got a nervous laugh of the kind comedians call "tension release."

One evening the director of the Little Rock Urban League, a black man not much older than I, arranged a meeting for me with what then passed for the black power structure in the city. I was there to explain the rudiments of the antipoverty program. We sat at a rectangular table. The director of the Urban League, opening the meeting, assured me that this was to be an informal session. "Gentlemen, allow me to introduce our new antipoverty director, Joe Epstein, to you. Joe, going around the table from your right, this is Reverend Fulks, Attorney Bledsoe, President Simpson of Philander Smith College, Dr. Wingate . . ." Informal? Everyone in the room seemed to have a title but me, which struck me as a comic reversal of old black-white roles that also carried a touch of the spirit of *Amos 'n' Andy*. After I had my say, the others spoke, each with a strong ceremonial flavor. There was something of a performance quality to the evening, with the proviso that everyone in the room except me had no doubt seen the performance scores of times before. What they said among themselves after I left, I cannot know. Some must, at a minimum, have felt a strong distrust, for the antipoverty program promised to shake things up—that, in any case, is how I sold it to them—and the men gathered in that room had actually all done quite well with things as they were. Potentially, they had something to lose if the antipoverty program succeeded. As it turned out, they needn't have worried.

My dealings with the authentically poor were hardly any closer. I visited segregated schools, where, especially in the

outlying areas, facilities had passed to the stage beyond dilapi-
dation, windows had no screens, and flies settled on lumpy
food in dark cafeteria kitchens. I accompanied my staff of field
workers through ramshackle houses where wooden stoves
gave off the only heat in winter and holes in walls were
plugged with rags and broken windows covered in cardboard.
On one such tour of a so-called poverty area, I mentioned to
a black woman who was the local school principal that it was
ironic all these sad houses seemed to have television sets. "Mr.
Epstein," she said, "please do not knock those old television
sets. Because of them the children in these homes hear what
little good English they are likely to hear before they get to
school." I recall attempting to explain to a young, bloated black
woman, the mother of four illegitimate children—not a welfare
racketeer, but someone who had had these children through
passive ignorance—how important voter registration was, and
noted that my explanation was greeted with the deepest, the
most hopeless, incomprehension.

Poverty in Little Rock was real, but was the antipoverty
program? It was certainly real in the sense that there were
offices and jobs and a man named Sargent Shriver in Washington who was the national director of the program, and checks
flying around for millions of dollars to pay for salaries and
services. But was it real in the sense of having any hope of
bringing about the social change it promised and of the kind
that I, as a local director, envisioned for it? Social change
entails the transfer of power, and the record would appear to
show that people who have power have not been known to
give it up cheerfully. Nor have there been many instances of
power being given to the powerless because the powerful feel
an aching sense of the world's injustice. People have to take
power for themselves. Was the delusion of antipoverty bureau-

crats such as myself monumental in thinking that we could transfer power that was not ours to transfer? Before I was on the job three months, I began to wonder about this.

All the grants I had hoped to apply for had behind them the dream of social change. Such roundly popular, non-controversial programs as the Neighborhood Youth Corps, which supplied teenagers with summer jobs and fattened everyone's payroll, and Headstart, which gave poor children a year of preschooling with free breakfasts thrown in, were no great problem. But I had it in mind to set up a legal-aid program (through which the poor would be able to sue for their rights), a birth-control program (which would at length lighten their economic burden), and a voter-registration drive (which, under the guise of registering poor people to vote in an election for the antipoverty board, would make them a political force). More exotic programs were available; I seem to recall chuckling at what seemed to me the pointlessness of something called "foster grandparents," which would give older people money to baby-sit for poor working mothers. But I had little interest in such things. Give the poor lawyers, condoms, and the vote, I thought, and you have given them a lot.

There was a minor problem or two. Lawyers, physicians, and local officials didn't quite feel as I did about these things. Everyone was worried about going too far too fast, and so such grants as I was able to apply for were rather piddling ones. Worse news, people to my left, on whose support I had counted, were not hugely impressed by the antipoverty program.

Now, nothing makes a liberal more nervous than not to have the approval of people to his left. In this case, the people to my left were the young men and women in the civil-rights movement, which, in Little Rock, meant the people in the Student Nonviolent Coordinating Committee (SNCC) office

in one of the city's black districts on 9th Street. Although I
never became close to any of the SNCC people, I greatly
admired them. What I admired about them was very simple:
their physical courage. They had engaged in sit-ins and pro-
tests in tough Arkansas towns like Pine Bluff and Jonesboro at
a time when they stood to have their heads bashed in for doing
so. The then leader of SNCC in Arkansas, a white man
roughly my own age named Bill Hansen, had put in much time
in jails across the South. Hansen was tall, slender, very political, and quite humorless. Once, after we had lunched together
at a small restaurant on 9th Street, he dropped a few coins for
a tip. "Why, Bill," I said, "Trotsky never tipped. He felt that
tipping only supports a corrupt system, you know." Hansen
picked up the coins.

Still, there was the physical courage, a fact not to be denied
or washed away by psychology. People with a bent for psychology used to say that Bill Hansen had arrived at the point
where he rather liked a good beating, which seemed to me a
crummy notion. You may not care for someone who has returned from the front, but you have to respect his having been
there. It was less easy to respect those kids, graduate students
most of them, who came down South from Columbia, the
University of Michigan, Harvard, Boston University, and elsewhere to spend their summer in the civil-rights movement.
They did odd jobs around the SNCC office; some of them
taught at Philander Smith, Little Rock's black college. I recall
asking a young man working for his Ph.D. at Columbia how
he liked teaching at Philander Smith. He told me it was usually
interesting, though there were some bad days, such as, in particular, when he had attempted to discuss the poetry of Paul
Valéry in class. I must say, I had not thought such naiveté was
possible in the world.

One sunny Sunday morning I drove out to the countryside

to attend a statewide meeting of SNCC, where I explained how the antipoverty program worked and how SNCC could apply for grants for programs of its own. But there was not much interest in what I had to say. SNCC was undergoing its own troubles. The organization had come into being during a time of great moral purity. There were segregationist laws on the books of the states of the South, and they needed to be challenged. Young SNCC kids, black and white, at the risk of their lives, challenged them. "In every social movement," Bayard Rustin once told me, "you need people who are willing to go to jail for their cause." But now the action seemed to be moving elsewhere. Protest itself seemed all but played out. On school integration, public accommodations, voting rights, and much else the segregationist South had in effect surrendered. Yet all SNCC knew was protest.

Not long after this, sitting in my office, I received a phone call from a young woman in the SNCC office who had come to Little Rock for the summer. She informed me there was to be a protest march on the state capitol building, and she thought I would want to be among the marchers. "If I were to march with you," I said, "you understand that my usefulness here would be at an end." "That's your problem," she said, and hung up. Around this time Stokeley Carmichael, with much fanfare, announced that "Black is beautiful," which really meant there was no longer any place for whites in the civil-rights movement. I sensed that my own time in the South was nearing its end.

Other, more personal items were involved. Petty inconveniences began to loom large. I had to wait a full day after its publication date to read the *New York Times; The New Yorker*, which I used to read on Tuesday in New York, didn't arrive until the following Monday in Little Rock. The town had no decent restaurants. The one Chinese restaurant in Little Rock, as an accommodation to the local populace, which was used to mopping up gravies, served slices of white bread with its meals. I no longer found it quite so amusing when, during the holiday season, local television announcers pronounced the word *Hanukkah* so that it sounded like *Chattanooga.* I longed for bookish conversation. I was growing tired of judging everyone by his views on race. I realized that I hadn't the temperament for compromise that is required of an effective bureaucrat. I was leaving the South in spirit, and when I was offered a job at roughly twice my then salary to become a senior editor at Encyclopaedia Britannica, Inc., in Chicago, I took it and left the South in person.

III

My chief link with Little Rock was snapped with my divorce in 1970. Without a Southern wife, there was no reason for trips to the South. Yet, having lived in the South during crucial periods in my life, I have subconsciously come to consider myself partly a Southerner—in a way that I do not consider myself partly a New Yorker. I know I generally feel at home among Southerners. Not long ago I met with a magazine editor from Mississippi, who told me he had returned home recently to be with his family and, as he put it, "to talk a little Southern"—the phrase reminded me of talking a little Yiddish. For him, clearly, the South represented something akin to the old country, and I have felt something of this myself.

By now long an outsider, I had nonetheless maintained a former insider's interest in Little Rock and in Arkansas generally. I noted the demise from the national scene of the bulldog-faced Senator John McClellan and the retirement of the urbane J. William Fulbright, who used to tell his constituents back home that his real interest in foreign policy concerned his attempt to sell Arkansas agricultural products abroad—both to be replaced by smooth younger men who might as easily have come from, say, Michigan. The glad-handed and politically powerful Wilbur Mills, then chairman of the Ways and Means Committee, who insisted on going directly to first names on the few occasions I met him, had long since met his political Waterloo in the company of a stripper in the Tidal Basin in Washington. Orval Faubus, at seventy-six, had mounted a last campaign for governor (after serving six terms), but had his hopes for a last hurrah snuffed out in a sound primary defeat. My own political ambition in Arkansas was to be appointed state boxing commissioner, a job which, since the state holds no boxing matches that I know of, would leave plenty of free time for other things.

A few years ago, I received a letter from a reporter on the *Arkansas Democrat,* a business letter, which ended by his re-marking, with Southern courtesy, that I was "a small legend in Little Rock." I answered that I did not know about the legend, but, being under 5'7", I would accept the small part. I also noted, to myself, that I ought to return for a visit. But to visit whom? My friend Jerry Neil had died; I had heard that Ruth Arnold, who had remarried and moved first to Washington, D.C., and then to Denver, had suffered a terrible stroke. Other friends and acquaintances were growing elderly; I was growing no younger. When I learned that Ruth Arnold and her husband had returned to live in Little Rock, I finally made the trip.

It had been twenty years since I last lived there, and the first thing I noticed upon arrival is that they had moved the airport on me. I remembered the old Little Rock airport as very small, almost cozy. Of major airlines, only Delta flew to the city, and one could never fly direct but invariably had to make a stop first either in Memphis or St. Louis. No longer. The airport

itself now looked like the airport in almost every other secondary city I have been in. The weight of time pressed down upon
me. The son who had called his younger brother "honey-chile
baby" was now working in San Francisco; the honey-chile
baby himself had graduated from college a month before.
Being in Little Rock again I felt as if someone had turned the
time machine abruptly forward—almost violently so.

Much of this feeling was owing to the fact that my old
mental landscape of the city had been altered. A new freeway
tore through the center of town. The walk down Louisiana
Street between my apartment and the recruiting station was
now interrupted by it; the recruiting station itself had been
torn down. Where I used to watch the revivalists, a small
shopping center was being built. Downtown Little Rock had
been transmogrified by several new skyscrapers, in which law
offices, insurance companies, brokerage firms, and psycho-
therapists did their business. Main Street shopping was now all
but dead, for downtown Main Street had been turned into a
mall, but a mall that was obviously a bust, or so, walking along
its deserted blocks at four in the afternoon, I gathered from the
preponderance of discount and cut-rate shops. Except at mid-
day, when there was some lunchtime traffic on the street,
downtown Little Rock felt like Wall Street on a Sunday. People drove in their air-conditioned cars into the air-conditioned
garages in the basement of their air-conditioned office buildings and then drove out again at night to their air-conditioned
homes. The white middle class was moving farther and farther
west, doing its shopping in suburban malls and plazas, sending
its children, where the money was available, to preponderantly
white private schools.

The old Marion Hotel had been razed. It was there that
politicians used to gather when the state legislature was in
session to do their drinking and make their deals. I used to have

my hair cut in the basement of the Marion by a barber then in his seventies who kept a portrait of Jesus Christ alongside his barbering tools and a pair of pajamas in his towel cabinet; the pajamas were there in the event that it snowed—which it did about once every three years—and he had to spend the night in the hotel. Where the Marion had been, a new glass-and-red-brick skyscraper hotel and convention center now stood. Across the street an old fleabag of a hotel called the Capital had been beautifully restored, its old marble and wood handsomely refurbished. I was taken to lunch in its restaurant, an absolutely up-to-the-moment, altogether elegant establishment, with waiters announcing the day's specials and rolling out the sweets trolley at the close of the meal. I heard that a French-Swiss couple had opened a place called Jacques and Suzanne a number of years ago, and a few of their chefs, having left them, had begun restaurants of their own. Refugees from Vietnam and Taiwan had also opened restaurants in town; the days of chop suey mopped up with slices of white bread were obviously over.

Stately mansions, in the antebellum style, once inhabited by single families, had been broken up into apartments, some of them sold as condominiums. The Arkansas Arts Center, built not long before my second stay in Little Rock, was currently housing a Surrealist show. On the way to see it, driving over in a rented car, I heard over the radio that the first cellular car telephones were now available in Little Rock. Some of the older homes on the east side were being expensively re-vamped—by, it was said, yuppies. Yuppies, car phones, trendy restaurants, Continental food, Surrealist shows, skyscrapers, freeways slicing through town, suburban malls—from one perspective progress, or at least modernization, seemed to be playing a strong hand in Little Rock.

From another perspective, it seemed as if nothing had

changed and some things had even worsened, giving that de-cline-and-fall feeling that overtakes us all at different times in contemporary cities. On the east side of Little Rock the houses of poor blacks appeared as desolate—and as desolating—as ever. A broken-down car, two wheels missing, rested exhausted at the side of a house whose porch was half collapsed; out front, three barefoot children and a pregnant mother who appeared to be in a stupor stood on a scraggly lawn. The scene might as easily have been set in 1932 as in 1986, awaiting capture by a photographer like Walker Evans. It would take more than snappy government programs to lift such a family out of its morass. And not even snappy programs were forthcoming. What was left of the antipoverty program, now run by a black director, was reported to be in tatters; there were even mur-murings of scandalous dealings in real estate on the part of program officials. The school system, too, was said to be in a parlous state, standards visibly slipping, mayhem in high school classrooms always a distinct possibility.

In Little Rock, blacks are currently in control of the city's welfare and educational establishments. The media, which normally adore scandal and exposé, have apparently declared hands-off. A friend of mine, a liberal and former Catholic priest who served on the antipoverty program board when I was the program's director, averred that he hadn't the heart to speak out about what he knows to be the truth. To speak out would be to court being called a racist, which, given Little Rock's heritage, is the last thing people of good heart can bear to hear. So people pretend—as they do in other cities, North and South—that it isn't there while hoping that, in time, the thing that isn't there will go away.

Progress, regress, *plus ça change, plus c'est la même chose;* on a three-day visit to a town I once knew well, I could not finally make up my mind in which direction Little Rock was headed. A moment when progress seemed to shimmer with promise was when I visited the downtown offices of a new journal to be called the *Southern Magazine.* It is one of a stable of local magazines, one a business weekly, another a monthly on the model of *New York* (Ten Best Places in town to get barbecue, ice cream, a hiatus hernia, etc.). What impressed me was the youthfulness of everyone in the office—the median age looked to be about thirty—and their go-ahead spirit. I was reminded of something told to me by Midge Decter, who had worked for the Mississippian Willie Morris when he was editor of *Harper's* and when that magazine had a great many Southerners as contributors. Those Southern boys could be hugely talented, vastly ambitious, Midge Decter had remarked, but they always seemed to want to stop for a beer. With the staff of the *Southern Magazine* gathered about me, I retold this story. "Remember this," I said, underscoring the moral, "and try not to stop for a beer quite so frequently."

The next day at lunch I joined the editors of the *Southern Magazine* for—what else?—a beer. They took me to what they said was the best barbecue restaurant in Little Rock, a black-run place on the far south side of town. A combination of soul and rock blared away on a radio turned all the way up. The barbecue was as good as advertised. We talked about magazines, with me, in this circle the wily old veteran, doing much of the talking. Outside it was up around 100 degrees. A walk sixty or so yards from the restaurant to the car was enough to set one's shirt clinging to one's back.

One of the chief editors of the new magazine, himself a Southerner who had worked for *Playboy* in Chicago and had now returned home to the South, drove me back to where I was staying. Through mists of heat, we drove past once grand and now rather exhausted-looking neighborhoods, over freeways with skyscrapers in the background, down thoroughfares festooned with franchise operations of every kind; and driving along we talked about his return to the South, the new South really, where he hoped to finish out his professional life.

When I lived in Little Rock, I now realize, the old South had been in its last throes. I hadn't much approved of it then and I was not at all that pleased with the new South now. What was I: a utopian, or merely a habitual complainer? Sometimes, in my imaginings, I had thought about returning to live in Little Rock, where life is less expensive, more scenic, calmer, rather out-of-it perhaps but not unpleasantly so. But this, I recognized on my recent visit, was sheerest fantasy. The city has changed and so have I; a chapter of my life—two important chapters, actually—are over, and there is no call for an epilogue or afterword. It isn't so much a matter of not being able to go home again, for Little Rock was never, strictly speaking, my home. It is more a matter of beginning to learn at long last that one of the things that makes the past so wonderful is that it cannot, finally, be recaptured.

The Man in the Green Hat

U NLIKE EVERY OTHER PARAGRAPH I have written in my life, this one I am writing while wearing a red fez. It is a serious fez, too, quality goods, purchased more than twenty years ago in Cairo and lent to me by its owner, a dear friend. I do not know whether I am wearing it correctly, but there it sits on top of my head, its black fringes dangling just above my right ear. In this fez I look like a man who has seen his share of the world's corruption and who is prepared to respond, strictly as a middleman you understand, to the most complicated murmurous suggestions. "A jeroboam of absinthe, a jade anklet, a male llama that understands Croatian, and a heavy-duty dry-cell battery?" I can hear myself saying. "Is not a problem, *effendi*. All four items will await you back in your room at the hotel within the hour."

I begin this paragraph in a green velour hat, a cross between a fedora and a trilby, its brim snapped down back and front. It is a handsome hat, in my opinion, but I am not in the least handsome in it. "Country Gentleman" is marked inside its crown. Wearing it, however, I look more like a city dog. Specifically, in this fine hat my face rather resembles the face of an oversized spaniel in a compromising position—apologetic, half embarrassed, distinctly mournful. This is not quite the fashion statement I wish to make. Yet I do require a hat, especially in Chicago, where from December through March the city usually does a nice imitation of Moscow on Lake Michigan. I grow old, I grow old, the top of my size 7½ long oval head grows cold. It also begins to grow a bit silly-looking in the caps I have taken to wearing in recent years as protection against the weather.

That I have gone through thirty-odd years of adult life in a cold climate without regularly wearing what I think of as an adult hat is a mildly interesting social fact. I have owned the green velour hat that gives me the fetching spaniel effect—in his memoirs, the musician Nicolas Slonimsky tells that, when still struggling with the English language, he once introduced Pablo Casals to an audience as a great cellist and "distinguished Spaniel"—I have owned this hat for better than fifteen years, and never once have I worn it out-of-doors. At one point, I gave it to my father, who shares my large head size. He did not look the least like a spaniel in it, but in time grew tired of the green hat, and I have since reclaimed it. I continued to admire the hat, so long as it didn't have my head in it. Then the other day I clapped it on while I happened to be wearing glasses—I also have grown a good crop of gray hair that now shows underneath the brim—and it looked rather better, or at any rate less ridiculous, on me. I may one day before too long wear the hat in public, I thought to myself, perhaps trying it out late at night in some quiet nearby suburb that doesn't have a leash law.

Mine is the first generation to give up wearing serious men's hats. Ours is the first generation for whom wearing a hat is no longer *de rigueur*, which, as the boys in the back room at *Webster's* will tell you, precisely means no longer "prescribed or required by fashion, etiquette, or custom: PROPER." Such hats as we wear tend to be slightly comic ones, parodistic versions of serious hats: little snap-brim jobs, or floppy Irish tweed numbers, or checkered lids of the kind to which the late Bear Bryant, football coach of Alabama, was partial. Early in the 1960s, men who worked for advertising agencies used to wear a short-brimmed hat known among themselves as the Madison Avenue crash helmet, but in no other line of work that I can recall did a serious hat seem, as they say in the army, "standard issue." Today a man walking the streets of an American city in a homburg, with its curled brim and high crown, is likely to attract more attention for his oddity than another man dancing a boogaloo in a deep-sea diving suit.

Not long ago I found myself seated at a small lunch party next to a man who had only recently retired as president and principal owner of a successful manufacturing company. We appeared to have nothing in common yet got on quite well. I don't recall any of the subjects we talked about, but our conversation flowed nicely, each of us establishing with the other that he was a man of gravity, good humor, and superior perspective—establishing that we were both, in short, men of the world. When at the end of the lunch we rose from the table, my companion told me that he much enjoyed our talk and asked for my card so that he might call me to arrange another meeting. I had only to admit that I had no card to feel the breeze from my fall in his estimation. I wrote out my telephone number for him, but it wasn't the same. A man without a business card was not, in his view, somehow a substantial fellow. He never called. In retrospect, I am glad that he didn't see the hat I wore that day, a herringbone eight-section cap that, even though carried by all the Anglophiliac men's stores with names like the Shropshire Lad, was worn by workers fresh off the boat and newsboys in Horatio Alger novels.

This man was of my father's generation, the generation of men for whom hatlessness was roughly equivalent to shoelessness. For these men, to go out meant to go out in a hat. When I was growing up, I cannot recall my father being out-of-doors without his hat. The least errand—down to the drugstore at the corner for a newspaper, for example—required putting on his hat. To this day he seems, out-of-doors, a bit undressed when hatless, which in any case he rarely is, though he no longer wears felt hats made by such firms as Dobb's or Stetson but instead dons the jauntier, more relaxed chapeaux of the kind befitting a man now retired from the business wars ("seamed all over with the scars of the marketplace," as Henry James once characteristically put it).

Men of that generation early formed their style, their conception of how a man ought to look, and not only went with it, as we should nowadays say, but stuck with it throughout their lives. Edmund Wilson's getup for socializing at the Wellfleet beach at Cape Cod, ably described by Alfred Kazin ("the too elegant cane, the stains so carefully preserved on the Panama hat, the absurdly formal long white shirts sometimes flopping over the bulky stomach in Bermuda shorts") is a reminder that men of a certain era had a fixed manner of dress. "I have only one way of dressing," Wilson told Kazin, and he apparently never felt the need of another.

I myself have several ways of dressing. I am at this moment wearing a high and weighty fur hat, purchased for me in the Soviet Union for roughly seventy dollars. The hat stands some six inches high; it has earflaps that tie together across its top; its fur is luxuriantly dark. I am very fond of this hat, though I tend to wear it only three or four days a year—on those days in Chicago when it is so cold that running a Jiffy Lube franchise on the equator seems immensely attractive. I would wear my Russian hat more than I now do but for the inconvenient fact that when people see me in it they tend to laugh. As they pass me, adults smile, as if to say, "Look at that clown." Kids, especially little kids, point and giggle. I think the problem is that the hat makes me appear top-heavy, so that I seem a pair of galoshes walking under a fur hat. Handsome and splendidly warm though it is, perhaps this hat is not the best headgear for anyone who is not very tall, very Russian, or very unself-conscious.

Hats have long been a stock prop for comedians. One thinks of Chaplin's and Laurel and Hardy's little bowlers, Keaton's pancake boater, the broken-down top hat of Harpo Marx worn at the back of his curly blond wig—props and trademarks all. Gangsters, according to the old movies, never went hatless; and I gather the fact that so many gangsters in the 1920s were photographed wearing costly hats, usually with extravagantly broad brims, drastically hurt the hat business. A cowboy without a hat is suitable only for bartending. A spy ought to wear a hat; so ought a detective, and an insurance man, and anyone whose job carries the title of commissioner. I would go a step further and say that all jobs that carry the title commissioner ought to come with a hat.

A number of other jobs should require a hat, and I mean a serious hat: a pinched-front, gray-felt, small-feather-in-a-black-band, I-kid-you-not, grown-up man's hat. As many jobs are nowadays referred to as "hard-hat" jobs, so ought there to be "serious-hat" jobs. A bank officer should wear a serious hat, and so should a chief of police and all judges (circuit court on up). No man should be hired for a university presidency until he is seen in such a hat; and if he looks ridiculous in one, then perhaps search committees would do best to find another man for the job. Perhaps something of the grandeur of the United States would be restored if senators volunteered to wear serious hats. Let's face it, there have to be some adults around here someplace.

Heads of state once wore crowns, but today they ought at

least to wear, as Mikhail Gorbachev, I note, did when he showed up in New York City, a gray-felt, two-inch-brim, suede-finish job. No American president has regularly worn a hat since Lyndon Johnson, and then he wore a Texas special (about six and a half gallons, by my rough reckoning). John F. Kennedy wore a top hat to his inaugural and a serious hat on rare occasions; Richard M. Nixon sometimes wore a hat. Ronald Reagan wore no hat, except a cowboy number when riding on his ranch in California, and the mere idea of a hat on Jimmy Carter—who brought the first hot comb and blow dryer into the White House—is laughable. President Carter was too carefully coiffed to wear a hat, and hats are hell on ambitious male hairdos.

Hat or hairdo, a man cannot have both, and thirty or so years ago, before the advent of male hairstyling, most men chose hats. A man's hat was, moreover, a thing to which he could easily become strongly attached. After all, it traveled with him day after day; it underwent the same heavy weather; it was part of his style and manner of addressing the world. If in time a man's hat came to look a little the worse for wear, so, probably, did he. Frank Sullivan, author of *The Night the Old Nostalgia Burned Down* and other works, in a piece entitled "A Man Never Drops a Hat," wrote about a twelve-year-old hat he was forced to relinquish: "I should never have deserted the faithful friend if there had been enough left of it to be true to." Sullivan recounts how hatcheck girls handled his hat "with disdain and tongs," while others made jokes about it. Still, he writes: "I grew to love that hat as only a man can love an old hat, and perhaps in its mute hatlike way it grew fond of me." Frank Sullivan was what is technically known as a humorist, but I am not altogether certain that he is kidding here.

Two ways to view an old hat: one is that it is beat-up and misshapen; the other is that it is nicely broken in. In the World

War II movies of my childhood, the ace American fighter pilots—frequently played by Dana Andrews, Van Johnson, Robert Taylor, among others—always wore leather-billed service caps with what was known as "the fifty-mission crush," meaning that they had survived a great many dangerous missions and, like their owners, had been through a lot. These hats always had a comfortable, marvelously natural look, especially when their wearers pushed them slightly to the backs of their heads. My own somewhat similar hat, worn while serving in the peacetime army in the late 1950s, had a no-mission non-crush, and its rigid leather headband invariably left a weltlike red mark across my forehead. Wearing that hat, which I did as seldom as I could, I always felt uncomfortable and unnatural, as if I were missing something large and important. Missing, I came to conclude, was a bus, for in that hat I felt less like a soldier than a bus driver.

The late Arnaldo Momigliano, the distinguished historian of the ancient world, wore hats that had the civilian equivalent of the fifty-mission crush, except that in Arnaldo's case the hat looked as if he had been shot down over enemy territory on each mission and had managed his various escapes through a series of swamps, bogs, deserts, and avalanches. Arnaldo dressed with that disregard for the niceties of haberdashery permitted only to the world's greatest thinkers and scholars. (Recall Einstein, who always dressed to the nines, negative integer.) Arnaldo simply did not care about clothes, except for the warmth they gave, and this showed nowhere more than in his treatment of his hats. Small, dark gray, not inexpensive—they were in fact Borsalinos—after being in his possession for only a few months they looked, as befitted an ancient historian, as if they had been on winter campaign with Hannibal. Traveling with Arnaldo by plane, I have seen him stuff his hat into an already fully crammed overhead compartment as if it were a scarf, or perhaps an envelope, then slam the compartment door shut without giving it another thought. Those hats paid a heavy price for riding on top of so interesting a head.

Arnaldo Momigliano knew very well the comic condition of his own hats. He once gave me a brief account of shopping at a rather swank Borsalino store in Milan, at a time when it had become plain even to him that another of his gravely mutilated hats must be retired. The Borsalino salesman evidently knew, if not precisely who Arnaldo Momigliano was, that he was a man of great distinction, and his respect for men of distinction easily eclipsed any contempt he may have felt for the professor's unpressed, only approximately fitted clothes. Great care was devoted to waiting on him, to making certain that this new hat—*il povero cappello,* what brutal treatment awaited it—was a proper fit. When the sale had been concluded, Arnaldo asked about his old hat. "Ah, *professore,* " said the salesman, with a slight bow, "not to worry. We have already taken care of it." Momigliano's wonderfully expressive eyebrows jumped slightly over his glasses, he smiled with his head bent slightly to the right, and the index finger on his right hand was extended to make an undotted exclamation point to close the unspoken sentence, "What exquisite tact!"

The earliest photograph I have of myself taken while wearing a hat shows a boy of three or four, in a tweed fingertip coat, clutching a bag of penny candy, standing on the balcony of an apartment in New York, ample cheeks puffed out by a forced-for-the-camera smile, sandy-colored bangs showing under a leather flier's cap that buttons under the chin and has goggles attached. One can read much into this uncandid snapshot. Here is a little boy who has had much love. He will require vast quantities of attention later in life. He will not be easily pleased. Figures to have dental troubles. May just develop a thing about hats.

When I was a boy, it occurs to me now, I always had one or another kind of hat. I recall a not very impressive Indian headdress and, later, a more impressive Daniel Boone coonskin cap with a real raccoon tail. I had a number of brightly colored stocking caps, some that trailed down my back with a tassel at the end. There was a white navy gob's cap and several dark blue watch caps. A thick wool red-and-black checked cap with earflaps that I lost, maybe on purpose. Various baseball caps came my way, especially in grammar school days, and I broke in the bills of all of them, shaping them tentlike, as soon as I acquired them, in imitation of big-league ballplayers of the day. I remember in particular a red hat, an amalgam of a baseball and a hunting cap, that gave me pleasure every time I wore it. At ten years old, I thought I looked terrific in that hat; wearing it lifted my spirits, which were not low to begin with, and made me feel I was (in the phrase of the day) an astonishingly neat guy. Odd, is it not, how a piece of clothing—a hat, a shirt, a necktie, or a jacket—can induce one to take the most generous view of oneself and can bring one more sustained happiness than a good idea.

A hat that brought me no happiness at all was the maroon baseball cap I wore for nine or ten weeks during the sixth grade when I had a bout of—even now the word brings back the smells and sensation of shame—ringworm. A certain amount of it was then, as they say, "going around." Children of my generation were told not to put their heads on the backs of their seats at the movies, for this was supposed to be the main cause for the spread of the infection. I don't know if I caught mine at the movies or elsewhere, but one night I began scratching my scalp fiercely, and the next day my mother took me to the dermatologist with the most powerful reputation in Chicago. With large, confident hands, he held my head firmly under an ultraviolet light. "Yep," he said, unmoved, "he's got it."

The consequences following from that "Yep" were that I had to have my head shaved and that each night my mother washed my scalp in some special solution that smelled like every hospital corridor I have since walked, after which she spread a vile-smelling purplish salve over the infection. I had to wear a gruesome stocking cap made out of an old nylon stocking, over which I wore my maroon baseball cap. Having ringworm seemed like having what we kids used to call "cooties," but to the highest power. It seemed to me at the time a humiliation and a damnation and a bloody embarrassment. I brought a note to school that told of my infection and explained that I would have to wear my hat in class. No one, as I recall, teased me, no one made me feel any more leperish than I already felt. But one morning, walking along the halls between classes, our principal, a little man in an invariably gray suit whose name was Herman Ritow, snatched the hat off my head, exclaiming angrily, "Young gentlemen do not wear hats indoors." I stood there, my nylon-stocking cap over my shaved head, feeling exposed and utterly ashamed. Realizing that he had made a mistake, he apologized, but I felt unmasked as I never have since and hope never to be again.

To contradict the estimable Mr. Ritow, young gentlemen nowadays do wear hats indoors. Occasionally, a male student will show up in one of my classes wearing a hat, which puts it up to me to decide whether or not to call him on it. Often, I do, though usually not directly, preferring the sly-dog to the head-on confrontational approach in such matters. "That hat, Mr. Swenson," I recall once asking a young man wearing in class the black-and-orange cap of the San Francisco Giants, "are you wearing it for religious reasons?" When—shocking to report—he allowed that he wasn't, I gently signaled that he remove it, which he did without fuss. In a larger class, on another occasion, I noticed a student sitting toward the back of the room wearing a tight wool watch cap. He was a superior student, and so I decided to say nothing about his hat until after class, when, stopping him at the door, I asked, "Mr. Weiner, why are you wearing that hat?" "I was late this morning," he replied, "and didn't have time to shampoo." He then removed his hat, which released a small violence of curly, kinky, and spiky hair, a live and mobile bramble patch. "Mr. Weiner," said I, "please put your hat back on before you put out someone's eye."

But it is not the young alone who ignore the etiquette of wearing hats. On an airplane to New York, I not long ago sat a few rows behind a professor from the University of Chicago who wore his hat—a suede sports-car cap—for nearly the entire flight. Men wear hats of all kinds in supermarkets and in department stores and on buses. A man who regularly tipped or even touched the brim of his hat when passing women or acquaintances would likely today be thought to have a tic. Baseball players still take off their hats when the national anthem is played, but I'm not sure many other men do. The seasonal rhythm of changing men's hats must by now be almost lost, so that a passage such as the following from Eudora Welty's *The Optimist's Daughter* will one day seem—if it does not seem so already—as obscure as an Aztec rite for killing poultry: "Back home, Judge McKelva had always set the example for Mount Salus in putting aside his winter hat on Straw Hat Day, and he stood here now in his creamy panama." What a charming detail! Here's mud in your eye, Judge, and none on that creamy panama.

As the etiquette associated with wearing hats has all but disappeared, the institutions once in existence to deal with the care and maintenance of men's hats have disappeared completely. Establishments that cleaned and blocked men's hats, once ubiquitous on the cityscape, are now quite as difficult to find as new castanet or phylactery repair shops. Presumably, nowadays when a hat becomes dirty or begins to lose its shape, one pitches it out, even though it is not uncommon for a good man's hat to go for more than a hundred dollars. Leather hatboxes, of the kind I imagine Proust, the Duke of Windsor, and other serious wearers of serious hats must have had, are simply no longer available outside of antique shops. Hatcheck concessions in nightclubs and good restaurants, manned (make that womanned, you sexist dog) by hatcheck girls (always called girls no matter how old they were), are distinctly a thing of the past, with the consequence that the care of one's hat when on the town is pretty much one's own lookout. Even such a reliable old figure of speech as "If I'm wrong about that, I'll eat my hat" no longer has any grip, since the chances are great that the man who has said it isn't wearing a hat.

"If you're right about that," men used to say in the heat of argument, "I'll buy you a new hat." I don't say it, nor does anyone say it to me, but that doesn't stop me from buying myself a new hat whenever I come upon one that strikes me as amusing or that might make me as suavely dashing a figure as I secretly have always felt myself to be. I haven't thus far found the latter hat, but I have acquired a fair number of the former. I have owned a deerstalker's cap (à la Sherlock Holmes) in a material of bold checks; a wide-brimmed soft white hat fit for a deeply tanned Davis Cup official in the glory days of amateur tennis; a World War II tanker helmet (which I used to play football when I was in grammar school); a dark blue cap, with lots of what in the military used to be called scrambled eggs across its bill, of the kind worn by astronauts aboard battleships after they have completed successful celestial cruises; and authentic replicas of the caps—the most chastely elegant in all of baseball, in my view—of the Boston Red Sox and the St. Louis Cardinals. I no longer own any of these chapeaux. I have given some away to people who expressed admiration for them, misplaced others, allowed all somehow to get away from me.

A hat I still own, one that even as I write this sentence sits on my skull, is a rich blue baseball-style cap with the interlocking letters *N* and *D* in gold thread woven across its front, which stands for Notre Dame. It cost fourteen dollars and is a fine piece of goods but for one flaw: it has a small piece of plastic belting at the back that allows one to adjust it to fit different head sizes. It is, in other dreary words, what is known as "one size fits all." One-size-fits-all must be a boon to cap makers, who no longer have to worry about sizing hats to the eighth inch, but it does take the notion of individuality away from one's hat. Would Henry James have worn a one-size-fits-all hat? Would Oscar Wilde? Or either of the Brothers Goncourt? Seems doubtful. Among literary men, perhaps only Tolstoy, who late in life fancied a floppy peasant's hat, and Walt Whitman, who affected a high-crowned, broad-brimmed hat for the frontispiece of *Leaves of Grass,* would have gone for it. Whitman might even have written a poem, one of those democratic dithyrambs he specialized in, entitled "One Size Fits All":

> Send me your fat-, your large-, and your lumpy-headed,
> Your crania quite narrow, most pointy, and small.
> America, where the shape of a head need not be regretted,
> Great Democratic land where one size fits any and all.

Max Beerbohm once wrote rather a better poem about his old man-about-town top hat, which he abandoned when he left England to live permanently in Italy:

> > Once I used to perch on Max Beerbohm's pate,
> > But now he's become Italianate;
> > So here in contempt and disregard
> > I moulder for ever at Appletree Yard.

A photograph of the Italianate and quite aged Max Beerbohm hangs on my wall, and in it he, the dear old dandy, is sitting upon a wicker chair on the balcony of his villa at Rapallo. At the time this photograph was taken, he must have arrived at his eighties, which did not impair his fastidiousness. In the photograph he is nicely turned out in a cream-colored soft flannel suit with white waistcoat and dark tie and dark socks. But the crown on this jewel of a man is his hat, a straw boater worn at what I believe used to be called a rakish angle. It is a fine finishing touch. My guess is that Max would wear this hat when alone, standing on his balcony staring out at the limpid blue Mediterranean. Many a deliciously impish, interestingly charming thought must have floated beneath that old straw boater.

I was myself last seen in Italy in a hat altogether un-Italianate. It is a cotton khaki number, with a soft crown and a narrow red-and-blue headband and widish brim that I usually wear pulled down all the way round. I try to wear it with panache, but I am fairly sure it doesn't come off; the general effect is a bit suburban, not to say public golf course. I was last seen donning this hat in Florence, in the Piazza Signoria, near the Palazzo Vecchio, a plaid short-sleeve shirt on my back, copies of Christopher Hibbert's book on the Medicis and Montaigne's *Travel Journal* in my hand, cleverly disguised as a simple, rather unworldly American tourist.

Among Europeans, the English were traditionally a notably well-lidded people. The Victorians and Edwardians had splendid hats in rich assortment. Winston Churchill was a hat man, and his hats, worn either on state occasions or in leisure, never disappointed; on him they all seemed very Churchillian. Rex Harrison made popular the soft checkered hat he wore as Professor Henry Higgins in *My Fair Lady*. Before his disgrace, Jeremy Thorpe, then leader of the Liberal Party, brought back the low-crowned, narrow-brimmed hat known as the trilby (named after the chief character in George du Maurier's novel *Trilby*). Bowler hats, which every Englishman who worked in the City used to wear, are nowadays much less in evidence in London. I'm not sure that today there is a characteristic English hat. A pity, I feel, though I am not exactly sure why I feel that it is. Room here for a theory? When a nation loses its empire, I wonder, does it also lose its hats?

The male beret, like the *baguette*, may seem a staple of French life, but one doesn't think of Frenchman as behatted. Charles de Gaulle is most readily recalled in his kepi, but recent French premiers—Giscard d'Estaing, Mitterand—balding though they are, have sought their own versions of *la gloire* pretty much bareheaded. Camus, Malraux, Sartre, the most famous French literary men of the past half century, were almost always photographed, outdoors as well as in, hatless. André Gide was sometimes photographed in his library wearing over his starkly bald pate a largish skullcap—Sainte-Beuve, a century earlier, wore a plainer version of the same cap—of the kind favored by the Sephardic Jews of North Africa.

Which brings me to my good friends the Jews—"Some of my best Jews," a rabbi who during the 1960s lost many of his congregants to Quakerism is supposed to have exclaimed, "are Friends"—whose males, according to Orthodox tradition, are supposed to keep their heads covered in the sight of God. Oddly, apart from the small skullcap called the yarmulke, the Jews have not invented any particular headgear that I know about. True, the Hasidic Jews of Eastern Europe wore, or at least the wealthier among them did, an extravagantly fur-trimmed circular hat. But otherwise Jews have worn the hats of the countries in which they live. Among the ultra-Orthodox, one comes upon small boys wearing black versions of what I have been calling serious men's hats, which adultifies them, and it always takes me slightly aback. Normally observant Jewish boys of college age, dressed in every other way quite as their contemporaries are, will wear doily-sized yarmulkes held in place toward the back of their heads with bobby pins. Coming out of the Princeton Club in New York a few months ago, I saw such a young man walking in. "Ah," thought I, "F. Scott Teitelbaum."

Having established by these remarks what in our touchy times will pass as my bona fides as a Jewish anti-Semite, let me double down, as they say in Vegas, and see if I can't win some points for being a racist by asserting that, for some while now, black men have worn hats with more flair than anyone else in America. Sidney Poitier looks dashing in a conventional fedora, and Walt Frazier, the retired New York Knick, looks as good in a more dramatic lid. (The word *lid* for *hat* is, I am confident, a black coinage, which reminds me that, at a pro basketball game, I once heard one young black guy greet another, who was wearing a wide-brimmed pearl-white hat with one side turned down, by saying, "Hey, man, where'd ya get that sky?") I never saw the inevitably elegant Duke Ellington in a hat, but it must have been a fine spectacle; Count Basie I saw in one of those Greek fisherman's caps, which I thought unworthy of him. I believe that many black men, perhaps a proportionately greater number than white men, understand that clothes can be not only stylish but witty, and that a hat can be the wittiest item of all, a real topper.

Fred Astaire knew that hats could be amusing, and he wore them well, even while dancing. Astaire chiefly wore the hat known as the porkpie, a low-crowned, circular, flat-topped number; so, too, did Dick Powell. Frank Sinatra was a sometime porkpie, sometime traditional-fedora man. Spencer Tracy wore no-kiddin'-around pinched-front hats in his movies and looked, consequently, like someone you oughtn't to kid around with. Very tall, generally husky men—John Wayne comes to mind—tend to overwhelm a conventional hat, which is probably why Wayne looked best in various wide-brimmed variations of cowboy hats, from cavalry colonel to Indian scout. Gary Cooper, whom one was used to seeing in full ten-gallon cowboy hats, played the part of a lawyer in the movie version of *Ten North Frederick* and was absolutely convincing in a lawyerly gray black-banded, pinched-front hat; I at any rate would have paid his no doubt high bill for legal services. It may be that to look serious in a serious hat you have to be a fundamentally serious person, which is one of the things that worries me about my not being able to wear my own green hat.

Three other hats—one an orangey red, the other a pacific blue, both made of linen and with long bills, and the third a one-size-fits-only-me Chicago Cubs hat—complete my collection of hats. A modest collection it is, too, if collection it can be called at all, since those hats that I own have not been acquired in any systematic way but only because they struck my fancy at the time I first saw them. Truman Capote, I recall reading, was a fairly serious collector of hats and was himself often photographed in one or another mildly exotic piece of headgear. Is there, I wonder, a hat museum? If there is, I should be delighted to attend it, there to stroll among the hats of the famous and the great: Roman and Viking helmets, crowns and headdresses, tricorns and shakos, German World War I helmets and sola topees, hats jaunty and solemn, cocked, flocked, billed, beaked, peaked, and festooned with feathers, flowers, and (alliteration out of control here, can't stop now) other fine flotsam. My guess is that the most interesting private collection of hats must belong to the Pope, who, in my opinion, looks good in all of them. But then he, the Pope, would probably look great in my green velour hat.

Unlike the Pope, Chekhov, otherwise a handsome man, did

not look very good in his hat, a black, somewhat high-crowned job that, worn with his standard black suits, gave off a slightly clerical, not to say Hasidic, effect. Kafka, with his large pointy ears and low hairline, looks more than a touch unnatural in the one photograph of him in a hat that I have seen: the hat is a too-small derby that makes him faintly resemble an organ-grinder's monkey. Somebody ought to write a story entitled "Kafka's Hat." Bernard Malamud wrote one entitled "Rembrandt's Hat," which shows its author to have been a man who knew his headwear (". . . Rubin had taken to wearing various odd hats from time to time, and this white one was the newest, resembling Nehru's Congress Party cap, but rounded, a cross between a cantor's hat and a bloated yarmulke; or perhaps like a French judge's in Rouault, or a working doctor's in a Daumier print"). Gogol, of course, wrote "The Overcoat"; a shame he didn't write "The Hat" to go with it. John O'Hara published a collection of stories entitled *The Hat on the Bed*, and one of his stories in another collection, *Assembly*, is about a man whose most salient characteristic, at the outset of the story, is that he wears a plastic rain cover for his hat. When, in Flaubert's novel, Bouvard and Pécuchet meet for the first time on the Boulevard Bourdon, they fall into conversation only because they discover that each has taken the precaution to write his own name into his hat. And what, in *Alice's Adventures in Wonderland*, drove the Mad Hatter mad, exactly? Clearly, we have here a rich subject: hats in literature. Perhaps we ought to open the canon, as they nowadays say in university English departments, where they always have plenty of loose cannons around, and let in Hat Lit.

I have recently had lunches with two men who wore serious hats and had serious titles to go with them: one a gray-pinched-front-wearing federal judge, the other a mellow-copper-shading-into-brown-trilby-wearing former ambassador.

Both lunches gave me much pleasure. But more to my oblique point is how correct these gents—one of whom is younger than I, the other older—seemed in their hats. Caps wouldn't have done for either of them, and to have gone bareheaded on the wintry days on which we met would have seemed foolhardy for men who had impressive responsibilities. How is it, I ask myself now, that they wore their hats while my green hat seems to wear me, leaving me standing there with the earlier-mentioned mien of an indisposed spaniel?

I think it is that though my hair grows grayer and thinner, my eyes pouchier and dimmer, though I realize that I shall never sing at the Carlyle, live in Paris, or be adored for my divine physical grace, though I rely heavily on my age and experience in teaching the young and am pleased to have lived through an interesting half century of history, even though and despite and notwithstanding all of this, I, in some part of my decreasingly agile mind, continue to think myself, if not exactly a youth, then nevertheless a young fella. "There's nobody too old to be young," Saul Bellow wrote in *The Dean's December.* "That's the present outlook." I wish it weren't mine. One afternoon not long ago, the more I thought about it, the more disappointed in myself I became.

I strode to the closet, put on a raincoat and scarf, and clapped the green hat on my head. It was late afternoon, but still light, and I had a few errands to run. I looked at myself in the mirror before I left and the effect, despite my determination, was still pure spaniel. So be it. I walked into the downtown section of the town in which I live, attempting to appear nonchalant while keeping an eye peeled for anyone who might be giggling at me in my hat. I walked two blocks at a brisk pace, looking at reflections of myself in store windows whenever I passed them. The green hat still seemed strange sitting there atop my head. But no one, near as I could make out, was laughing or gazing upon me with a look that implied, "Catch the turkey in the green hat!"

A young woman asked me for directions to the local YWCA, which in my green hat I gave and she took with a perfectly straight face. In the stores where I shopped, and in the library where I picked up a book, I removed my hat, but no one seemed to think it odd that I was carrying such a hat. True, I met no friends or acquaintances, who might have remarked witheringly on my new headgear, but I kept moving through that cold and drizzly midwestern afternoon, eager to return to my apartment without being jolted by odd or hilarious looks.

When I was back in the apartment, I left my hat on, with its now single-mission crush, to see if I looked any different in it. In the mirror I looked not like a spaniel but like a boxer—not a prizefighter, that is, but the breed of dog: my eyes under the hat were red-rimmed and a touch rheumy from the cold and I seemed to myself rather jowly. Well, a boxer is not yet an adult male of mature years but it does beat a spaniel, at least in my view. It's a start. I intend to make further outings in my hat. If you happen to see a smallish man in a green velour hat, stroke his back, scratch him behind the ears, give him a biscuit if you have one on you, but whatever you do, please don't laugh at him. He's only trying to act his age.

A Few Kind Words for Envy

> *Well, though many an arraigned mortal has in hopes of mitigated penalty pleaded guilty to horrible actions, did ever anybody seriously confess to envy? Something there is in it universally felt to be more shameful than even felonious crime.*
>
> —*Herman Melville*

Y OU MAY AS WELL KNOW the worst about me, Doctor: I have not coveted my neighbor's wife in years, and I certainly do not want his Rolls-Royce, his duplex, or his shiny new fax machine. The young walk by, with their lithe limbs and clear minds, the years and years stretching out leisurely before them, and I feel no longing to change places with them. Neither do I desire to be a United States senator, a university president, the benevolent dictator of a small, mineral-rich country nestled in a lush setting in a lovely mild climate. I have no longing to enjoy the emoluments of the editor of the *New York Times,* the president of L'Académie Française, or Magic Johnson. Please do not understand me too quickly here, Doctor. I am not, I assure you, expressing complacency, smug (isn't *smug* the inevitable adjective here?) self-satisfaction with my own lot in life. No, something deeper, more mysterious, is going on. I am, not to put too fine a point on it, losing my capacity for envy, and I wonder, Doc, what can it mean?

I suppose none of this would worry me if, for so many years, I hadn't envied so widely, so thoroughly, so energetically. Many were the mornings I woke envying and many the nights I retired to envy, with time off for several little breaks for envy during the day. I read somewhere that one of the few benefits of growing older is that, in one's psychic economy, envy is replaced by admiration. I am not sure what I currently do with the time I once lavished upon envy, but I am quite sure that I do not pay it out in admiration. Can it be, too, that, now that I envy less, I shall grow fatter, for Horace, in the *Epistles*, remarks that "those who envy others grows thin despite vast wealth" (of envy, he adds, "Sicilian tyrants could never have contrived a better torture"). Is my loss of envy, then, likely to result in substantial weight gain? Am I, by envying insufficiently, endangering my health, Doc?

To begin my life not quite with the beginning of my life, the first thing I can remember envying was the parents of two boys I grew up with named Sammy and Billy Cowling. I loved my parents a very great deal, you understand, but on paper they just didn't stack up next to the Cowlings' parents. For openers, their father, Sam Cowling, Sr., was on the radio; he was the comedian on a then immensely popular radio show called *The Breakfast Club*, where, among other things, he did a bit known as Fiction and Fact from Sam's Almanac. Even at five years old, I knew that being on the radio was pretty hot stuff. He also happened to be a friendly man, kindly and thoughtful to children, and a good athlete. Sam Cowling, Sr., owned baseball spikes. I knew of no other father but the Cowlings' who owned spikes. Mrs. Cowling was feminine, beauti-

fully so, and named (are you quite ready for this?) Dale, which
was the name of Roy Rogers's wife. The Cowlings seemed so
wondrous to me as a child that, in those days, I shouldn't have
been surprised to learn that they kept a flowing-maned
palomino in the dining room of their two-bedroom apartment.
I don't want anyone to think that I envied the Cowling kids
their parents so much that I would have traded my own for
them. I would never finally have done that, but before deciding
not to do it, I believe I would have had to give it considerable
thought.

The second thing I remember envying was Catholics. For
a time, from roughly age four to seven, I thought the United
States was a Catholic country. This was owing partly to there
being a preponderance of Catholic families on our block and
partly to the movies of those years, a large number of which
seemed to feature Bing Crosby, Barry Fitzgerald, Spencer
Tracy, and Pat O'Brien playing priests. I envied the rigmarole
of the Catholic church, at least as it came across to me in the
movies and in the bits and pieces of it I was able to pick up from
families such as the Cowlings. Nothing theological or even
religious about this, for I was in fact rather like Valéry, who
felt that the Protestants had made a big mistake and should
have gotten rid of God and kept the pope. I liked the lighting
of candles, the confessional, the prohibition against meat on
Fridays, the clothes of priests and the extraordinary get-ups of
nuns. "May I offer you my seat, Sister?" I used to say whenever
the opportunity presented itself on Chicago streetcars or el
trains. "Excuse me, Father, but would you care to have my
seat?" I would announce with just a slight hint of an Irish
brogue. Any fisher of souls who knew his business could have
had me in the net in those days in fewer than thirty seconds.

I keenly envied friends who had hair of a kind that could
be combed to resemble the hairdos of Gary Cooper, Cary

Grant, Clark Gable, John Wayne, Errol Flynn, and other movie stars of the day. My own hair was thick, curly, thoroughly disobedient. It resisted pompadours, widow's peaks, and wouldn't even tolerate a simple part. "My goodness," I remember my mother once saying to me, "that part in your hair looks like Milwaukee Avenue," a reference to a lengthy diagonal street in Chicago that every so often juts sharply to the left or right or takes a surprising turn. I longed for precisely the kind of hair I didn't have—for lank hair that bopped up and down rhythmically when I ran and that I would frequently have to brush back out of my eyes with my hand. When crew cuts became the haircut of choice for Midwestern boys between twelve and eighteen, my hair wouldn't allow a serious flat-top crew cut either. All my attempts to obtain a crew cut ended in my coming away with an extremely short haircut that, mocking the power of prayer and pomade, would not stand up. Wishing to look like a brutish Big Ten athlete, I merely looked, as I am told an immigrant woman in Princeton once put it, like "a nice boy clean and cut from the Ivory League."

None of this, I realize, quite sounds like the envy that has had such a poor historical press. I refer to the envy that Balzac, in *Lost Illusions,* described as "an ignoble accumulation of disappointed hope, frustrated talents, failures, and wounded pretensions"; that Orwell called "a horrible thing," which "is unlike all other kinds of suffering in that there is no disguising it"; that the Austrian novelist Marie von Ebner-Eschenbach rated beneath hatred, noting that "hatred is a fertile, envy a sterile vice"; and that Gore Vidal, a writer scarcely known for specializing in the goodness of humankind, cites as "the only credible emotion, isn't it?" The motive for Cain's slaying of Abel was envy. Melville's splendid *Billy Budd* shows the horror that envy acted upon can achieve. "The vilest affection,"

Francis Bacon called envy, "and the most depraved," and in cataloging by type those frequently obsessed by envy, he writes: "Deformed persons, and eunuches, and old men, and bastards, are envious." Not, as I say, a good historical press.

Envy is apparently more easily felt than defined. Semantically, the word provides a thicket out of which only a philologist in a pith helmet and carrying a magnifying glass is likely to emerge with his spirits intact. Envy and jealousy, envy and emulation, envy and invidiousness, envy and ambition, envy and desire, the distinctions, the connections, the shades of meaning, the contextual nuances, all these things, if tracked down and carefully considered, could keep a fellow off the streets till well after the turn of the century. As there are some faces only a mother could love, so are there some books only a German scholar could write, and just such a book, *Envy: A Theory of Social Behaviour,* has been written by a Professor Helmut Schoeck, but it, on the matter of definition, plunges one back into the thicket. The standard dictionaries, I fear, are not very helpful on this troublesome word either. I have, therefore, decided to supply my own definition: envy, I say, is desiring what someone else has—a desire usually heightened by the knowledge that one is unlikely to attain it. This definition nicely accommodates my feelings about Sam and Billy Cowling's parents, the Catholic church, and tractable hair.

My homemade definition leaves out the dark elements of spite, hostility, ill will, and begrudgment that most definitions of envy usually include. These elements cause the Parson, in *The Canterbury Tales,* to call envy "that foul sin . . . the worst sin there is"; these elements give envy its unenviable status as one of the seven deadly sins. Yet there is also a milder, even approbative sense of envy that is free from all malice, as when the Reverend Sydney Smith, writing to Francis Jeffrey, remarks: "I envy your sense, your style, and the good temper with which you attack prejudices that drive me almost to the limits of sanity." I don't think that Sydney Smith, who chose his words punctiliously, misused *envy* here and that he really meant *admire*—he not only admired these qualities in Jeffrey but wished he had them himself.

Along the same line, I recall several years ago, awaiting a table in a restaurant, sitting in a bar in which a man was hired to play, on a small electric organ, such sappy songs as "I Left My Heart in San Francisco," "The Way We Were," and "Raindrops Keep Falling on My Head." The unspoken consensus in the bar was that plainly this man loved his work too much, for he was banging away at his instrument with a fervor almost religious in intensity, making conversation just about impossible. Then, during a brief pause between numbers, a smallish, well-dressed man, a customer sitting only a few seats away from my own, walked over to him, handed him a hundred-dollar bill, and told him to take the rest of the night off. How I not only admired but envied that gesture, the rightness and not least the largeness of it! The fellow seemed pleased with the money, which was probably more than his regular night's wages; the room settled down into calm talk; and I felt a tinge of envy for what I had just witnessed, knowing that, had the notion even occurred to me, I probably would have offered the man a mere twenty bucks to knock off for an hour or so.

Not that I haven't felt my share of rich purple envy, the kind mixed with lots of malice and generally grudging feeling. But I don't recall feeling much envy of this kind when young. Such envy as I did feel was instead rather impersonal. I envied the freedom and wider experience of kids older than I; I envied boys who had the knack of winning the affection of beautiful girls; finally I envied those who had the unfailing ability to make themselves enviable. Being born to parents of middling wealth and being oneself of middling talent is surely to know envy more comprehensively than otherwise, for it permits envy of those both above and beneath you. From my earliest adolescence, I recognized that there were families who lived better than mine—in larger houses, with more expensive cars, and more capacious habits generally—and felt them, somehow, luckier than I. But I also felt envy for those born without my advantages, and the constraints that went along with them, and I remember reading, in high school, a series of novels with slum settings—*A Stone for Danny Fisher, The Amboy Dukes, The Hoods*—that made me feel that people who grew up in slums grew up more interestingly, sexier, luckier than I. Envy perhaps begins with the attribution of luck to the next fellow, for it seems that people with a real flair for envy—of whom I was clearly one—almost always sees the next fellow as, somehow, luckier than themselves.

Very little about my youthful envy was subtle, and this, I believe, was owing to my having grown up in a family in which snobbery was almost nonexistent. Delicate, and even rather bulky, calibrations in status were of no concern to my parents, who did not bother to make many social distinctions beyond noting that some people were pleasant and some nasty, some rich and some poor, some gentile and some Jewish. Not at our dinner table were you likely to hear discussions about the fine distinctions between Williams and Amherst colleges, a Brooks Brothers and a J. Press suit, the Budapest and the Julliard string quartets. The Midwest was my milieu, and Midwestern the outer limits of my view. In both my own high school graduating class and in the class that preceded mine, only two students went to Ivy League schools—both, as it happened, to Harvard—and neither was a boy it would have occurred to me to envy. For envy to take on interesting twists, shadings, and dark refinements, a little knowledge—always, as the old maxim has it, a dangerous thing—is required.

Three writers who did, I think, know a good deal about envy, young and at first hand, were F. Scott Fitzgerald, John O'Hara, and the journalist George Frazier. Fitzgerald, who lived in the poorest house on a very good block in St. Paul, Minnesota, learned about envy as a boy and had this knowledge honed as a young man who ran the gauntlet of snobbery at Princeton. The great event of John O'Hara's life turned out to be a nonevent, his not going to Yale, which, wise though O'Hara was in so many other ways, he appears never to have gotten over. George Frazier, who came from the Irish neighborhood in Boston known as Southie, went to Harvard but with the certainty that, as an Irishman in the early 1930s, he could never hope to make the best clubs or quite cut it with students who came from the best families and prep schools. Frazier was an admirer of the fiction of Fitzgerald and O'Hara, and all three men were immensely, intensely interested not only in style but in stylishness. Frazier even wrote a column in *Esquire* under the rubric "Style," which tended to be about people who had it and people who didn't. The three men also shared Irishness, at a time in our history when being Irish did not carry the comfortable, vaguely comical connotations it does today. I think they never got over the feeling of being boys and young men with their noses pressed to the glass, outsiders looking enviously in. Too keen an interest in style, I have come to suspect, betrays an early life of longing and envy.

The best-known method for combating envy is to arrange to acquire everything you want in life. Unfortunately, it often takes the better part of a lifetime to decide what, precisely, it is that you do want, which leaves damnably little time to acquire it. "I suppose you must be well," wrote Virgil Thomson to Paul Bowles, "you had everything there was when you were young; nothing left to have, I suppose." An odd error, in so worldly-wise a man as Virgil Thomson, to think that wanting ever ceases. So long as avarice, lust, the appetite for glory, and snobbery continue to play as main attractions in the human heart, there is unlikely to be any serious shortage of wanting.

The sorting out of one's wants, especially when one is young, can be nearly a full-time job. I believe it was so for me, for, as I look back upon my young manhood, there was scarcely anything I didn't want and hence didn't vaguely find myself resenting in those who had it. I had only to see a beautiful woman with another man for my mind to jump to the question—the injustice, really—of why she was not instead with me. I would drive by suburban estates, walk past plush Park Avenue apartment buildings, and readily imagine myself happily ensconced therein. A Rolls-Royce convertible would tool by and, the resentment string in my heart plucking discordantly, I would not wish its owner well. (Not long ago, being driven in heavy traffic in a flashy raspberry-colored Cadillac Seville, I suggested to the car's owner, an intelligent woman who takes the world as it is, that she put out her arm to request a break in the traffic so that she could get into the next lane. "I'm afraid," she said, "that in a car like this people tend not to give you many breaks.") When I was young all I really wanted from the world was money, power, and fame— and, naturally, the little perks that went along with them.

The problem, I have long since concluded, is that I spread my desire too thin. I merely wanted everything—but nothing, evidently, greatly enough. I also hit a lengthy detour in my desirousness—I am, apparently, still on it—when I developed this strange passion for acquiring the knack of writing interesting sentences. Although this passion freed me from the comprehensive generality of my desires, it concentrated my envy.

For the first time, my envy lost its character of general longing and took a turn toward the particular, where envy usually gets unpleasant. What I now envied, with some intensity, was people of my own generation—I was then in my early twenties—who wrote better than I. Since I did not write all that well, my envy was given a wide berth and a fine chance for regular workouts. Around this time I can recall reading, in a biographical note, that a contributor to *Poetry*, a magazine I much admired, was born in 1940, which was three years later than I, a fact that registered like a rabbit punch to the kidneys. I didn't write poetry, you understand; nevertheless it seemed to me offensive for this young woman, three years my junior, to publish in a place in which I should have loved to publish had I written poetry. If this sounds a little crazy to you, not to worry; it only sounds crazy because it is.

The first of my contemporaries of whom I felt envious was a fellow undergraduate at the University of Chicago who had published a short story at the unconscionable age of sixteen. He had published it, moreover, not in some vulgar popular rag such as the *Saturday Evening Post* or *Redbook*, but in a then immitigably highbrow journal called *New World Writing*, where it appeared alongside work by the likes of Federico García Lorca and Wallace Stevens. I, who dreamed of publication, of seeing my name not in lights but in very small type, and who knew that publication, with luck, was still several years off, looked upon this boy and felt the sting of the world's terrible injustice. I also felt toward him a simple desire to exchange lives. I do not say that I despised him—he was very amiable, without the least air of superiority—but I should have preferred he matriculate elsewhere, so that his presence not remind me of my own drearily slow progress. Strangely, so far as I know, he never published another thing. Did some personal tragedy intervene, I wonder, or was his petering out owing to his own lack of sufficient envy?

Writers and musicians tend to be rivalrous, which means, inevitably, envious and jealous. (Jealousy, Professor Schoeck holds, "remains the passionate endeavor to keep something that is one's own by right," whereas envy has to do with wanting something belonging to another.) Painters, for some reason, seem less envious of one another, or at least I, with limited knowledge, can think of more genuinely comradely behavior among painters than among musicians and writers. (All exceptions granted: John Morley, for example, said that Matthew Arnold "had not a spark of envy or jealousy.") Envy figures to be deepest at the top. Isaac Stern is famously generous to young musicians, but is he, I wonder, sound on the subject of Jascha Heifetz? At a dinner party in heaven, I think it probably a good idea not to invite, on the same evening, Shakespeare, Goethe, and Tolstoy; nor would I recommend seating Leonardo and Michelangelo next to each other. Having achieved great fame, having garnered all the world's great prizes, does not necessarily slake envy. Nor are scientists free from envy. "Don't call X this morning," a friend once advised of a scientific acquaintance of ours. "The Nobel Prize was announced, and since he didn't win it again this year, he's likely to be in a foul mood." The joke here is that, a few years earlier, X had already won it.

But then artists and scientists have no monopoly on envy; it is merely that their often monstrous egotism tends to display it in high comic relief. Academics are very good at envy, too, and it takes so little to get their envy into gear: the slightest advantage or advancement gained by a colleague will usually turn the trick. Modern corporations, sociologists and journalists have been claiming for years, are scarcely more than envy organized. Freud contended that all women, to lesser or greater degree, were envious, because of the absence in their own anatomy of a certain male appendage—as sweeping a generalization as our century has to offer. And as long as we're talking appendages, Melanie Klein, the Freudian psychoanalyst, maintained that envy is learned, literally, at the breast, and in a paper entitled "Envy and Gratitude" she rattles on at depressing length about "the primary envy of the mother's breast." As a member of a generation whose parents felt breast-feeding was bad form—we, so to speak, dined on takeout—I feel disqualified from commenting on the persuasiveness of Dr. Klein's argument. I suppose, as the saying is, you had to be there.

Such theories—and I, for one, do not envy anyone who subscribes to them—gain currency chiefly because envy appears to be so universal a phenomenon that an equally universal theory seems to be required to account for it. No known society, from simple tribes organized around a belief in magic to large industrial nations organized around a belief in communist equality, has ever been entirely free from envy, and in many societies—those that are fearful of the evil eye of envy, those that through competition encourage envy—it has been dominant. Envy has long been considered a theological problem, with its power of sowing discord, especially where it abuts its sister sin of pride, for even among saints it is possible to imagine one envying the other's greater spirituality. Spiritual envy is often the subject of the novels and stories of J. F. Powers. The great political (Churchill, de Gaulle), spiritual (Gandhi, Martin Luther King, Jr.), and scientific (Freud, Einstein) figures of our century were none of them without envy in their lives. The pope, I am prepared to believe, is without envy, but was he before he became pope? Mother Teresa of Calcutta is the only person alive today that I can think of who appears to be utterly free from envy. Doubtless there are others, but if they were to meet in a convention I don't think one would need to reserve all the rooms in the Helmsley Palace to accommodate them.

I hope no one thinks that because I began this essay by saying I was running out of envy, I imagine myself approaching the spiritual trim of Mother Teresa. "I have never known life without desire," remarks the hero of Italo Svevo's *Confessions of Zeno*, and neither, I must report, have I. And where there is desire, be assured, nearby envy lurks. I thought, for example, that I had long ago made my peace with money and material possessions. The terms of the treaty, set by me, were entirely in my favor. I liked having money, respected money, had not the least doubt of the importance of money in human affairs. Yet I long ago decided that I would never knowingly truckle for money, or, if I could help it, expend great energy on projects whose sole result was pecuniary gain. Insofar as possible, I felt, everything I did should either amuse me or contribute to my intellectual progress—preferably both. My mind, in this scheme, would dwell in the clouds, my bottom never rest for long on the bottom line.

In exchange, I agreed to surrender all fantasies of real wealth: the country estate, the Paris apartment, the limousine, the staff of unobtrusive but absolutely reliable servants. Such fantasies ought to have been easily enough surrendered, for fairly early in life it became evident to me that I should never be rich. Part of my problem is less an antipathy than an inability to concentrate for long on money. It isn't that my mind is too fine to be violated by money matters, but instead that I haven't the attention span to learn the fundamentals of the stock, commodities, options, and other markets, or even to learn how to get the best out of the smallish sums I am able to save. Part of the problem, too, is that I could never quite imagine myself rich, with all the world's objects within my grasp. You are rich, says Henry James in *Portrait of a Lady*, when you can meet the demands of your imagination. My imagination, that nag, would never allow surcease in its demands, so that even with billions I could not, by Jamesian prescription, qualify as rich anyhow.

Do I, I ask myself, envy the very wealthy their riches and what they have brought them? I like to think not, and yet I do find myself taking a perhaps uncommon delight in hearing stories about burglar alarm systems going off in homes with serious art collections and spoiling otherwise gracious meals. Why does my spirit jump a notch when I see a large Mercedes being towed ignominiously off to Rolfe's Auto Repair? Can it be that we have a case here of *Schadenfreude,* that little subdivision of envy that *Webster's* allows itself the rare luxury of going alliterative to define as "malicious merriment at someone else's misfortune"? La Rochefoucauld gives *Schadenfreude* a genuinely hideous twist when he turns it very personal and remarks that "we always find something which is not displeasing to us in the misfortunes of our best friends." That is not envy, though—it is merely pure human viciousness. But there is, I think, a national *Schadenfreude* that is excited by revelations about the ostensibly very fortunate—the rich, the beautiful, the immensely talented—living in great emotional squalor. Howard Hughes supplied the country with Schadenfreudic titillation that lasted for months when it came out that his having a fortune in the billions of dollars did not prevent his living, poor devil, at the emotional level of a rodent. On its dark side, a democracy enjoys few things more than the spectacle of the rich undone, the beautiful besmirched, the talented penalized. See any issue of the *National Enquirer, People,* or *Vanity Fair* for confirmation.

Whatever their other deprivations, academics, intellectuals, and artists find no shortage of occasions for *Schadenfreude* or straightforward envy. The promotion denied, the manuscript rejected, or the dead-on devastating review can put the ugly little curl into the sympathetic smile of the colleague one had thought, until now, civil enough and not displeased with your success. "The Book of My Enemy Has Been Remaindered" is the title of a poem by Clive James whose refrain lines run: "And I am pleased." "And I rejoice." "And I am glad." Attend the honest *Schadenfreude* note amusingly played by Mr. James exulting at the defeat of a book by a rival poet:

> What avail him now his awards and prizes,
> The praise expended upon his meticulous technique,
> His individual new voice?
> Knocked into the middle of the week
> His brainchild now consorts with the bad buys,
> The sinkers, clinkers, dogs and dregs,
> The Edsels of the world of movable type,
> The bummers that no amount of hype could shift,
> The unbudgeable turkeys.

In intellectual life, awards and prizes are no longer quite the efficient swizzle sticks for stirring envy that they once were. Pulitzers, Guggenheims, NEHs, NEAs, honorary degrees— too many of all of these have by now been given out, and to too many mediocre people, for them any longer to carry much prestige, and hence to excite much envy. One award, though, can still do the job—narrow the eyes, quicken the pulse, dry the palms, send a little black cloud across the heart—and this is a MacArthur Fellowship. "It isn't the principle of the thing," my father used to say when attempting to collect bad business debts, "it's the money." And so with "Big Macs," as they are known in the trade, it isn't the prestige—too many not very impressive MacArthur Fellows already walk the earth—it, too, is the money. To win a MacArthur Fellowship is to go on a five-year ride at as much as $75,000 a year, for a total score of nearly four hundred grand. Nowhere near the kind of money that a switch-hitting second baseman can bring down these days, true, but still a nice piece of change.

My own carefully considered view of the MacArthur Fellowships was, I believe, similar to that held by most intellectuals, artists, scientists, performers, and inventors: sheer resentment for just about every nickel that did not go to me. I could understand the foundation's need to come across for a Navajo underwater architect or a woman weightlifter who is making a series of documentary films based on the Talmud; there are, after all, political reasons for such awards. But I failed entirely to understand the reasoning behind all the awards to literary men and women, none of whom, when you came right down to it (which I did rather quickly), seemed nearly so fit for a MacArthur as I. I won't go into my qualifications here, except to say that they seemed to me damn near perfect: my work was unusual and various; from the outside, I must appear overworked; and, like 99 percent of my countrymen, I could use the dough. What was more, a MacArthur Fellowship was one of the few such awards I had any hope of winning, for I had long ago determined never to apply for a grant or prize. If people wished to give me these things, splendid, but I was raised to believe that you didn't ask strangers for money.

So I went along from year to year, happy enough in my mild resentment, gaily mocking each year's fresh crop of MacArthur Fellows, until it was revealed to me that I had myself been nominated for a MacArthur. Good friends even sent me thoughtfully inflated letters of recommendation they had been asked to send in on my behalf. The envy in my soul now had to make room for its first cousin, greed. I thought a goodly amount in an unconcentrated way about what I might do with the money such a fellowship would bring in. If I had long ago agreed to forgo the large luxurious things, I had a decided taste for the small luxurious things: the German fountain pen, the Italian loafers, the dish of raspberries in midwinter. With my MacArthur Fellowship, there would be more of these things, much more. And, while at it, I ought to acquire some really good luggage. Most of the money, I thought, I would pocket away in some high-yield bank account, perhaps with an eye, at the end of the fellowship's five years, to plunking it all down on a modest house on Fiesole overlooking the red roofs of the city of Florence. The Big Macs were announced, I knew, sometime in the summer, and so about June first I began opening my mailbox in anticipation of finding that envelope from the John D. and Catherine T. MacArthur Foundation informing me that I had won a fellowship and might now, baby, let the good times roll. I thought, too, with some glee, how discouraging my winning a MacArthur Fellowship would be to my enemies. Alas, no letter arrived; it was not to be; and now, with the printing of these last few paragraphs, it isn't ever likely to be.

Had I won a MacArthur Fellowship, of course, I should have stepped across from the shady to the sunny side of the street—from being an envier to being envied. Even without a MacArthur, I might, it occurs to me, already have crossed that street. In the eyes of many, I am among the world's lucky people. And so—I knock wood here, lest the evil eye fall upon me—do I generally think myself. I have all the essential things: work that amuses me, excellent health, freedom, the love of a good-hearted and intelligent woman. Ought not that be sufficient? It ought, except that, human nature being human nature—or is it instead my nature being my nature?—it hasn't been sufficient to diminish envy; or at least it hasn't been until recently.

Within the past few years, two acquaintances, roughly my contemporaries, have written books that have made them millions of dollars. Despite the fact that my most recent royalty check was for $2.49, I found that I did not feel the least wisp of envy for either of these fellows; nor do I now. Not long ago I went to dinner with a political columnist who appears regularly on television, and our meal was interrupted by a request for his autograph; on the way out of the restaurant he was twice stopped by strangers and congratulated for recent work. I thought this fascinating, but my envy gland, usually so sensitive, gave not a twitch. True, for my own writing, posterity and not prosperity is the name of my (slightly embarrassing to admit) desire; and rather than widespread fame, I prefer to have a good name among a select audience of the genuinely thoughtful. But none of this is a convincing reason not to have felt envious. What good is longing, after all, if you can't long for contradictory things: the pleasures that riches bring and a life of simplicity, fame and privacy both? If you are going to force envy to be consistent, you're likely to put it out of business.

Many people would, of course, prefer to see envy go permanently out of business. Arthur Rubinstein, in his memoirs, remarked that at bottom anti-Semitism was owed chiefly to envy, and that the anti-Semite's "real hatred is concentrated on the Jews who possess the highest standards of ethics, intelligence, and talents, on those who, whenever allowed to compete, become prominent in all possible fields like science, art, or economy." On the other side of the ledger, envy is a foe of drab leveling. L. P. Hartley has written an anti-utopian novel entitled *Facial Justice* in which equality is known as Good E and envy as Bad E; what makes envy Bad E is that it arouses people's passions for discrimination, degree, difference, all the things that give life variety and make it interesting. Without these differences, Hartley's novel argues, life is scarcely worth living.

Perhaps the problem lies in the word *envy* itself. There is a good envy, of the kind that encourages dreams and aspiration, and a bad envy, based on disappointment and hatred. Perhaps a new word is needed, one that falls between envy and admiration, to describe the positive qualities of the former and strip it of traditional pejorative meanings. But the language, as Flaubert remarked in a very different connection—he was trying to convince his mistress of his love for her by describing its intensity—the language, as Flaubert remarked, is inept.

Meanwhile, my own problem, I begin to realize, is that I am becoming more discriminating in my envy. What I am discriminating against is the world's larger, more obvious prizes: wealth, fame, power. Glittering though these prizes are, and as they once were to me, I now find them mainly glaring, and in my own life even a little beside the point. I still envy large things, among them genuine achievement, true religious faith, real erudition. I justify envy of these things on the ground that surely there is no point in envying things you can actually have and that it is only the unattainable that is worth a serious person's envy.

The only expensive item I continue to envy is a small, well-made house with a fine view of water and of a naturally elegant landscape. For the rest, I envy things on which a price tag cannot be put, many but not all of them fairly trivial. Permit me to list them. I envy anyone who can do a backward somersault in midair from a standing position. I envy men who have fought a war and survived it. I envy people who speak foreign languages easily. I envy performing artists who have the power to move and amuse audiences to the point where the audience wants the performance never to end. I envy people who can travel abroad with a single piece of carry-on luggage. I envy people who have good posture. Above all, I envy those few people who truly understand that life is a fragile bargain, rescindable at any time by the other party, and live their lives accordingly.

Waiter, There's a Paragraph in My Soup!

---

*Do not read, as children do, to amuse yourself,
or, like the ambitious, for instruction. No, read
in order to live.*

—*Flaubert*

GEORGE BERNARD SHAW, who in a long life said so
many things, said that "[I] could remember no
time at which a page of print was not intelligible to me, and
can only suppose I was born literate." I wish I could suppose
the same—I wish, now that I am at it, that I could have called
Shaw "Bernie," which might have taken a bit of the helium out
of him—but I cannot. I can recall, quite precisely, the excitement of learning to sound out words on the page and that the
page in question was one from the Sunday comics, or what
used to be called "the funny papers." I can recall as well the
time when it began to be clear that reading would be not only
a source of heightened pleasure for me but indubitably the
central experience in my life. In fact, I tend to spend something
on the order of five hours each day reading. By my rough
calculations, this means that if I live on to my middle seventies,

I shall have spent something like eleven and a half years, of twenty-four-hour days, with a book or magazine in my hands.

It would be more if I hadn't come to books rather late in life. When I did I was already twenty and precocious in the ways of the world while retarded in those of the mind. Reading reports about the shameful condition of our schools, I smile the furtive smug little smile of the man who has gotten away with something. When I learn that only a very small percentage of seventeen-year-olds in America have read *Tess of the D'Urbervilles*, or know why *The Federalist* was written, or can locate Yugoslavia, Greece, and France on a blank map, I confess that I neither read nor knew how to do any of those things at seventeen, and I am none too confident about other such items that appear in these reports now that I am in my fifties. An extremely happy childhood in which books played almost no part and an indolent adulthood of the most desultory reading have made this possible.

My passion for reading showed up in the dark winter of my junior year at the University of Chicago. That winter, because all my classes met in the morning hours, I decided to sleep days and stay up nights, on the model, I subsequently learned, of George Sand. I would return from class at eleven in the morning and sleep until dinner at six or so. After dinner I played poker or gin, watched television, went to the movies, schmoozed, and engaged in other such character-building activities until nearly midnight. Then, when everyone else had turned in, I spent three or so hours doing my various school assignments. That left four or five utterly quiet, altogether solitary, absolutely delicious hours for reading exactly what I pleased.

What I pleased to read was not all that elevated. Elevation to heights where oxygen equipment would come in handy was already available in the classroom, for the curriculum of the

University of Chicago offered only great books for study. I had no argument with that; I still don't. But I, for my own personal reasons, had a simultaneous hunger for merely good books and even for a few rubbishy ones. So there I sat, in a small but immensely comfortable armchair purchased for five bucks from the Salvation Army, in my robe, a blanket over my lap, smoking cigarettes and drinking coffee or Pepsi-Cola, reading the novels of John O'Hara, Christopher Isherwood, Aldous Huxley, Henry Miller (in the plain green paperback covers provided by the Olympia Press), J. D. Salinger, Truman Capote, and I forget what others, awaiting the sunrise, feeling flat-out, deliriously, pig-heaven happy.

The hook was in, deep down, permanently planted. Henceforth one of my life's perennial problems was how to clear a decent bit of time for that lovely, antisocial, splendidly selfish habit known as reading. In *The Principles of Psychology*, William James remarks that "the period between twenty and thirty is the critical one in the formation of intellectual and professional habits," which certainly proved true in my case. I was fortunate in being able to indulge my newfound habit in a big-time way by being drafted for two years into the peacetime army, where reading, in the fastnesses of army posts in Texas and Arkansas, seemed far and away the best if not the only game in town. Early in my time in the army—in, specifically, basic training—no books, magazines, even newspapers were allowed, and, though this lasted only eight weeks, I can distinctly recall feeling it as a genuine deprivation, like withdrawal from cigarettes or sweets. Later in the army I found myself living alone with occasional stretches of seventy-two hours with no responsibilities and no money for sporting diversions and nothing else to do but read, which I did, at three- and four-hour uninterrupted clips. Too much of a good thing? William James, in his chapter on habit in *The Principles of*

Psychology, suggests that "even the habit of excessive indul-
gence in music, for those who are neither performers themselves nor musically gifted enough to take it in a purely intellectual way, has probably a relaxing [by which James meant a
bad] effect upon the character." But I took care of this little
problem by determining to become a writer. No other occupation, after all, would begin to justify such a voracious appetite
for reading.

Not long after this decision, I moved to New York, which,
say whatever you like against it, is a fine town for reading.
What makes it so fine is that New York has the best bookstores;
better yet, the best used-book stores; the greatest availability of
serious magazines and journals—and all of this in the most
generous abundance. Shortly after I arrived in New York, I
found a shop near the public library that sold back issues of
Commentary and *Partisan Review,* and some days, rather than
look for a job, I took five or six such back issues to the park
and read the day away. Later, when I found a job, it turned out
to be near lower Fourth Avenue, which in those days had an
impressive array of used-book stores. Walking along Fourth
Avenue, I always felt like a sailor in port at Macao; temptation
lurked everywhere, and so, prudent fellow that I was, I often
left my wallet in my desk back at work, lest I blow money
meant for telephone and electric bills on, say, a complete set
of John Ruskin. A hazardous city for an innocent reader, New
York.

While living in New York I acquired the habit of rarely
going out without tucking a book or magazine under my arm.
Vibrant and fascinating though New York can be, it has so
many parts and patches that are best read through: riding
subways, standing in bank lines, arranging any sort of bureaucratic business, sitting through traffic jams. New York probably offers more good reasons to avert one's eyes than any other

city in America, and where better to avert them than into a book? To this day, though long removed from New York, I still usually walk about with a book in hand, and I keep a book or two in my car, often getting in a quick paragraph at a stoplight. If you happen to be behind me, please don't honk when the light turns green, for I could be coming to the end of a paragraph.

Sometime in my middle twenties I began to review books, which, as a reader, I looked upon as the equivalent in sports of turning pro. The notion of being paid for reading was exhilarating. To be sure, the money was poor, but the hours were long and the fame quite fleeting. As a youthful book reviewer, I was apparently able to do a convincing impression of an intelligent and cultivated fellow, and so I was soon asked to review books intrinsically much more serious than I was. Would I care to review the most recent volume of Bertrand Russell's autobiography? Yes, I rather should. An English translation of Thomas Mann's letters is about to be published, and would I be interested in writing about it? Actually, I would. The memoirs in four volumes of Alexander Herzen have appeared, and did I have time to read and write about them? Not, I allowed, a problem. (Who, exactly, was Alexander Herzen, I recall thinking after agreeing to write about him, and I rushed to an encyclopedia to find out.) Yet I worked hard on these reviews, reading lots of other books in connection with them, in no small measure because I was fearful of making a jackass of myself by committing some horrendous error. This, I believe, is what is known as getting one's education in public. Whether it is also known as fraud is a question I prefer to let pass.

As a reviewer, I took notes on my reading and made light vertical pencil markings alongside pertinent passages that I wanted either to quote or to reread. It was all a bit like being a student again, which was not my idea of a jolly good time. One of the reasons I was so eager to be out of school—and knew with a certainty that graduate school was not for me— was my ardor to read what I wished and in precisely the way I wished to read it: not to read for examination or to acquire someone else's sense of a book. My temperament led me away from concentrated study. An expert—on anything—was the last thing I wished to become. If not in life then at least among books, I was a born roamer. Boswell reports that Samuel Johnson's mind was "more enriched by roaming at large in the fields of literature, than if it had been confined to any single spot," adding that "the flesh of animals who feed excursively, is allowed to have a higher flavour than that of those who are cooped up." If desultory reading was good enough for the Doc, I figure it is plenty good enough for me.

But to read desultorily, to be an intellectual roamer and grazer, luxurious though the freedom of it is, carries its own complications. Certain reading habits require a commensurate reading habitat. Multiple have been the definitions of the intellectual, that professional dilettante, but any realistic definition should include the unfailing identifying mark of his living amidst a vast welter of paper. In the abode of the intellectual, books, magazines, newspapers are everywhere. The splendidly sensible Sydney Smith, in composing a sketch for a cheerful room, suggests that tables "should be strewn with books and pamphlets," but he elsewhere warned that, to preserve oneself from becoming completely swamped by books, one should never "suffer a single shelf to be placed in [a room]; for they will creep round you like an erysipelas till they have covered the whole."

In my own apartment, books and magazines are currently in every room, including the kitchen. I am married to a woman whose tolerant love for her husband has caused her to repress her natural (and quite reasonable) penchant for order, which I try, with uneven success, to respect. I shiver at the thought of what my apartment would resemble if I lived alone. Harry Wolfson, the great Harvard scholar, who was a bachelor and a man of wide interests, is said to have kept books in his refrigerator. A pity microwave ovens weren't in wide use in Wolfson's day—he died in 1974—for one would have perfectly accommodated his Loeb Classics.

The home of any serious desultory reader has to be a shambles of odd reading matter, chiefly because such a reader has no useful principle of exclusion. By the very nature of his reading, his interests tend to widen not to narrow, to exfoliate endlessly, like a magical rose. Ten or so years ago I could have confidently said that I had no interest, as a reader, in space travel. I have since taken a very elementary course in astronomy, and so books on space and astronomy come into our apartment, as does a subscription to *Astronomy Magazine.* A recent trip to Italy has brought modern Italy into the already crowded list of subjects I now read about regularly. An essay in the British magazine *Encounter* on a writer I had not hitherto heard of named Julian Jaynes caused me to acquire a copy of Jaynes's book *The Origin of Consciousness in the Breakdown of the Bicameral Mind.* It begins brilliantly. Another bookmark in yet another book; another book atop yet another pile of books—one of several—with bookmarks in them. It is endless, absolutely endless—and I must confess that I wouldn't have it any other way.

Having too much to read isn't the worry; having too little to read has been on occasion. In paucity, never profligacy, lies fear. Sir James Mackintosh, the journalist and jurist who wrote for the *Edinburgh Review,* used to travel around the country with so many books in his carriage that he couldn't pull down the windows. S. N. Behrman, the American playwright and memoirist, used to travel with a portable library, a smallish leather case that contained twenty-five or thirty books. To people who do not require ample dosages of print, taken daily, this will seem excessive, even foolish. I myself think it shows eminent good sense. Abroad, in the town of Ravenna, I had read my way through the books in English that I had brought along. Sheer panic set in. I discovered a shop off the Piazza del Popolo that sold British paperbacks. I bought two novels of the insufficiently amusing British novelist Simon Raven, at the scandalous price of ten dollars a shot, which at least calmed me down until I returned home.

I don't mean to imply that anything at all will satisfy my hunger for reading. I have never, for example, been able to read detective stories or spy thrillers, no matter how elegantly composed, though I enjoy both kinds of story in the movies or on television (which I often watch with a book or magazine in hand). Wherever possible I prefer books that amuse me; this comes down to meaning books that were written with style. I would rather read a stylish book than a style-less more scholarly book on the same subject. I have of late been reading Sacheverell Sitwell's *Liszt.* Doubtless more serious books on Liszt have been written. Yet Sachie, as Sitwell's friends called him, seems to me to have written a fine book because he knew what was interesting in life, knew how to tell an anecdote well, knew how to put a lot of spin on his sentences. He was, in two words, no dope. I prefer not to read dopes. I prefer to read writers who know more about the world than I do, and to steer clear of those who know less. I discover more of the latter as I grow older, but the growth of my own wisdom is not proceeding at so alarming a rate that I fear running out of things to read.

Although reading is a solitary act, it need not be done in isolation from other acts. In his chapter on habit, William

James cites a man named Robert Houdin who could read while juggling four balls. (I assume he wasn't reading Immanuel Kant.) A husband and wife conversing behind their separate sections of newspaper over breakfast is an old cartoon set piece. Lots of people—I am among them—read while watching television, sometimes during commercials or through the more trivial news items or awaiting a weather report or sports scores. Reading while watching baseball on television is especially fine and, given light reading, is easily brought off with the help of instant replay. Why do one thing at a time when you can do two? And between the two done simultaneously, light reading and watching television, the former almost always wins out.

People commonly read while bathing and sunbathing. In my time I have done a good bit of both, but I may have been pushing it when in my early twenties I brought a copy of *The New Yorker* to read in a steam bath. It was in fact my first visit to a steam bath, and once inside I proceeded to clamber to the topmost bench, nearest the ceiling, whence the heat exuded. I must have been sitting there reading *The New Yorker*'s racing writer Audax Minor no longer than three or four minutes when I felt an odd pulsating in my forehead. I touched my hand to it and discovered a good-sized vein. I next looked down to find that one of the pages of the magazine had raveled itself round my wrist, the humidity in the room causing it to cling to my forearm. Head pulsating, arm now wrapped in dampened slick paper, body wound in a sheet, in panic I fled, never again to make the mistake of treating a *shvitzbud* as a substitute for the Reading Room of the British Museum.

Reading not in the bath but in the bathroom is a subject that, in any earnest survey of reading habits, cannot be avoided. ("It's alimentary, my dear Watson.") Recently asked for permission to reprint an essay I had written, I in turn, never shy of the vulgar question, asked if there was a reprint fee provided.

There was none, I was told by the editor, but he hastened to add that his journal was ardently read by its subscribers. "Really," he said, "they take it to the john." I had not hitherto thought of that as a standard, but it is unquestionably true that one tends to take only reading matter that one is genuinely interested in to the bathroom. (The same goes for the hospital.) Whether an author thinks it beyond the dignity of his work to have it read in the bathroom is another question. As a bathroom reader myself, I should feel honored to have others read me in the room that the English, in a notable euphemism, used to call "the House of Commons."

Books for bathroom reading oughtn't be too heavy, in any sense of the word—neither too large nor too densely argued. What is wanted is writing that can be read in short takes, easily abandoned and returned to at a later time without losing the thread. Diaries and journals and collections of letters fill the bill nicely; so do wittily written novels of modest length. I read a volume of Tocqueville's letters in the bathroom; I am currently reading selections from James Agate's amusing diary *(The Selective Ego);* and some years ago, over a two-year stretch, I read through the twelve slender novels that comprise Anthony Powell's *Dance to the Music of Time.* More recently, I read three volumes of Frank Sullivan's humorous writings, and I continue to read, intermittently, two books by Arthur Koestler on scientific subjects: *The Case of the Midwife Toad* and *The Watershed,* a biography of Johannes Kepler. But then everyone will have his own notions about what makes for the most commodious reading.

Reading while eating has its own complexities. Eating alone, especially in a restaurant, one's solitude seems redoubled. One notices, as one rarely does when dining in company, the lengthiness and noisiness of one's chewing, the slight awkwardness with which one handles one's cutlery, one's ineptitude with lettuce. Dining in solitude renews one's sense of the necessity of company to the enjoyment of food. A book at the side or in front of one's plate takes one's mind off all that, serving as a screen against the public when dining out, as a companion when dining alone in one's own home. I do not like to eat in restaurants when I am alone, and avoid it whenever I can, but when I cannot I always come armed with a book or magazine. I eat most of my lunches alone, at home, and automatically pick up something to read while eating lunch.

Here the problem is never what to read but what to eat—more specifically, what kind of food can be efficiently eaten while reading. (Taking the opposite tack, Edmund Wilson once remarked that the Marquis de Sade was the only writer he couldn't read along with his breakfast.) Soup, for example, is very poor stuff while reading. Not only does it require concentration on its own, not only is it potentially messy, but it doesn't allow one much pause between spoonfuls to read a paragraph or so. Of more solid foods, pastas, stews, club and other sandwiches that require two hands to manipulate are rather more than is wanted. A plain cutlet is nice, or a cold breast of chicken; so is cheese (if you can afford the cholesterol) and fruit—one takes a bite of food, chews deliberately, reads a paragraph, returns to the plate, and then returns to the page, which sets up a nice little rhythm of reading and eating, reading and eating. Certain sandwiches can be quite good, too, a cold turkey sandwich, say, or a ham sandwich, or any other cold cuts that are without greasiness, which will inevitably find its way onto the page, as the jelly from a peanut butter and jelly sandwich inevitably will. It's a deep problem, and Reading Lunches, on the model of TV Dinners, may be the solution. I hope to get around to packaging such lunches for mass consumption once I complete the proposal I have been writing to Ted Turner about my idea for turning some of the great

Hollywood Technicolor extravaganzas—*The Ten Command-
ments, Gone with the Wind, Fantasia*—into black and white.

I hope nobody is gaining the impression that, merely because I seem to be reading all the time, I get much reading
done. I don't, or at least it doesn't feel as if I do. Perhaps the
chief reason I don't is that, apart from being an unmethodical
reader, I am also a fairly slow reader and have been ever since
I made the decision, in my early twenties, to become a writer.
As a writer, I don't claim to read more penetratingly than
others, but I do find that I ask certain questions while reading
that nonwriters need not ask. Anyone reading an interesting
passage in a book asks, if often only subconsciously, Is what I
have just read formally correct? Is it beautiful? What does it
mean? Do I believe it? Along with these questions, a writer asks
two others: How technically, did the author bring it off? and
Is there anything here that I can appropriate (why bring in a
word like *steal* when it isn't absolutely required) for my own
writing? Reading not alone for meaning and pleasure but also
for style, in which further meaning and pleasure are usually to
be found, can surely keep a fellow from being able, as the
speed-reading schools all promise, to sit down early of a Saturday afternoon to read through the collected works of Werner
Sombart and still have plenty of time left over to enjoy oneself
at the big dance.

If I were a fast reader, I have sometimes thought, it might
only be the worse for me. My reading ambitions might have
doubled. I might have been unhappy—felt guilty—if I didn't
read at least a book a day, as the literary critic Stanley Edgar
Hyman once told me that he did. As a fast reader, too, I should
have often been tempted to stay up all night to finish a stirring
book—a thing I have done only twice in my life, both times
with novels: once, in my adolescence, with Willard Motley's
Knock on Any Door, and a second time, in my twenties, with

I. J. Singer's *The Brothers Ashkenazi.* H. L. Mencken is said to have been a blazingly fast reader. Samuel Johnson may have been, if not faster, more efficient, for according to Adam Smith's account as retold through James Boswell, Johnson "had a peculiar facility in seizing at once what was valuable in any book, without submitting to the labour of perusing it from beginning to end." It was Johnson who thought Henry Fielding's novels a waste of time, who said that no one ever wished *Paradise Lost* longer, and extended this remark by once asking Mrs. Piozzi, "Was there ever yet any thing written by mere man that was wished longer by its readers, excepting *Don Quixote, Robinson Crusoe,* and the *Pilgrim's Progress?*" Johnson's own method was to begin a book in the middle and if he felt the inclination to read more to go back to the beginning.

My own present modus operandi is to begin a book at the beginning and, for one reason or another, often to bog down somewhere near the middle. On a quick search of our apartment, I find twenty-three books with bookmarks in them, and this does not count books I am reading for professional reasons. Jumping from one book to another, reading lots of magazines in between, sometimes I go a week or two without actually finishing a book. Every once in a while, out of sheer frustration, I sit down and finish reading two or three books, if only to get some minor sensation of completion in my life. All these half-read books, taken together, form no pattern, show no evidence of anything resembling coherence. Here, for example, currently resting half-read on the coffee table in our living room is the following pile of books: *Max Weber,* a biography by his wife Marianne Weber; *Words in Commotion: And Other Stories* by Tommaso Landolfi; *Collected Poems, 1919–1976* by Allen Tate; *Fast Company: How Six Master Gamblers Defy the Odds—and Always Win* by Jon Bradshaw; *A Part of Myself,* the autobiography of the German playwright Carl Zuckmayer; *A*

Distant Episode: The Selected Stories by Paul Bowles; and *Conducted Tour: A Journey Through Twelve Music Festivals of Europe and Australia* by Bernard Levin. One distinctly feels the want, in this brief list, of a slender volume of instruction on needlepoint for left-handers and a Rumanian cookbook for heterosexual men who like to entertain at home, which would round things off nicely.

What admirable catholicity of taste! I can imagine some people saying in response to this confusing little pile of books. But then I can as readily imagine others saying, What a mushbrain the man must be! Myself, I incline toward the latter camp. If I had to extrapolate the personality of the man from this pile of his half-read books, I would posit a man without much discipline, an intellectual clearly, but also a hedonist of the intellect, who gives way to his every whimsical interest. He may be a man who has come to feel that not only is reading a significant form of experience but in some respects is rather more efficient and pleasurable than actual experience. He is a man—no *may* about it—who was much taken with the following brief passage, in a review by Mark Amory, in the British *Spectator:*

> Reading about bridge has several advantages over playing it: no waiting, no cross partners, you do not lose money, you can stop when you want to, it can be done in the bath, every hand has a point. Best of all, you can visit above your station, and at least appreciate the skill of others.

Each of us will have his or her own list of words or phrases that can readily be substituted for *bridge* in that passage. Mine would include *boxing, Third World travel, complicated love affairs.*

As widespread and central an experience as reading is, seldom is reading mentioned in novels. We are told that Don

Quixote's imagination was inflamed by reading too many trashy novels; so, too, was Emma Bovary's, much to her ultimate chagrin; and Jane Austen occasionally makes plain that one of her characters is victimized by his or her reading. But the only novel in which a character actually appears sitting down in a chair reading, at least to my knowledge, is Somerset Maugham's *The Razor's Edge*. The narrator of the novel comes upon the young American Larry Darrell, sitting in his club reading William James's *The Principles of Psychology* and at the end of the day he is still there, having finished reading James's nearly fourteen-hundred-page tome in a single sitting. This small bit of reporting has always seemed to me to place in peril Maugham's reputation as a writer in the realist tradition.

Visual artists have done better by the subject of reading. Renaissance painters would occasionally paint a monk or saint at study. Persians would paint a caliph or scholar in a garden with a volume of verse in his hand. A pity, I have always thought, that Rodin didn't put a book in the other hand of *The Thinker*. The nineteenth-century painter Gustave Caillebotte, who was much interested in the life of the mind, has at least three paintings that I know of in which people are reading: in one, a man in a high straw hat, a loose white blouse, and espadrilles is reading with his back to the viewer, while his wife pauses in their lovely garden; in another, three women are doing needlework while a fourth reads from a small book, perhaps containing poems; and in the third, a man is reading a newspaper as his wife, whose back is to us, nevertheless expresses forlornness as she looks out a heavily draped window onto a Parisian street. I thought Edward Hopper might have painted people reading, but, on further thought, given Hopper's penchant for the subject of loneliness, it is unlikely, for no one absorbed in a book is really lonely.

On Reading is a charming little book of photographs,

chiefly taken in Paris and New York, by the Hungarian photographer André Kertész (1894–1985). Many of these show people reading in public places: parks, churches, libraries, fire
escapes, standing on city streets. However public the setting,
a person reading, these beautiful photographs make plain, is
engaged in a private act. One also grasps that reading, though
far from a passive act, is nonetheless a reposeful one. Reading
may provide most of us all the repose we obtain outside of
sleep. Whether he is photographing an elderly vagrant reading
a newspaper just fished out of a trash can or a well-set-up
gentleman in his book-lined, wood-paneled study in Paris,
people out of motion, at rest, in repose, are Kertész's true
subject in this book. Repose ought, in some part, to be the
intention of all readers.

   Some reading, of course, is more reposeful than others. The
least reposeful for me is that provided by the newspapers.
Many people make a meal out of a newspaper, chewing and
swallowing every morsel; I can't find the makings for the
lightest of snacks. I read only one, the *New York Times,* and
that only six days a week, and, like the prostitutes of Athens,
never, never on Sunday. A wise man whose name I cannot
recall said that one picks up newspapers in anticipation and
inevitably sets them down in disappointment. I no longer feel
the anticipation. I chiefly consult the newspaper to get a feeling
for the heft and slant of current political opinion and to discover—the only real news—who has died. I scan the letters
column in the (usually) vain hope of finding a man or woman
after my own heart. I take a pass on the editorials, unless they
promise to be especially cowardly, and quickly check the
sports. I glance at the reviews and absurdities on display in the
pages given over to the arts. I merely glimpse the general news,
and read only to the end articles about scandal. I prefer to have
the whole deal out of the way in something under twenty
minutes, and generally do.

I suppose I justify being so cavalier about reading newspapers because I put in so much time reading magazines, which provide me with a vast quantity of information about current events, social trends, and what is the going thing in art and much else. Something like twenty-five magazines come into this apartment, all but four of them American. I love magazines, and shall never forget the excitement when in my last year of college I discovered such intellectual magazines as *Commentary, Partisan Review,* and *Encounter.* Around the same time I began reading *The New Yorker,* which I have continued to do for more than thirty years, and other magazines—the *New Republic, Harper's,* the *Atlantic*—for nearly as long. There are times when it feels as if *all* I read is magazines, other times when the backlog of unread magazines rises perilously high and getting through them seems an impossibility. At such times, I hope that the magazines that continue to arrive will have nothing in them of interest to me: that the *New Republic* will give an issue over to a symposium on arms control, that the *Atlantic* will run a thirty-two-page essay on global soil erosion, that *The New Yorker* will begin a seven-article series on growing surprisingly large radishes in canoes in southwest Canada by John McPhee. I earlier mentioned not reading the *New York Times* on Sunday, but a friend saves the *New York Times Book Review* and the *New York Times Magazine* for me, and I pick them up from him in clumps of eight or ten copies of each. Having all these copies there before me all at once is a wonderfully effective way of warding off any chance of my reading, say, a review of the memoirs of a woman who grew up in the home of a reform rabbi in Las Vegas or a lengthy account of industrial development along the banks of the Gogra in Nepal.

But lest anyone get the mistaken notion that I have become even mildly discriminating in my reading habits in my middle years, let it be known that I am a subscriber to *Vanity Fair.*

There is nothing about *Vanity Fair* I like, but I find myself reading a large amount of each issue, doubtless with a stricken look upon my face, for it is filled with articles written by people, about other people, all whose ideas on what constitutes the good life are so far distant from my own as to make it almost seem as if we are of different species. I also alternate subscribing to *Esquire, Gentlemen's Quarterly,* and a newer, more malicious magazine called *Spy.* Any one of the three is quite sufficient, for their main purpose, at least in my personal reading diet, is to remind me how far behind the times I am falling—and, given the times, how pleasant is the fall. As if to underscore this, *Spy,* to which I currently subscribe, prints a good deal of material in a minuscule type that I cannot read without strain. Continual reading, surely, has contributed to the fact that I now wear glasses almost full-time. "Professor," a student said to me the other day, "I didn't recognize you not wearing your glasses." "Ah, my dear," I wanted to answer, "I do not recognize myself wearing them."

My eyesight does not figure to improve, nor does my appetite for reading figure to diminish. I wish I could settle down into fixed reading habits—like the man I know who reads a chapter of *Pickwick Papers* every evening—or begin now to devote myself to rereading many of the important books I read badly because I read them too early in life the first time around. But I think this is unlikely. If anything, my reading has become more desultory than ever. Only recently have I begun to read about music in I won't say a serious but in a fairly large-scale way. Once musical notation is put on the page, I am a goner, but I do enjoy reading about the lives of the great composers and the memoirs of the great performers. I always read a great deal of literary criticism, but now I read more music, art, and dance criticism. I like to read criticism, to watch a man or woman stand and deliver his or her understanding of how art works and how well a particular artist has brought it all off. The only criticism I do not read is that having anything to do with the Brontës. Why, you ask, exclude the Brontës? I don't really know, except that they are all so gloomy, and excluding one small body of writing makes me feel as if I have drawn at least one line and am in some sort of control of my reading life, which of course I am not.

As one grows older, reading becomes an even keener pleasure and an ever greater comedy. Part of the pleasure derives intrinsically from the activity itself; and part from its extrinsic rewards, not the least of which is knowing that there will always be plenty to read and so superannuation presents no real fear. (Great readers have this advantage over great lovers.) The comedy of reading is owing in part to one's memory, which in the natural course of things retains less and less of what one reads; and in part to that oldest joke of all, which Dostoyevsky insists comes to each of us afresh, I speak— hushed tones please—of death, which among other erasures rubs out all that one has read over a lifetime.

Still, as addictions go, reading is among the cleanest, least harmful, easiest to feed, happiest. As an addiction, however, one shouldn't underestimate its power. If reading has presented me with many of the most delightful moments in my life, there have also been times when I should rather read than be with a friend, or when reading about life has seemed more attractive than life itself, and I happen to be extremely fond of life. My heavy reading schedule keeps me from thinking too much about an afterlife, but it occurs to me that in the various descriptions I have read of heaven, no one ever mentions a library or bookstores there. Can it be that there will be no books or magazines in heaven? (Hell, I assume, will be full of newspapers, a fresh edition of each published every thirty seconds, so that no one will ever feel caught up.) If there is nothing to read in heaven, I am not sure I want to go. But should I ever be invited, I trust that whoever is sent to fetch me will at least have the common courtesy to allow me the few moments required to come to the end of my last paragraph.

Entre Nous

HAVE YOU A MOMENT to hear the most aesthetically pleasing piece of gossip I have heard over
the past decade? It was told to me by an English friend, who
is something of an insider in the rather enclosed affair that is
English intellectual society and whose word I have good reason to trust. It was this same friend who told me that the
novelist Salman Rushdie and his American wife were about to
break up their marriage just before the publication of Rushdie's
The Satanic Verses forced him to run to ground. To have to hide
from your potential assassins in the company of a wife you no
longer care for, or who no longer cares for you, this, I recall
thinking at the time, was a torture worthy of one of Dante's
lower circles in hell—like having your lower lip sanded off
while a Gila monster lunches on your ankle bone. But was the
story true? Several months after I first heard it, Reuters, the
European news agency, reported from London: "Salman
Rushdie, the British author who has been living under an
Iranian death threat since February, and his American wife, the
novelist Marianne Wiggins, have separated." So there you
have it: a pretty peachy piece of gossip from a practically
unimpeachable source.

Well, anyhow, and other pregnant pauses, this same friend

told me that the very left-wing wife of a then dying English writer was having a love affair with—gossip, don't you agree, ought to be bestowed like a small but charming gift, hidden for a moment or so behind one's back—with, yes, Fidel Castro. Forgive me for not supplying more names, but I feel I cannot mention the name of the now dead writer, lest I dishonor him, or of his widow, lest she sue the spats off me. As for Fidel, diplomatic nonrecognition being what it is, I gather that he can't lay a legal glove on me. But even without all the names, what I find aesthetically pleasing about this story is that it has all the ingredients of gossip at its most delectable: it has sex, celebrity, decadence, a touch of international politics, lots of steamy matter for the imagination to work upon, and, finally, it cannot be checked.

Not, you understand, that learning of Mr. Rushdie's domestic troubles or of Dr. Castro's amorous amusements came anywhere near making my day on the particular days I was told about them. But I must confess to having been a mite pleased to come into possession of both these stories. Chalk it up to my morbid curiosity, if you like, or to my low and prurient taste. I myself think, though, that the true source of my pleasure in such stories is that they put me, in however peripheral a way, in the position of being an insider, a man in the know. I was permitted a glimpse behind the scene that was not available to everyone. I was being offered the news before it was news, which is the only time that the news is generally worth having. Evelyn Waugh has a journalist in *Scoop* put the same point rather more bluntly: "News is what a chap who doesn't care much about anything wants to read. And it's only news until he's read it. After that it's dead." Gossip, then, is the news while it's still alive.

Most definitions of gossip do not talk about news at all, but instead feature slander, betrayal of secrets, invasion of privacy,

and backbiting. Detraction, libel, and malice get a good workout, too, in the standard definitions. Gossip has not had a very
good press in dictionaries, going from "idle talk, groundless
rumours, tittle-tattle" *(The Concise Oxford Dictionary)* to—considered as a verb—"run about and tattle; to tell idle, esp. personal, tales" *(Webster's New International,* second edition). For
a long while gossip was described as an activity chiefly of
interest to women. Trivial stuff, gossip, for the vast most part,
except where it is held to be plain vicious, which in many
quarters it of course is. Stendhal once famously remarked that
the only thing wrong with ice cream is that it isn't a sin (which,
given contemporary concerns with calories and cholesterol, it
has since become). But I sometimes wonder if the only thing
wrong with most gossip is that it is considered a sin. Or is it
the sense of its (usually) modest sinfulness that lends gossip a
pleasing touch of tarragon? I think of gossip whose intention
is not obviously mean-spirited as sinful at the level of, say,
overeating or some other mildly forbidden activity in which
one hesitates briefly before muttering "What the hell!" and
pitching in.

Very little of the gossip I am privy to is at the Fidel Castro
level of celebrity. None of it has to do with show business. Big
business and high finance, too, are excluded. I have friends
who are themselves friendly with men and women in important political places, though this has never been a rich or amusing source of gossip, with the exception of the story I heard
not long ago about a U.S. senator whose serious drinking has
caused his staff frequently to put off callers by saying that the
senator cannot come to the phone just now because he is on
the floor. I don't ever hear Jackie Onassis stories. No, most of
the gossip I hear is about writers and editors, publishers and
academics, folks in my own line of work. Much of it has to do
with foibles—pathetic thrusts of ambition, sensuality out of

control, acts of intellectual cowardice, examples of fetching hypocrisy—almost none of it calculated to remind one of the deeply ingrained dignity of the species. The gossip that comes my way falls under the category of what the writer Isaac Rosenfeld, who himself had a strong appetite for gossip, used to call "social history," a term that lends gossip a bit more standing.

The only famous figure in artistic or intellectual life who apparently eschewed gossip, at least to my knowledge, was John Dewey, although my guess is that Wittgenstein, too, was able to live without it. According to Sidney Hook, Dewey "never gossiped, and although with the exuberance of youth I used to press him hard on men and events he had known intimately, except once or twice he never gave way." Bertrand Russell, Hook reports, gossiped with great enthusiasm. Justice Holmes used to say that to find the general in the particular is the chief difference between philosophy and gossip, which is very smart, yet his own letters—to Harold Laski, to Sir Frederick Pollock, to Lewis Einstein—are from time to time nicely laced with gossip. The Duc de Saint-Simon, in his *Memoires,* created a classic work of literature out of chronicling gossip at the court of Louis XIV. Henry James and Marcel Proust were great connoisseurs of gossip and both made fine artistic use of gossip in their novels. (Recall Proust's narrator's aunt, in Combray, who, through the good offices of her maid Françoise's regular rounds in the village, is able to acquire an encyclopedic knowledge of everyone else's business without ever leaving her own invalid's bed.) E. M. Cioran has somewhere remarked that two of the most interesting things in the world are metaphysics and gossip; that they are the *most* interesting, I do not know, but the two do at least share the qualities of being often fascinating, sometimes believable, and usually unascertainable.

The affable Reverend Sydney Smith, founding editor of

the *Edinburgh Review,* was always eager for gossip, never more so than when living in the country, far from London or any other large city. He was never above requesting of his corre-spondents—among whom were several of the most clever Englishwomen of the first half of the nineteenth century—that they "refresh my Solitude with Rumor's agitations." To one correspondent he writes, "I am panting to know a little of what passes in the world"; to another, "I long to know the scandal"; and to Lady Mary Bennet, "Pray send me some treasonable news about the Queen . . . and don't leave me in this odious state of innocence, when you can give me so much guilty information, and make me as wickedly instructed as yourself." In the realm of gossip, it is understood, only those who give can hope to receive. "I will send Lady Grey the news from London when I get there," he writes to Lord Grey. "I am sure she is too wise a woman not to be fond of gossiping; I am fond of it and have some talent for it." And, decidedly, he did, as when he provided J. A. Murray, who worked on the *Edinburgh Review,* with this small nugget:

As I know you love a bit of London scandal learn that Lady Caroline Lamb stabbed herself at Lady Ilchester's Ball for the love of Lord Byron, as it is supposed. What a charming thing to be a Poet. I preached for many years in London and was rather popular, but never heard of a Lady doing herself the smallest mischief on my account.

Gossip tends to be most plentiful in capital cities. In the United States one of our problems—it is not a very pressing one—is that we have more than one capital: Washington for politics, New York for art, no one special place for learning and intellectual life. I am insufficiently interested in politics to find the gossip of Washington—the "guilty information," in Sydney Smith's fine phrase—of much interest. Stories about

Ted Kennedy, no matter how rococo the details, bore me. Which journalist is napping with which ambassador's former wife doesn't do it for me either. I consider every sentence that has the initials CIA in it at the level below that of gossip. At a large dinner party in Washington I once sat next to an Englishwoman who seemed a bit bored and who I later learned wrote a gossip column called "Ear on Washington." Had I known her occupation I would have regaled her with stories about congressmen cavorting with giraffes in condominiums overlooking Rock Creek Park owned by Saudi furriers.

They order these things better in Manhattan, where the gossip tends to be less exclusively politically and generally livelier. Perhaps this is owing to artists and intellectuals being intrinsically more amusing in their foibles than politicians. (My own favorite short definition of gossip, self-devised, is two people happily agreeing on the foibles of a third.) It may have something to do with New York itself, where the crowdedness and costliness of life would on first sight almost seem to preclude the fertile conditions of clandestinity necessary to carry on gossip-worthy activities. Manhattan today is not Versailles under the Sun King, which provided the perfect soil for gossip—namely, many brilliant and ambitious people living together at close quarters—but Manhattan is an island, where nothing is easily hidden and news travels fast, and, somehow, everyone seems to know everyone else's business. All this may not be one's idea of a sensible way to live, but it does make for a vast quantity of spirited talk.

Nowhere else am I treated to so rich a feast of gossip as in New York. "Heaven for climate," as Mark Twain used to say, "hell for conversation." Before the day is done all the great gossipy subjects usually get covered: money, sex, dereliction, bad character, the conjugal jungle. I learn that a not very good writer has been given a publisher's advance of $200,000 on a book that he is ill suited to write and will probably never finish; that a painter, a married woman of fifty or so, mother of four, has declared herself a lesbian and moved in with another woman; that the son of a powerful publishing executive has been found guilty of selling drugs; that a famous feminist is the "great good friend" (as *Time* magazine slyly used to put it) of a big-time real estate operator. But the spirit of gossip in New York has always been best summed up for me by an anecdote about a poet who, during a reading at the 92nd Street YMHA, read a poem in which he allowed that he was both homosexual and Jewish, and to whom, after the reading, W. H. Auden is supposed to have remarked, "Why, Jeffrey, I had no idea that you were Jewish."

Gossip is impressive in its variety. It can run from entertaining chitchat to genuine viciousness. It can claim to be factual or sheerly speculative. It can be trivializing, reprehensible, and absolutely vital to know. (Gossip differs from rumor in being exclusively about people, while rumor is frequently about such events as wars, economic trends, forthcoming business decisions.) Aquinas, Kierkegaard, and Heidegger all attacked gossip, though the latter had good reason to fear it, in both his public and private life. One recent writer on the subject, Patricia Meyer Spacks, speaks of "serious" gossip, whose "participants use talk about others to reflect upon themselves, to express wonder and uncertainty and locate certainties, to enlarge their knowledge of one another." Sissela Bok, the ethicist, who devotes a chapter of her book *Secrets* to gossip, after contemning it for the standard reasons, goes on to say that "the desire for such knowledge [as gossip brings] leads people to go beneath the surface of what is said and shown, and to try to unravel conflicting clues and seemingly false leads." I myself tend to think of gossip as an entertainment of a literary kind, in which life is understood to be a vast novel, with hundreds, even thousands of characters passing through, none of whom can be altogether measured by what he or she wishes to reveal about him or herself, so that gossip, when it is available, supplies additional evidence that must itself be carefully measured. At the outset it has to be understood that this novel may never yield a definitive meaning, but merely provides endless small surprises and the suggestion of revelation that never quite arrives, which, as Jorge Luis Borges once said, is perhaps the essence of the aesthetic phenomenon.

Revelation suggests secrets, yet not all gossip is about secret information. Some has to do with information not yet confirmed—has the poet really left his fourth wife? has the university president really agreed to take a job with the foundation?—but that, sooner or later, one way or another, will be known. Much gossip does have to do with secrets, or rather and more precisely with secrets broken. Someone swears you to secrecy about an item he ought not to be telling you but nonetheless feels you should know, thus paying you the high compliment of assuming you can keep a secret when he has just demonstrated that he himself cannot. Often gossip of this kind will come with specific instructions: it is strictly *entre nous;* or it's between you, me, and the lamppost; or this is to go no further lest my cassoulet be truly cooked.

I do believe that I am among that portion of humanity—how small a minority are we?—that can keep a secret. Self-deceived in all the standard ways, I do feel on this count I know my man. I am one of those people La Rochefoucauld must have had in mind when he indited his Maxim 120: "We betray more often through weakness than through the deliberate intention to betray." As a man with a taste for gossip, I have felt most stirringly the urge to pass along an interesting bit of "guilty information," to earn myself easy intimacy at the bargain price of putting the next fellow in possession of some inside knowl-

edge that will delight him and cost me nothing, except a reinforced knowledge of my own weakness. Not wishing to be
reminded of this weakness, I stifle the impulse, choke the urge,
and stow the information in a small Ziploc bag in my mental
freezer. Those who are able not to give a secret away, live to
gossip another day.

None among my friends, far from being morally opposed
to gossip, is above enjoying a bit of gossipy information. Some,
true enough, have a keener appetite for it than do others and
do go in for it in rather a big way. A common taste for gossip
is not enough to build a friendship upon, but the exchange of
gossip is an intimate act, or at least can be, and the extent to
which one can gossip freely with a friend is one measure of the
depth of intimacy in a friendship. I refer to gossip here in the
full range of its activity: passing along socially classified material, speculating on other people's base and sometimes neurotic
motives, being candid and usually comic about the pretensions
of one's acquaintances. Gossip, you might say, and I believe I
shall, is candor at other people's expense.

Obviously, one doesn't wish to be candid in this way with
just anyone about everyone. In the line of gossip, I am ready
to go just so far and no further with some people only on
certain subjects. Apart from my wife, to whom I do not even
bother to hide my most inchoate thoughts, I have one dear
friend with whom I feel I can say anything about anyone. It
is a very great luxury to have such a friend. In our gossiping,
this friend and I do not moralize—being perfectly attuned to
each other's views on morality, to do so would be superfluous—though I assure you we can be perfectly scorching on
people we agree in finding disagreeable. Our real pleasure is
instead in the human circus. We delight in the spectacle that
human conduct provides when gossip reveals secret ambitions,
pointless perversity, and sheer jolly wackiness. The true behav-

ioral sciences, as they are studied neither in Palo Alto nor Cambridge, Mass., are what fascinate us.

As a man with a healthy appetite for gossip, I have naturally considered the possibility of having myself been the subject of gossip—putting in a cameo appearance as a small red-nosed clown with large yellow floppy shoes in the human circus just mentioned. I fear I may have led a too-quiet if far-from-blameless life. As a subject for gossip, I prove disappointing in the realm of money (I haven't enough to be interesting), sex (I am entirely monogamous, if you can believe such a striking confession as the twentieth century draws to a close), and am without secret ambition (I am, occupationally, without complaint). Only one event in my adult life might generously be construed as mildly scandalous: in my early thirties, I underwent a divorce. Since I talked about the details of this divorce with no one, did friends and acquaintances, I wonder, speculate upon the causes for the breakup of my marriage—Borgian cruelty? gruesome sexual incompatibility? petty-cash disputes?—as I would doubtless have done upon theirs?

As it happens, I went semi-public with this event in my life by writing a general book on the lugubrious subject of divorce, concentrating on its bitter ironies, unresolvable injustices, and ultimate sadness. In this book, I devoted several passages to my own emotional condition while undergoing the humiliations, little and large, that await anyone who goes through a divorce. I quite deliberately left my ex-wife out of the book, since I did not want it to turn into an act of personal grievance against someone I once loved and who was in no position, literarily, to defend herself against a professional writer. The problem arose, however, when the book's publisher informed me that there was wide interest in the book, and asked, in the gentle hammerlock way of a certain kind of publisher, if I would agree to a bit of publicity about it, which meant, in the nature of the case, a bit of publicity about me, which really meant that, if I was clever, here was a chance to gossip about myself for fame and, the hope was, immense profit.

Never a man to go after a main chance enthusiastically, I grudgingly agreed to go ahead with the publicity. In for a dime, as I frequently say, in for the dolor. So I went on the road, without Rosinante you may be sure, visiting seven cities in six days. This took place some fifteen years ago, and much of it is now rather blurred, but then it all seemed even more blurred when I was actually going through it. I appeared on several extremely dopey local talk shows, both on television and on radio, and underwent a number of newspaper interviews that struck me as distinguished by the high degree of insincerity shown on both sides. I was the Divorce guy, not as interesting as the Transsexual who had passed through town the previous week, but a little better than the woman who wrote the book on what's wrong with our public schools. I especially recall showing up at 6:30 A.M. on a rainy morning in Cleveland, where a goateed and potbellied disc jockey, wearing a red turtleneck and pants with a flowery print on them, announced, "Hey, WIXY weather in five minutes, but right now we got Joe Epstein down here to answer all your questions about divorce."

Around this time, *People* magazine sent out a woman journalist in a green Mercedes with a Hungarian photographer in tow. The Hungarian addressed me straightaway by my first name and walked off to snoop through my apartment for photo possibilities. The journalist began pumping me with a series of questions all meant to elicit the true lowdown about my private life. Two such sessions were held along with a number of telephone calls between us. A problem, clearly, had emerged. It was that, from *People*'s standpoint, I didn't appear to have much of a life, or at least none that could be told strikingly in seven or eight hundred words and three or four photographs spread across two or three pages. I had made it a condition that my two then young sons, who lived with me, were not to be photographed. A woman I was then seeing had too much natural refinement to wish to appear in the pages of *People*, so there would be no shots of us holding hands, walking dreamily down the misty beach.

There was only me, who wrote and read and watched a certain amount of television and whose life had no discernible dramatic turns or twists. The journalist took me to breakfast and pleaded for my ex-wife's address, but it was no sale. The whole story, from the journalist's point of view, wasn't working out. When the piece finally ran in *People* there was a photograph of me sitting on a bed reading a biography of Chekhov and another, shot from behind, of me standing before a bathroom sink, the whole pictorially suggesting a campaign for getting plenty of rest and remembering to wash your hands. If I hadn't realized it before, I had to know it now: to a journalist devoted to digging up rich dirt, I was hopeless, a loser, a real dog—plain bad copy. But, then, as the disc jockey at WIXY in Cleveland might say, "Hey, I can live with that."

What I live rather less easily with is the extent to which gossip has come to take over larger and larger stretches of contemporary life. The pervasiveness of gossip today—on television, in journalism, through books—is making gossip, one of life's minor pleasures, something of a major nuisance. Much investigative journalism is based chiefly on gossip, which is to say on "leaks"—and what else is a leak but betrayal or machination by gossip—and an exposé is scarcely more than a bit of gossip gone public. Gossip-ridden books by former cabinet members and the wives of presidents are the new form of contemporary national history. Gossip remains delightful only so long as it remains private; once gossip goes public, it is inevitably degrading.

"Until quite recently," the critic John Gross has noted, "gossip was by definition what *wasn't* printed and what *wasn't* televised." Gossip columnists had long been on the scene: Hedda Hopper and Louella Parsons in Hollywood, the egregious Walter Winchell in New York, with his infamous "blind" items ("Communists, your meeting, originally planned for the Roosevelt Hotel on January 9, has been canceled"). The magazine *Confidential,* which specialized in go-for-the-groin scandal, made a great loathsome splash in the 1950s before being brought down by lawsuits. But all this was understood to be peripheral, strictly freak-show stuff, and never quite permitted under the big tent. Now, somehow, it has become center-ring.

People, Us, Vanity Fair, Entertainment Tonight, and *Lifestyles of the Rich and Famous* are only a few of the magazines and television shows devoted nearly exclusively to purveying gossip. "She's outrageous, off the wall, and full of gossip," ran a recent promotional ad for the television talk show of the comedian Joan Rivers. The phenomenon of people appearing on talk shows to gossip, in effect, about themselves is now a commonplace one. At first only fairly garish show business folk did this—starlets and specialists in the embarrassing such as the actress Shelley Winters—but soon politicians, businessmen, and serious writers began to do so. Truman Capote was masterful at milking a bit of gossip on a television talk show. I once saw John Cheever, over television, inform Dick Cavett (and a few million other people who happened to be watching) that he had for years been an alcoholic. Poor Cheever, his own children finished the job for him, when his daughter wrote a book that went into ample detail about his being homosexual and, later, his son edited a collection of his letters that confirmed his sister's scandalous stories. If my children were ever to do anything even remotely similar to me, I should greatly regret, from my grave, not having beaten them sufficiently when they were young.

"I'm a very private person" is nowadays something one usually says only to a journalist or a talk-show host. No one, once he or she reaches a certain level of fame, is permitted much in the way of privacy. The more famous one is, the less is privacy permitted. The three most-gossiped-about people in the United States today must be Jacqueline Onassis, Frank Sinatra, and Elizabeth Taylor, which probably means that they are also the three most famous people. Even in death, Marilyn Monroe and the brothers Kennedy continue to do a brisk business as the subjects of gossip. "Marilyn Pregnant by Kennedy at Death" runs the headline of a gutter-press tabloid I glimpsed in the express line in my local supermarket. Cyril Connolly once said that his ambition was to write a book that could still be read ten years after its original publication; perhaps for a celebrity a comparable ambition might be to continue to be gossiped about twenty-five years after his death.

People conspiring in gossip about themselves is another new phenomenon. I was reading along rather uninterestedly in an *Esquire* article about the television news anchorman Peter Jennings when I came across the intelligence that Jennings's wife had allegedly had a love affair with a Washington columnist. The story was apparently initially revealed in the newspaper *USA Today*, but in the *Esquire* article Jennings and his wife evidently do not mind speaking further about it. ("Their marriage, Marton [his wife) will say later, was 'kind of on automatic pilot.' ") Friends joined in to give the *Esquire* journalist further information. Jennings, we learn, "was humiliated, angry, grieving," and "nothing mattered to him more, he decided, than keeping his family together." Why are this man and his friends agreeing to talk to a journalist about such private matters? Surely this doesn't come under the rubric of the public's right to know. Can it be that Jennings thinks that candor about such material will make him, a man who makes vast sums for reporting nightly disasters to the country, seem more human? With knowledge of the man's marital difficulties in mind, now, when he has finished reporting upon oil slicks, the breakup of the Communist empire, the rise in crime, the decline in the GNP, now is one supposed to wonder, "And at home, Peter, everything going all right at home?"

How famous does one have to be to be worth gossiping about? Doubtless the more famous the better. If it is to be gossip of the kind carried in the mass media, one must be easily identifiable. This in practice probably means that one ought to earn one's living in show business, politics, sports, television, or the arts. One might make it, too, if one is related to the immensely rich or the vastly famous or the socially well connected. In England a royal-family connection will ring the gong every time. A story recently appeared in the *New York Times* about a relative of Queen Elizabeth, a young woman who is twenty-fourth in the line of succession to the throne, publicizing a dispute with her parents about her out-of-wedlock pregnancy. The young woman—she is twenty-three—pleaded over BBC television for her mother not to pressure her to marry. Her gentleman friend, a professional photographer, told the press that he doesn't "agree that Marina should be pushed up the aisle into, as such, a shotgun wedding."

What an old-fashioned phrase "shotgun wedding" now seems! When I was young, it cropped up with a modest frequency. Now, when one hears it at all, it has a positively antique ring. So many couples living together unmarried has put a prominent dent in it, and the passage of stricter gun control laws outlawing the ownership of shotguns ought to finish it off linguistically. But not so long ago a bride going to the altar pregnant carried, in the realm of gossip, real punch. Let me see if I can recollect other items that did. Many among them in the middle-class neighborhoods in which I grew up had to do with failure, usually in business, sometimes with children who didn't turn out as planned or otherwise went astray to graze in those pastures set aside for black sheep. I knew about a man who went to prison for a year for draft evasion during World War II: he was supposed to be working at a job in a defense plant and sent someone else to work at it in his place; when he was caught it was considered a sad disgrace for his family, who stood by him. As an adolescent, I never heard true-life stories of philandering or cuckolding, though there were of course endless jokes about both. As for homosexuality, it, to my youthful knowledge, had not yet been invented.

Tame stuff all this might now seem, but it left plenty of room on the margins for scandal, and hence for gossip, to thrive. Contemporary standards of behavior, by contrast, have all but annihilated scandal. It isn't that the world has run out of scandalous behavior, merely of behavior it chooses to consider scandalous. As a notable example, I notice a practice allowed extremely successful male artists of fathering illegitimate children: Woody Allen and Mikhail Baryshnikov have both taken this to be among great success's generous perks. Where a single divorce used to seem mildly scandalous, now three or four marriages seem unremarkable and thus scarcely worthy of gossipy remark. *The New Yorker*, once a bastion of cultural prudery, whose regular contributors had to find other magazines to publish their sexier material, is now open in its support, at least in criticism, of pornography in visual art; and not long ago one of its critics calmly proclaimed her lesbianism in its pages. Eustace Tilley, not to speak of William Shawn, would have fainted dead away.

The consequence of the annihilation of former categories of scandal has been not to eliminate gossip but instead to raise its stakes. Where once upon a time there might have been gossip about whether or not an actor or writer was homosexual—and I recall vividly a time in the early 1960s in New York when such gossip was used as a strong smear tactic, the social equivalent of McCarthyism—now the gossip is more likely to turn on whether or not such men have AIDS. One saw this in the general flow of gutter-press gossip about Rock Hudson before his death; it operated even more vigorously in the case of Roy Cohn. In the less glaring intellectual world that I inhabit, it had for years been said of a young writer, a gifted man from a distinguished artistic family, that he was dying of AIDS. When he died, at forty, no mention was made of that dread virus in connection with his death, at least in any press or personal accounts I read, and so people are left to speculate upon it. The moral here is that, though scandal would appear to be eliminated, gossip doesn't die. It only finds new subjects.

Gossip contains a built-in intensifying element. It has to provide not merely ever-fresh but ever-more-amazing information. One of the more hideous gutter sheets on display in my supermarket illustrates the way this works. Along with running rather standard stories about Elvis, John Lennon, and Hitler still being alive, about UFOs, miracle drug cures for cancer, and monstrous animals, it occasionally carries headlines about fantastic pregnancies, such as "Girl Six Pregnant" or "Great-Grandmother Eighty-two Pregnant." The other day, waiting to have my groceries checked through, I noticed the headline "Two-Headed Woman Pregnant." (I assume that the paper even now has an ace reporter out searching for the extraordinary man who caused this pregnancy.) Given the new openness of behavior, and the degree to which the once-scandalous appears in many quarters to have become normalized, regular human gossip sometimes seems to be approaching the stage of "Three-Headed Woman Pregnant with Antelope."

Not that I in the least worry about them, but it occurs to me that it probably isn't easy to be a gossip columnist in this new scandal-free atmosphere. The day is long past when Hedda Hopper could hold Hollywood in thrall, or Walter Winchell could terrorize anyone in politics, sports, or show business by threatening to run a mischievous item about him. Today one must have to reach, stretch, invent to find items that truly titillate. I do not now read a regular gossip column, but if I did, so mad has the world of professional gossip become, I think I should just as soon read one that was purely imaginative. It would contain items like "Trump Buys Bessarabia," "Barbara Walters Contemplates Sex Change," "Oprah Dates Donahue Son," "Cher Undergoes Face Transplant." Let 'er rip.

Yet most people with an interest in gossip, myself among them, continue to survive on the scraps from the *ancien régime* of middle-class behavior. A man in his seventies marries a woman forty years younger than he, and the telephone rings, sly smiles are passed along with the bread across the lunch table, and the heads of women shake knowingly. A local basketball coach is fired without explanation after a winning season, and the telephone rings, and a friend reports that he heard from another, well-placed friend that behind the firing is what is euphemistically known as a "conflict of life-style," which dysphemistically means that the coach had been bonking the daughter of one of the team's owners. My interest—disinterest really—in such matters does not seem to slacken.

A bit of gossip is a datum, a report on ostensibly hidden

doings, evidence that the old Adam has been let loose or some fresh Adam has invented a new twist in what one would have thought was a game in which all the possible twists had already been wrung. A man is discovered slipping around town with his ex-wife, an enormously successful playwright demonstrates pathetic vanity about his rather wretched poetry, a woman worth millions never neglects to remove the extra soap and to steal at least one ashtray whenever she stays at a hotel. I love to hear about all such human zaniness. Not only is it rich material in and of itself, but it shows that finally the last word can never be said about our peculiar species. So splendidly peculiar are we that I have this unavoidable suspicion that, despite my carefully attending to all the observations available in books and through art, despite my full-time attempt to be a man upon whom nothing is lost, I still ain't heard nothing yet.

Money Is Funny

"IT IS FUNNY ABOUT MONEY," wrote Gertrude Stein, who thought money "a fascinating subject," adding that it was "really the difference between men and animals," and concluding that "everybody has to make up their mind if money is money or if money isn't money and sooner or later they decide that money is money." For Miss Stein the decision came later rather than sooner, when she was fifty-nine, to be precise, and had achieved a nice little financial score with *The Autobiography of Alice B. Toklas*, which she claimed to have written one beautiful autumn in Bilignin in a mere six weeks. With this, her first serious infusion of cash, she bought a new eight-cylinder Ford, a costly made-to-order coat at Hermès, and two studded collars for Basket, her poodle. A few more items were added, such as the telephone she installed in her famous quarters at 27 rue de Fleurus, on which to talk with her literary agent, and two servants, a married couple, where previously there had been one. Miss Stein had made up her mind that money is money all right, and she seems to have enjoyed it hugely and without the least complication.

I knew that money was money quite a bit earlier than did Gertrude Stein. Aided by the instruction of parents whose early maturity was rudely interrupted by the Depression, I grew up with an emphatic sense that money was important—very, very important. I continue to believe in its importance, but not, apparently, with sufficient ardor. Keen though I am for all the swell things money can buy—food and finery and, in some circumstances, even freedom—I am, evidently, not keen enough. Certainly, I have never been able to concentrate for long on ways to acquire it, or to devise other ways to make what little of it I have multiply at an impressive rate. Far from being proud, I am rather embarrassed about my ineptitude with money. A man of many winters, I should by now be initiated into its secrets. I am not only of mature years but Jewish into the bargain, and Jews—consult the long-standing stereotype on this—are supposed to be especially adept with money. That I am not is a shame, really; so long as there is anti-Semitism in the world, I figure I ought at least to show a small profit.

I don't mean to poor-mouth. In fact, my financial condition approximates that of the old gentleman hit by a bus, then laid gently on the sidewalk by bystanders, his tie loosened and head resting on the overcoat of one among them who, while awaiting the arrival of an ambulance, asks him if he is comfortable. "*Comfortable* I don't know," says the old gentleman. "I make a nice living." So do I make a nice living. I make it, moreover, doing almost exactly what I wish to do, which makes me a very lucky fellow indeed, even if I do work 364 days a year (and under the bed on Yom Kippur). Yet, happy in my work though I am, not believing myself generally underpaid, of late I have begun to think myself something of a piker.

It isn't that I earn too little money; it is that so many other people seem to be earning so much more. Immense quantities of the stuff—"long green," as they used to call big money on the fairgrounds—is flowing across the land. A young lawyer fresh out of Harvard Law School may be good for eighty or ninety grand a year; a physician who doesn't turn more than a quarter of a million a year qualifies as an altruist; painters of not even dubious quality ring up obscene sums for their daubings; any professional athlete currently making less than a million a year must view himself as a hopeless mediocrity; movie stars and rock singers I don't even want to discuss. One would not have been able to discuss any of this until relatively recently, when salaries and earnings generally became a significant part of the news. The sports pages, I am not the first to remark, today often resemble the financial pages. So, too, do the cultural pages. The clink, the positively deafening roar, of gold pouring into other people's coffers has become more than a little distracting.

Why, though, I ask myself, need I feel at all distracted? A friend recently reported the death of an elderly relative, and mentioned that, along with several other members of his family, he would be in for an inheritance—not a huge but a substantial one. How nice, I thought. Yet I also thought that he and I were at a time of life, middle age, where our habits were so fully formed that only a momentous sum of money could radically change our lives. As for myself, no matter how momentous the sum, I should continue to work at the same things, live in the same place, wear the same clothes (though I might spend more for socks, which have gone up alarmingly in recent years). Perhaps I would travel more, going absolutely first-class, but then I recall that, as it is, I really do not like to be away from my work for much longer than two weeks, so how much traveling would I be likely to do? More and more, in this respect at least, I am beginning to resemble the poet Philip Larkin, who said that he would like to see China only if he could return home that evening.

Is the poverty of my imagination showing? Am I beginning less to resemble Philip Larkin than the man I saw several years ago on a morning television show who had just won one of the first big state lottery jackpots—for $40 million, I think it was—when that kind of story was still national news. The man was Italian, working-class, in his fifties, modest to the point of seeming more embarrassed than happy about his extraordinary good fortune. The television *nudnik* interviewing him asked what he planned to do with all the money that would now be his. "Well," said the man, "I think I'll get a new car." "What kind of car?" asked the *nudnik*. "Well," said the man, "I kinda like the look of these new Buicks." That shook me from my morning torpor. Forty million dollars in the till and this fellow's imagination did not extend beyond a Buick. I hope the car he bought had whitewalls.

"I call people rich," Henry James has a character say in *The Portrait of a Lady*, "when they're able to meet the demands of their own imagination." By this standard the lottery winner in the preceding paragraph didn't need anywhere near $40 million. How much Henry James himself needed is not known; what is known is that he never came close to attaining it. Owing to James's extreme refinement, it is often assumed that he was quite well-off, living perhaps on family money, and well above the vulgar concern of earning his own way. In point of fact, Henry James, unlike so many of the characters in his novels, was compelled to earn his living, and money worries were never for very long off his mind. Throughout his professional life, James operated as a free lance, and usually on a close margin. The greater his financial hopes, the likelier they were to be disappointed. His first royalty statement for the New York Edition of his work, on which he had put in an enormous amount of work, showed author's earnings of $211. When his friend Edith Wharton once informed him that she had bought her costly Panhard touring car with the proceeds from her first novel *(The Valley of Decision)*, James replied that he had bought a handbarrow on which to cart guests' luggage with the proceeds from his last novel *(The Wings of the Dove),* adding that "with the proceeds of my next novel I shall have it painted."

Above the ruck in almost every other way, here, in the realm of shekels, Henry James, in his disappointment, joined the large and far from uniformly distinguished fraternity of his fellow writers. "No man but a blockhead ever wrote, except for money," Samuel Johnson famously remarked. But Johnson himself can scarcely be said to have broken the bank with his pen. Perhaps his remark needs to be revised to read that few men who set out to write for money do not wind up feeling like blockheads. Fantasies in the realm of gold are most common among writers. I believe I have had almost all of them myself: fantasies of my books selling at stratospheric prices at auction, to book clubs, to mass-market paperback houses. Accountants must be called in to see that my income is properly deferred so that the government does not take an unseemly bite out of it. I am instructed by obsequious lawyers on tax shelters. My Italian publisher—charming chap, you'd adore him—tells me that he knows of a duplex along the Arno, ownership of which would save me millions of lire on my Italian royalties. . . . I could go on, and in my own mind I assure you that I have. But I am brought up by the painful recollection of the likeness of my own condition to that of Max Beerbohm's friend Reggie Turner, who once said that among his own novels the truly rare copies were the second editions.

Sometimes I think that very easy money is not meant to fall into my pocket. A few years ago I received a phone call asking me to speak for half an hour before an educational association in Indianapolis. I replied that I was hesitant to do so. I was told that in previous years speakers had included George Plimpton and Art Buchwald. I sniffed long green. "Besides," I added, "my fee is rather high." When asked what I charged for a talk of half an hour, I crossed my fingers, closed my eyes, and said, "Three thousand dollars." "Not," said the man on the other end of the phone, "a problem." Damn, I thought, low-balled myself again; should have asked for five.

Still, three grand was three grand, and not to be gainsaid, sneezed at, or kicked out of bed. I toted up the take at $100 a minute. I wrote out my talk, rehearsed it, and the morning of the "caper," as I thought of it, I felt the exhilaration of a man embarked on a perfect crime. I felt I ought to give the talk in gloves, even though it was spring, so as to leave no fingerprints.

I arrived to find O'Hare Airport even more bedlamic than usual; hazardous weather conditions had for the present canceled flights throughout the Midwest. One, two, three hours went by. Mine was to be the keynote talk at this meeting. I phoned Indianapolis in the hope of reaching my contact there, but he could not be reached. Four, now five hours went by. I returned home. I finally reached my man in Indianapolis that night. I told him what had happened and that I would be willing to give my talk on the following day. Unfortunately, he said, there would be no room on the schedule. "Ahem," said I, clearing my throat to make way for the vulgar subject, "about my fee . . ." He told me that he was sure some equable arrangement would be made. Equable (like comfortable) I don't know. The final arrangement was that I, rather in the position of a blind date who didn't work out, was sent a check for my cab fare. Easy money.

Allow me to move on to a subject having to do with a lesser sum and much greater emotion. When I was in my early twenties I worked for a small company in the East. Three of us were responsible for putting out the company's product. One of the three was officially the boss, no doubt about that, but there was supposed to be a sense of partnership, all three of us engaged upon a common enterprise. The job entailed long hours and didn't pay very well, yet the work was interesting, and I felt that I was learning a good deal that might pay off in its own way later.

I wasn't on this job long before it became clear that the sense of partnership among the three of us existed only in my mind. Not only was the man in charge eager to exert his authority, and in a way that was unpleasant in so small a shop, but the other man on the job had plainly decided that he was going to do a good bit less than the minimum necessary. Much of the work he didn't do fell to me; I not infrequently found myself working until ten or eleven at night, running odd errands, doing double duty on the purely onerous work that nearly every young person's job requires. Somehow, though, I didn't mind. The work had to be done; I thought myself a team player; what the hell, no big deal, and so forth.

At the end of the year, the man in charge called me in to tell me how much he appreciated all I had done. Without me, he said, the company would have been in serious trouble. My co-worker had proved a great disappointment. He could count on him for nothing, which made his being able to count on me all the more important. And I had come through—splendidly. He wanted me to know that and he wanted me to know, too, that he was grateful. He was giving me a raise of $800; he wished it could be more, for, as he said, I deserved more, but there were severe constraints on the budget.

Roughly a week later I had lunch with the third man in the office. He told me that, if I hadn't guessed it already, he had long been looking for a new job. He had had it with the man in charge, and he had had it with the work, which seemed to him a dead end in every way. "Do you know," he said, "last week I was given a paltry raise of a thousand bucks?"

From the moment the figure of a thousand bucks hit the air, I was, in spirit, out of there. I felt a sucker, a chump, a patsy, a fool. Before the week was out, I, too, began looking for a new job.

I know a successful salesman who once told me that he didn't mind being made a fool of from time to time. "Keeps me on my toes," he said. This is reminiscent of the educational views of the father of John D. Rockefeller, Sr. "I cheat my boys every time I get a chance," he is reported to have claimed. "I want to make 'em sharp. I trade with the boys and skin 'em. I just beat 'em every chance I get." That's all very well for those who have good business instincts to begin with, but for those of us who do not, being made a fool of is—if I am in any way representative—demoralizing at best; at worst, it is depressing and humiliating. Or so at least it is to me.

I have not been made a fool of often, true enough, but then neither have I much ventured out and thereby given the world many clear shots at me. Although I grew up with what can only be called a commercial background—my father was a salesman, then owned his own small business—sometime in my late adolescence I caught intellectual fire and chose not to enter the financial wars. My father might have said, parodying John Adams, "I must study the market for handkerchiefs, tablecloths, costume jewelry, and imports from Taiwan, so that my son may have the liberty to study Montaigne, Tolstoy, and T. S. Eliot, so that his son (as it turns out) may go happily back into business." Unlike Allen Ginsberg, I have seen the best minds of my generation go to law school and medical school and take the CPA exam. I was by background scheduled to have gone and done likewise, and probably would have, had I not taken the turn down that bumpy road marked Serious Cultural Pretensions.

The mind is a great wanderer, as one scarcely need tell anyone who owns one, and my own frequently wanders into thoughts—daydreams is perhaps closer to it—about what my life might now be like if I had not taken that turn. Such mental wanderings are most likely to occur to me when I drive along Sheridan Road, outside Chicago, along the lengthy and lush strip of real estate known as the North Shore. Houses on Sheridan Road on the North Shore run from half a million to three or four million dollars in current value. I shall never occupy one, which is fair enough, but might I have done so had I become a lawyer or cardiologist or commodities trader? I see myself driving in a tan Mercedes, on the car phone to my broker, headed to a house I was clever enough to buy fifteen years ago for $125,000 and that is today worth $750,000. I am wearing an Italian suit, a fifty-dollar haircut, a thin gold watch, a gold bracelet, and a tasteful diamond ring on the little finger of my right hand—what a wag I know once called a Sammy Davis, Jr., starter set. I cannot tell you much about my wife, except that she has a terrific tan. My son is away at school at Tufts, my daughter at Taffeta. (If there is a Tufts, why not a Taffeta?) I have season tickets to the Bears games, on the forty-yard line. It's not a bad life.

Mockery perhaps, but not completely mockery. I do not despise that man I might so easily have been, and a part of me even admires him. He has a certain mastery of his world, and I am fairly sure that it is more complete than my mastery of my own world. I am impressed, too, by his savvy. He may not have a deep understanding of the nature of money—or even have much curiosity about it—but he knows a lot about the power of money and how to acquire it. One of the oddities of being a man in America—and this may soon apply to women, if it doesn't already—is that whatever one's other attainments, there remains a nagging touch of doubt if one hasn't also demonstrated one's ability to earn what I think of as serious money. On the other side, if one has imagination, to have earned serious money, even great high mounds of it, does not on its own and alone seem sufficient either. "It's a complex fate being an American," Henry James once said. As the man behind the wheel of that tan Mercedes might reply, "Tell me about it, Hank."

Such money as I have made for the vast most part I have made by grinding it out. I work at three jobs: writer, editor, teacher. Encouraged by an unfortunate self-deception I seem unable to shake, I frequently, to my chagrin, take on still more tasks; the self-deception I refer to is the belief that I am a fast worker. The truth is that I am a pitiably slow worker. (I write this now, but I shall soon enough forget it.) Give me an opportunity for yet more "easy money"—ask me to deliver a lecture for $5,000 or write an article for a dollar a word—and I am sure to be able to find a way to perform the job with an efficiency of a kind that will have me end up, on an hourly basis, making somewhere just under the minimum wage.

On only one occasion can I recall things working out delightfully otherwise. The editor of a college reader who wished to reprint an essay of mine, for which he offered a reprint fee of $300, added that he would pay me $600 more if I would write a thousand or so words about some problem connected with the writing of the essay. I told myself I would do so if I could write these thousand-odd words in less than an hour. And so, extraordinarily (for me), I did. I found the feeling of accomplishment gratifying. I was suddenly transformed in my own mind into a $600-an-hour man—up there with certain famous trial lawyers, allergy specialists, group therapists, if not yet with plastic surgeons, network television anchormen and women, and established major-league pitchers. (Orel Hershiser, of the Los Angeles Dodgers, earns $600 a pitch.) True, I could do with four or five such hours a day, every day, but a single hour gave me a taste of real earning power.

The only ways I might become a regular $600-an-hour man, with such unlicensed talent as I possess, is through writing for the movies, or having an amazing run of luck in writing advertising copy, or hitting the best-seller gong by writing a book that no one needs but lots of people might buy. But I fear that it is too late for me to do any of these things. A number of years ago, I met a successful developer in San Diego who told me that, when he arrived on the West Coast after World War II, the opportunities in real estate were such that he made so much money he never had to do anything immoral in his entire business life. My own professional morality has similarly remained intact, but for quite different reasons.

I am no sellout, but then, in order to sell out, you have to have buyers, and I, pathetic truth to tell, never have had any. I am one of those fortunate people the iron of whose integrity has never been put to the fire. Had it been, the iron might have turned out licorice; that is, I am not so sure it would have come through, though now that I think about it, I am less and less certain nowadays about what constitutes coming through. (When I was younger, I knew precisely, one might even say pedantically.) If one had embarked on a career in culture, there were several things one didn't do for money. Corrupters, their fists full of cash, were felt to be everywhere. Long before I came on the scene, Edmund Wilson proclaimed that the two great destroyers of talent in America were Hollywood and Henry Luce, publisher of *Time, Life, Fortune,* and other publications that swallowed potential artists and spat them out mere journalists. But then writing for *The New Yorker,* or any of the so-called slicks, was considered selling out, at any rate among the intellectual monks with whom I hung out. If not outright poverty, then a genuine absence of interest in wealth was felt to be an assumed vow for anyone who had taken up the life of art or intellect. Not only young purists like yours truly believed this, but ring-wise, squinty-eyed realists felt there was something to it. Orwell, for example, wrote: "Serious writers, I should say, are on the whole more vain and self-centered than journalists, though less interested in money."

That there are some things writers and other artists ought not to do for money is apparently a fresh notion to the current generation of the young. More than once, when teaching a course in the sociology of literature to undergraduates, I have brought up for discussion an ad that appeared in *The New Yorker* in which, alongside a line drawing of John Cheever—who was then alive and had to have given his permission for the ad—there ran a paragraph of high-sheen ad copy likening the craftsmanship of a Cheever story to that which goes into the making of a Rolex watch. What, I have asked, is wrong with this advertisement? Not much, feel the students, all of whom have been in the class by dint of their aspirations to be poets or novelists. Freud said that the artist gives up fame, money, and the love of beautiful women for the sake of his art, through which he hopes to win—you guessed her, friend— fame, money, and the love of beautiful women. But I rather doubt that my students have Freud in mind when they feel that any artist is entitled to turn a buck any which way he can. I make the point that writers, working with words, have a responsibility not to allow their names to be linked with the insubstantial words of a glossy ad. But I don't think I have ever successfully sold this point; I think that when I have tried to make it, students think me kind of a quaint old guy, nice enough and not entirely stupid, but maybe a touch wacky.

Attitudes toward money seem to change with every generation. Certainly, the numbers, the sums, change, and one of the signs of becoming older is that one is almost perpetually shocked by the increased cost of things. "My mother was amazed to learn," a friend recently reported, "that I paid more for my car than she paid for her house." The numbers of one's early adulthood set one's expectations, and, later, a slight shock comes at having them jarred. In my early adulthood, for example, a good shirt (at Brooks Bros.) cost $7.50, a suit (at the same place) was less than $100, $10 bought an excellent dinner, and $30,000 an impressive house, corner lot. I remember thinking, when in my middle twenties, that if only I could get my salary up to $10,000 a year I could breathe more easily.

I am often surprised at current prices, but people in the generation before mine tend to be frankly astonished by them. They simply cannot comprehend how anyone would pay, say, $1,800-a-month rent for a small and rather shabby apartment in a good neighborhood in San Francisco, or $270 for dinner for two in Manhattan, or $900 for a raincoat. And now that I have written out these prices, I realize that, though I can comprehend them, I nonetheless find them appalling. They give off bad vibrations, they feel wrong, they are in some fundamental way in bad taste. More than appalling, I find them, somehow, immoral. No matter how much money one has, to spend it thus is in some sense to destroy it. As a minor character in *The Mansion*, the last novel in Faulkner's Snopes trilogy, puts it, in a passage that has stuck in my mind more than twenty-five years after I first read it: "Only the gauche, the illiterate, the frightened and the pastless destroy money."

Although I have a taste for nearly every luxury going, I find my appetite for the good high life often curtailed by my monetary morality. Some things it sorely pains me to spend money on—frequently very small things. In Jerusalem recently, I wished to read Josephus's *The Jewish War*, which I had never read, and what better place to read it than at the scene of the subject! But at bookshops in Jerusalem they asked the equivalent of $15 for the Penguin edition that in the United States sells for $7.95. I could not bring myself to buy it. At our very comfortable and otherwise reasonable lodgings, the laundry service wanted $1.15 to do a handkerchief and the same price for a pair of socks. I washed out my own handkerchiefs and socks. I know a man who gives away tens of thousands of dollars to students, friends in need, and good causes from which he gains no personal renown, but who will not order a glass of wine in a restaurant—no matter who is paying—because the price is at least double and usually triple what the same wine costs in a shop, and he feels this is wrong. I quite understand; a peccadillo would be entailed. Money, being funny, is filled with such peccadilloes.

At the same time that I have grown morally sniffy about what seem to me vulgar expenses, I also happen to admire enormously the type once known as the "sport." I have never walked into a bar and said, "Drinks for everyone—on me," or been in a bar when someone else said it. But I do like a man who picks up a check, and I hope that in my time I have picked up my share. A friend once complimented me on a necktie I was wearing, and I straightaway slipped it off, saying, "It's yours." Once, in a barbershop, a stranger said he liked my shirt; I told him his was damn fine, too; and since we happened to be roughly the same size, we exchanged shirts then and there—close but not quite the same as giving the man the shirt off my back. I contribute modest sums to charities and to cultural institutions—music festivals, classical music radio stations, public television, poetry associations—which gives me the illusion that I am a large-hearted guy. But whenever I begin to think this, I am reminded that the true measure of generosity is not how much one gives but how much, after giving, one has left over.

If no true sport, certainly not in any grand sense, I qualify, I hope, as generous; I would even settle for the syntactically awkward "not ungenerous." It would pain me to have myself thought cheap, tight, a skinflint, a man from whose wallet moths have been known to emerge. Literature is full of misers, life of cheapskates. Thrift is a virtue, but I knew a man so careful with money that he was able to put something by when living on unemployment insurance, and did it, what is more, living in New York City. Cheapness is sometimes amusing, but more often it is contemptible. Putting too great a value on money is the sign of a dull mind and, possibly, a shriveled heart, or so one would be inclined to think. Yet who knows what dreams of security, independence, love, glory, and fear lurk in the mind of the true tightwad. "Money is human happiness *in abstracto,*" wrote the beetle-browed Schopenhauer; "consequently he who is no longer capable of happiness *in concreto* sets his whole heart on money."

Only the deeply religious and the wildly insane are above the influence of money. Culture does not generally lift one above it; and Freud, in the paper titled "Further Recommendations in the Technique of Psycho-Analysis," maintained that the psychoanalyst ought to understand "that money questions will be treated by cultured people in the same manner as sexual matters, with the same inconsistency, prudishness, and hypocrisy." Written in 1913, that still seems largely true, except that nowadays people do talk a great deal about money. Not to mention money in any connection was once thought a sign of good suburban breeding. It may be that people currently talk about it too much. Again, as with sex, so with money—it remains a subject about which there remains a distinct curiosity. *New York,* a magazine never noted for its delicacy, used to publish the salaries of prominent people, and my guess is that this was probably as widely read as anything in its pages. I would be greatly offended to have my own earnings made public in this or any other way. Several years ago, to accept an honorific place in a small government agency, I had to undergo a security clearance and to set out my earnings and financial holdings. I didn't so much mind the FBI asking friends and colleagues in the various cities I have lived and worked in if I had a drinking or drug problem, but I did find that it badly bugged me to list my earnings and financial holdings for strangers. Prudishness, if that is what it was, may not yet be dead in money matters.

Two conditions lead one to think about money almost endlessly: having none and having an immensity of it. Falling well in the middle ought to put one in a position to achieve the golden mean, or so one might think. But it usually doesn't. (That this Aristotelian concept should be expressed in the universal currency of gold is itself interesting; a silver mean, clearly, wouldn't do the job.) A cool perspective on money is almost never easily achieved. When I was young and made the quite conscious decision not to go for the dough, in my most financially strapped days I felt that when one didn't have to worry about money, one had enough. I don't worry about it all that much anymore, but I continue to think about it. What I mostly think about is what my life might have been like if I had had a great deal more.

If I were to have had any more money, it would not, I think, have been a good thing for me to have had it young. I would have found a way to screw it up, blow it, possibly turn my good fortune into a felony. A neighbor not long ago told me that her husband was one of eighteen nephews and nieces of a man who at his death left a trust that gave them, when they turned twenty-one, an annual income of $60,000 each. Apart from her husband, who went on to medical school, not one of these legatees finished college. The result of their uncle's generous benefaction was to breed a set of drug addicts, full-time beach bums, ne'er-do-wells, and other human disasters. Listening to my neighbor's story, I could not help but imagine what

I would be like today if I had had a trust of that kind. Had I been able to depend upon such an income from the age of twenty-one, I should now, at the age of fifty-three, probably be in shorts on the porch of my house in Majorca, putting the finishing touches on my first, quite unpublishable novel.

Although it was something I disdained when young, money, the brute fact is, was then a powerful and even useful goad to me. I wrote not alone for pleasure and out of vanity, but under economic necessity. I had a terrific "nut," as small businessmen used to refer to their overhead, and I needed the green to maintain it. Today I would write what I write for nothing, but getting paid for it makes it all the jollier, even if the sums involved do not send me scurrying for tax shelter. Even a small fee—something, say, in the high two figures—is better than none.

Money has its own reality, and justice in its distribution does not seem to be a part of it. Sometimes remuneration seems logical and fair; but in an economy that appears to be on goofy pills, often it does not. I was discussing with a friend the salary of an inept fellow worker who, in a strange conjunction of economic facts, makes way more than he deserves, which gives him less than he needs to live on. Above all, one must never expect even the roughest justice in connection with money and skill or money and the importance of a particular job to society. Besides, opinions differ on what work is important to society.

I once told a conservative economist the joke about the airplane that is in grave trouble and, overweighted, will crash unless one passenger agrees to jump out. The pilot and the crew have decided that they must ask that person among the passengers to leave who is of the least importance to society. At which point, the punch line of the joke goes, a disc jockey and a used-car salesman got up in the aisle and began fighting. "I would like that joke better," said the economist, "if, instead of a disc jockey and a used-car salesman, a psychologist and the curator of a museum of contemporary art got up in the aisle and began fighting."

One's outlook on money is likely to be greatly conditioned, if not altogether determined, by whether or not one grew up with much of the stuff. Growing up without money can make one eager, even anxious, to acquire as much of it as possible, though it can, conversely, cause one to disbelieve in one's chances of earning much of it and so render one content to live modestly. Growing up with a great deal of money can cause one to lose interest in it—if one is political-minded, even to feel guilty about it—though it can also make one wish to outdo one's parents and so be all the more furious in pursuit of it. I grew up with enough money to feel fairly secure about it, but never so secure as to be oblivious about it or its importance. All I want now, I suppose, is lots of money without having to give any thought or specific effort to getting it. Why do I feel that this isn't going to happen?

It might have something to do with the fact that my imagination has begun to shrink. I want only not to have to worry about money, from either side of the tracks, rich or poor. Great wealth would be an inconvenience, at least it would be for me, for I have no wish to think about the stock market, the prime rate, or any of the rest of it. I have no use for a limousine, live-in servants, or even a secretary. I don't say, with the old song, give me the simple life, which, even if it were available, would probably bore me blue. Yet the life I live, which requires purchasing things to sit upon, wear, and eat—not to speak of various tickets and books and a chance to get out of town every once in a while—does not permit my ignoring money for very long. Like the lady said, money is funny, and the biggest laugh may be reserved for those of us who are clownish enough to believe we can rise above it.

Dancing in the Darts

"As long as you have your health," say the Jews, fairly frequently. For all I know the Armenians, the Bessarabians, the Patagonians, and the Macedonians say it, too. If so, I wish to go on record here as saying that they are all bang-on-target correct. Over the past few months, I seem briefly to have lost mine—my health, that is—and it quite threw me. Not to be alarmed. I have suffered no heart attack, no cancer has been discovered lurking within me, no stroke has struck. Instead something much more trivial and undignified has hit. I have a disorder of the intestines; it is, technically, a disease. I prefer, out of personal pique, not to name it and therefore give it any publicity. In a book written for sufferers of this disease it is said that its cause, and therefore its cure, is unknown. It doesn't necessarily shorten one's life; it merely makes it more irritating—the hope is, if carefully watched, not too much more irritating.

I have come to refer to it, in Irish fashion, as "Me Troubles." For a while, these seemed quite serious. Me Troubles caused me to lose weight; grow anemic; fail to retain protein, vitamin B_{12}, also vitamin D; and for a while it was thought that it had done something to my liver that I do not quite recall, probably because I am of that portion of humanity whose members prefer not to know that they have a liver (or a gall-bladder, kidneys, pancreas, and spleen, not to speak of the islet of Langerhans, which I'd rather think of as a charming ski resort near Stockholm). But enough of this organ recital. The main point is that for three or so months I felt well below par, under the weather, not myself, plain lousy.

Perhaps complicatedly lousy comes closer to describing my condition. Feeling plain lousy would not have been sufficient to drive me into the hands of a physician, for I am—or at least up to now have been—a nearly pure type of the inverse hypochondriac. By this I mean that, in a reversal of the hypochondriac, I believe I am never ill. If I bleed, I wait until the bleeding stops; if I swell, I wait until the swelling goes down; if a rash appears upon my skin, I wait until it disappears—and, lo, it always has: stopped, gone down, disappeared. I am fearful that if I appear in a physician's office complaining of ear ache, he will put me through a battery of highly technical tests that will determine beyond all doubt that I must have two toes removed. I prefer to retain the ear ache and the two toes. Rather like a misogynist bachelor who enjoys hearing stories about marital failure that serve to confirm his own actions and views, I have enjoyed, perhaps unduly, jokes that deflate the authority of physicians: jokes about migraine headaches caused by too-tight underwear, about psychoanalysts who cannot be bothered to listen, about physicians being regularly astounded by the marvels of their patients' sex lives. I had begun to think myself a Jewish Scientist, on the model of Christian Science, so set had I become on avoiding all commerce with the saw-bonely trades.

I had been able to do so fairly successfully owing to the good luck of being in possession of solid if not always ebullient health. Let the record speak boringly for itself. When I was four or five, I had my tonsils removed; at nine I chipped an

elbow and wore a cast on my arm during a particularly hot
Chicago summer; at thirty-seven, at the Los Angeles airport,
I sprained an ankle and for a week walked with a cane; in my
mid-forties I acquired a mildish case of mononucleosis.
("Mono?" asked a terse friend at the time. "At his age are they
certain it isn't Meno?") Twice during the past two decades, at
the request of my wife, I have had general physical examinations, with delightfully empty results. And, oh yes, once about
eleven years ago, I discovered blood in my stool. I contemplated the possible meaning of this for some sixteen or eighteen
weeks—wondering from time to time if I hadn't ought to get
my rather unimpressive estate in order—then arranged an appointment with a gastroenterologist. A laconic man, he put me
through an examination that steadied me in my already firm
resolve to spend all my days as a heterosexual, had me knock
back a cup of barium for purposes of X-rays, and finally sent
me packing with some red pills that stopped the bleeding. Most
healthy—and therefore most happy—fella.

The only comfort I derive from Me Troubles is that it
confirms my general views about health. These views, I realize,
are arbitrary, unconventional, wholly unscientific, yet they are
mine own and hence precious to me. I believe that health is a
dart game in which darts descend from the sky, randomly
hitting some persons and leaving others untouched. (If you,
child of the Enlightenment, wish to call these darts "genes,"
be my guest.) Cause is not entirely disassociated from effect in
this view, and if you smoke fifty or sixty Camels every day or
have liberally lubricated your interior with a vast quantity of
alcohol over several decades, you really oughtn't to look up in
disbelief when told your lungs or liver are in bad shape. In
health, I believe, vice is punished, though not evenhandedly,
but virtue generally goes unrewarded. How else explain the
too-frequent illness, crippling, or death of the young, the inno-

cent, the good, and the magnificently in-shape? Viruses, genes, strange malfunctions, you say. Darts, say I, darts diabolically descending. Please recall that I speak with the authority of a man with a mild disease that has no known cause and no known cure.

Although the symptoms of Me Troubles are said to include fatigue, irritability, and depression, the last-named, depression, is not a condition I have ever been able to sustain for very long—owing, I have generally assumed, to an insufficient attention span. But in this instance I did feel distinctly down, and what put me there was the recognition that I could no longer be as heedless, as hitherto I have always been, about my health. Perhaps the sweetest luxury that health confers is removing one from thinking about health at all; it lets you live, so to speak, outside your body. Now I suddenly found myself thinking about it all the time: about diet, about sleep, about keeping up with a regular regimen of pills. (I, who once aspired to be known by certain nightclub bartenders, am now beginning to be known by certain drugstore pharmacists.) Resiliency, the easy snapping back from exertion that the healthy can count upon, could no longer quite be counted upon by me, at least not in the same deliciously careless way. Not that I wished to do power lifting or compete in a triathlon in Alaska, but I do from time to time like to break into a rather pathetic Fred Astaire imitation. ("You see," Fred himself says in the movie *Top Hat*, "every once in a while I find myself dancing.") I still do my Fred Astaire, but not quite full out. One thinks a bit before cutting loose with a dart in one's foot.

So far nothing has surfaced in the medical literature that I have seen, but I wonder if Me Troubles do not also cause a decided weakness for steep and risky generalization. Since Me Troubles, I have decided that the world is divided into two kinds of people. Robert Benchley, may he rest in peace, once said that the world is divided into two kinds of people: those who divide the world into two kinds of people and those who don't. Benchley's division, I suspect, is uneven, for most of us do so divide the world at one time or another, and at this particular time I happen to see it divided into those who have and those who do not have their health. Sheer solipsism on my part, perhaps, but I see a plenitude of evidence for it all around me, much of it on the very block on which I live.

From the chair in which I now sit, I can see a portion of the awning of a health club on the street below. Into this club, from six in the morning until ten at night, mostly young men and women come and go, and I am fairly certain they do not talk of Michelangelo. In sweatpants and tank tops, in sweat-shirts and spandex pants, they go at it, grunting and groaning, lifting weights, hoisting coiled machinery, dancing aerobi-cally, running treadmills, putting themselves through various other tortures in the name of staying in shape. Calisthenics of a low- or high-tech kind has never been my idea of a good time, but the people who depart from this health club seem beyond doubt happy in their work. Do they ever, I wonder, as they emerge, let their eyes fall on the very next door to the south, which is a physical therapy clinic, treating people recovering from serious illnesses, accidents, injuries, breakdowns? As do all ironists, I have a taste for stark juxtaposition, but this—a health club placed next door to what is in effect a sick club—is a bit heavy-handed, even for me.

Yet this neighborhood seems to be zoned Ironic. At the corner, a large apartment building and parking garage has been under construction for more than a year. "That," as Yeats said in a strikingly different context, "is no country for old men," and the young men working the construction jobs, through steamy summers and blasted winters, seem not merely healthy but at the stage beyond healthy. The normal rules of health seem not to apply to them. They smoke cigarettes without physical complication or social compunction, eat their fill of precisely the kind of food that appeals to them, appraise the passing young women with a jeweler's eye and a burglar's conscience. On a particularly cold day during a low ebb in my own health, I happened to be walking alongside one of these young men, who sported a modified version of a Nietzschean mustache—thick, auburn, and tinted with ice—and I thought to myself that there is perhaps more vitality in that mustache than I feel just now in my entire body. Sheer health envy, of course, which is a thing I had never felt before.

Near the other end of the block is a retirement hotel. Round the corner and a block to the east there are three other such institutions. A block to the west is an eight-story building filled with physicians' offices. Two blocks to the north, meanwhile, is a university with its large population of the young. Such a neighborhood makes for blatant contrasts. On one side of the street a blue-rinse-haired dowager, a touch tremulous with palsy, using a metal cane, trepidaciously takes the air, walking slowly, bringing one foot up to the other; while across the street a clean-limbed Chinese boy in silky blue shorts, a red baseball cap, and a gray University of Virginia sweatshirt seems not so much to be running as gliding by. Two male college students study, from behind, the walk of a splendidly aeroboticized young blond woman in a ponytail and a black velour Fila warm-up suit on her way to the health club, as she walks past the medical building. Before the building stands a gaunt man leaning on the contraption known as a walker, as his daughter, who herself looks to be in her sixties, pulls the car up to the curb before confronting the always tricky adventure of negotiating him into the backseat of the car. Yes, this neighborhood is quite nicely set up to make one think that the world is divided into two kinds of people.

Is the self-pity knob turned up too high here? I suspect that it is. (I cannot recall who said that self-pity was the only consistently believable human emotion. Whoever it was, the old boy was on to something.) Perhaps it is only that I have not yet quite grown used to finding myself on the unhealthy side of the great divide. The novelty of it may have me over-stimulated. I remind myself of Joachim Ziemssen, Hans Castorp's cousin in *The Magic Mountain,* the same Joachim Ziemssen who would have been "distinctly handsome if his ears had not stood out. Up to a certain period they had been his only trouble in life. Now, however, he had others." I find, moreover, that I tend to enjoy talking about my illness, even though until now I have been rather selective in whom I have told about it. I have not yet met anyone else who has it, but many people I know seem to know someone—a neighbor, a cousin—who does. I should be delighted to meet such a person—ah, *mon frère, mon semblable*—so that we could gas away unstintingly on what, at the moment, seems to me my favorite subject: my very own little disease. This, I realize, is what used to be called "sick."

What is sick about it was stated plainly enough by Seneca, who said that "no man can have a peaceful life who thinks too much about lengthening it." One has to respect that sentiment coming from a man who was forced to commit suicide for participating in an alleged conspiracy against his emperor and is said to have philosophized while in the act of opening his own veins. On the other hand, it strikes me as altogether natural to want to prolong an agreeable life, and to have, as a Henry James character in *The Europeans* puts it, "perhaps a selfish indisposition to bring our pleasure to a close." I am mightily grateful that my own disease, if carefully watched, is not supposed to shorten my life, for early death would make me feel like a buoyant child put to bed just when the party seemed really to get going. In longevity, as in so many other spheres of modern life, we now all live in a revolution of rising expectations. A full three score and ten, let us face it, does not, to most of us, any longer feel all that full. Those of us greedy for life prefer not to peg out until at least eighty, and well beyond. Of most people who survive to die beyond the age of eighty and who have not otherwise had a painful life, I find myself often saying, upon learning of their death, that they have had a pretty good roll of the dice. But my guess is that most among them would have liked to stay at the table at least a little while longer.

I suppose the crucial question is what you are willing to pay to live as long as you can, assuming that a dart does not get you young. A great many Americans just now seem to me to have organized their lives around the idea—the hope, more precisely—of making it to, say, ninety-seven, with good digestion, remaining sexually active, staying fairly nice-looking. They will achieve this through a combined program of exercise (a thing hated, as the Reverend Sydney Smith once remarked, by every person of sense and talent), diet, and sensible moderation. Ah, the hopeful ones, dreamers of the impossible dream. I note vast numbers of them, many middle-aged and far from athletic in bearing, jogging along the lakefront near where I live. Faces contorted in grimaces, limbs often bandaged or splinted, flesh flushed, they pound on—no gain, as the platitude has it, without pain—in anticipation of longer life, lots of it, right here on this earth.

Others hope to achieve a nearly endless life through diet. I see some of the most fanatical among them when, in need of some item forgotten at the supermarket, I repair to a nearby health-food market. Everything in the joint, I need scarcely say, is organically grown. This market sells chickens, I once heard it reported, whose feet have never been allowed to touch the ground—the only time in my life I can recall feeling a stab of pity for a chicken. Half an aisle in this market is given over to pills and various compounds. Granola abounds, sprouts proliferate, the fiber in the place is so high you can practically incur a nosebleed. It is not, in short, a good spot for picking up a five-pound assortment of Whitman's Samplers or a full slab of ribs for the barbee, as the Australians call it.

Yet for all the concern about achieving health through food, the health-food set in this shop, customers and employees both, look to me to be in very bad shape. So many of the women seem to have furry faces and sunken cheeks; the young men, wispy beards and reedy arms. All have a solemn air about them. They are people who treat their bodies as temples, but, like the old joke about the radical Reform Jewish temple, these bodies seem closed for the holidays. Not that I would consider telling a joke in this market, whose denizens sometimes seem to me from another planet. George Orwell, in *The Road to Wigan Pier*, wrote that "the food-crank is by definition a person willing to cut himself off from human society in hopes of adding five years to the life of his carcass; that is, a person out of touch with common humanity."

"And this man Orwell," I can hear one of the pale stock boys at the health-food market ask through his sprout-like beard, "how long exactly did he live?"

"Hmmm," I clear my throat before answering. "Died at the age of forty-six, actually."

The explanation would probably not go down well in these quarters, but in fact George Orwell caught a dart, the one called tuberculosis. That particular dart hit a large number of twentieth-century writers; Franz Kafka, D. H. Lawrence, Simone Weil, Albert Camus, Anton Chekhov, Katherine Mansfield, and André Gide, among others, were consumptives. Such names are almost sufficient to grant tuberculosis the status of the literary disease *par excellence.* Earlier, writers and artists tended to contract illnesses lower down in the anatomy. Montaigne suffered sorely from kidney stones, one of which eventually killed him. (Piranesi, too, died of a kidney ailment, in his case one he neglected.) Edward Gibbon himself became history as a result of an infection caused by an operation on his hydrocele, or accumulation of fluid around the testicles. None of these sound like graceful ways to make one's final exit.

But then writers seem not ever to have been famously healthy. One Dr. Tissot, in a book titled *De la Santé des gens de lettres* (1768), included in his list of illnesses that afflicted writers: diseases of the nervous system, tension, poor eyesight, palpitations, dizziness, defective digestion, lassitude, melancholia, gout, hair loss, tumors, aneurysms, insomnia, apoplexy, dropsy, flatulence, constipation, ulcers, impotence, and more. Not an unimpressive little list, taken all in all, especially for indoor work.

The tendency of writers to dramatize does not always make them the most reliable witnesses on the state of their own health. To hear some among them tell it, no work is so perilous as that of a career in art. Baudelaire's infamous remark about practicing any of the arts not being good for one's sex life— *"Plus un homme cultive les arts, moins il bande"*—is but one giddy example. Then, too, not a few writers have been hypochondriacs. Working alone, living in their minds, exercising their imaginations much more than their bodies, writers find plenty of time to invent diseases, illnesses, maladies both subtle and flamboyant. (Bachelors, in my experience, are also talented at hypochondria; it is a condition that requires a certain amount of free time.) T. S. Eliot's letter to his cousin Eleanor Hinkley nicely hits the cheery note of writers on their own health: "My teeth are falling to pieces, I have to wear spectacles to read, and from time to time I am contorted with rheumatism—otherwise I am pretty well." The Old Possum was all of thirty-five when he wrote that.

H. L. Mencken, who publicly posed as a genial rowdy mildly boastful of his boozing as a younger man, and who was philosophical about the fragility of *Homo sapiens* as an older man, Mencken the robust, Mencken the skeptical, this same Mencken turns out in his private life to have been a quite vigorous hypochondriac. His *Diary* is filled with reports on his ailments, which are not only various but numerous. Mencken had the distinct disadvantage, which all serious hypochondriacs seem to acquire, of possessing a vast store of medical information. A number of physicians at Johns Hopkins School of Medicine were among his friends, and doubtless he pumped them for all the latest medical scuttlebutt they had. Mencken watched himself with the most sedulous care, on the *qui vive* for some new symptom, some minor malfunction, some fresh shred of evidence that the entire human machine was about to collapse. He even thought that he might one day "add an appendix to my magazine chronicle [a book he never got around to writing] giving my medical history," a thing no other writer had done, "though all books by literati are full of complaints of illness." In a nice twist, Mencken attributed his own relative longevity to his bad health:

When I was 40 I had no expectation of reaching 65, and in fact assumed as a matter of course that I'd be dead by then. My father died at 44 and my grandfather Mencken at 63. Perhaps I have lasted so long because my health has always been shaky; my constant aches and malaises have forced me to give some heed to my carcass. To be sure, I have worked too hard and maybe also drunk too much; but on the whole I have been careful.

Eventually, of course, all hypochondriacs prove correct; that is, they do, in the fullness of time, sicken and die, as H. L.

Mencken did, at the age of seventy-five, seven years after a stroke that cruelly left him, most word-minded of men, unable either to read or to write.

To be a hypochondriac is to combine the compulsion toward perfection with the imagination for disaster. This combination, as will be quickly apparent, is not a guaranteed recipe for psychological ease. The hypochondriac wants everything about his health to be perfect—"I, for one, have never in my life come across a perfectly healthy human being," says Dr. Krokowski, second in command at the International Sanatorium Berghof in *The Magic Mountain*—and yet is endlessly finding flaws, danger signs, clear reasons for panic and terror. Hypochondriacs tend to be widely knowledgeable not only about illness and disease but about physicians, local and national. While they may not be found smiling there, they are often happiest in a doctor's office. They require lots of attention. Seven or eight hundred well-placed hypochondriacs could probably bring down socialized medicine, so great are their demands. Paradise for an earnest hypochondriac is not perfect health but a month at the Mayo Clinic, during which he is the sole patient and none of the staff is off on holiday. A true hypochondriac, say this much for him, is rarely without something to think about.

Evelyn Waugh was not a hypochondriac, but I have long been impressed by a story his friend Christopher Sykes, who was also one of his biographers, tells about visiting Waugh in a London hospital after his recovery from an operation for hemorrhoids. Sykes heard Waugh out on the pain the operation had caused him and on the suffering the subsequent treatment brought. In an attempt to cheer his friend up, Sykes suggested that at least he would now be relieved of much chronic pain, and in any case the operation must have been necessary.

"No," [Waugh] said, "the operation was not necessary, but might conceivably have become so later on."

"Not necessary? Then why did you have it done?"

"Perfectionism."

After reading that, Evelyn Waugh's hemorrhoids have become a symbol for me, in medical, dental, and other spheres, of the kind of job that doesn't need doing. "A clear instance," I say, "of Waugh's hemorrhoids."

Everyone needs all the symbols, talismans, uplifting stories, strings of garlic, and anything else he can use to ward off the hypochondria that now encroaches upon us all. So many elements in contemporary life conduce to make one more than a little nutty on the subject of health, and not least among them is the abundance currently loosed upon the world of what is known as "health news." Most television news programs in large cities now have someone called "a health reporter" or "our health editor." His or her job seems to be to recount stories of dramatic transplants ("Steelworker rejects liver of llama"), goofy diets ("Man loses fifty pounds in eleven days on smoked piranha"), and new causes, gastronomical and environmental, of cancer, heart attack, and stroke ("Marriage may cause stroke—tonight at eleven"). Who among us with a normal greed for longevity—or, if you prefer, an insufficient death wish—has not felt a bit jerked around by contradictory stories about cholesterol, fiber, caffeine, aspirin, and a great many other items? The morning it was announced that decaffeinated coffee, too, could adversely affect serum cholesterol levels, the man who reads the news on the classical music station I listen to sighed, then wistfully said: "Can't smoke, can't eat, now I can't drink coffee. Oh, well, there's still music."

What, I wondered the moment he said it, if classical music were found to cause cancer? I suppose the story would break, inevitably, in the *New England Journal of Medicine,* playing the next day on all the front pages and television news programs in the country. Soon thereafter researchers at the Erasmus University Medical School in Rotterdam determine that the most dangerous music of all to listen to is that provided by stringed instruments, especially violoncello and bass. (This finding will later be refuted by a study done at Pennsylvania State University; listening to a viola for twenty minutes, Penn State researchers find, is roughly equivalent to standing for the same length of time behind a bus without pollution controls whose motor is running.) The American Heart Association, meanwhile, announces that wind instruments—particularly the trumpet, French horn, trombone, and tuba—are bad for the hearts not only of those who play them but of those who listen to them. Music played by plucked instruments, according to a study at the Harvard Medical School, presents no health danger whatsoever. A well-organized program in the public schools teaches children about the dangers of chamber music; the First Lady gives her full support to a campaign among the young whose slogan is "Say No to Mozart."

What the infusion of a vast quantity of half-baked medical information appears to have done is to make everyone more jittery about his health. We now have an increased awareness of all that can go wrong with the human body without a commensurate awareness of what can be done to avoid some of the more horrendous of these possibilities. The great fitness craze, the careful eating mania, have not, I suspect, made people any less anxious about their health; quite the reverse. By objective measures, people are now more healthy than ever before, and the most convincing of these measures is that we live much longer: at the turn of the century, life expectancy for American men was 47.3 years; today it is 74.7, and 78.8 years for women. Death rates for the great killers of the day—cancer, heart attack, stroke—have all tended to go down. Why, then, aren't we happier?

Because, my guess is, greed for long life with unbroken

good health cannot finally be satisfied. Those of us who wish to live as long as possible—in, I need scarcely add, fine physical and mental repair—are living a hopeless dream. If one succeeds in living long, avoiding the crueler darts through cautious living and great good luck, in the end one will likely only have lived long enough to be visited by one of the two terrors most of us fear above all: cancer or senility. Sorry to put a damper on the party, but we really are all in the condition of the man in the cartoon who has just fallen out of his twentieth-story office window and who, ten floors from the ground, calls out, "So far, so good."

Still, the view on the way down is not without its charms. Or, to switch and gently mix metaphors (stirring lightly), even more than halfway out to sea with a rent sail, I myself find the shore full of fascinating fauna. Physicians, for example, who until now I have managed to elude, have come to me as a fresh phenomenon. My doctors, for one thing, are younger than I. This is excellent from one standpoint, in that it means they are likely to outlive me and thus will be around to help me shuffle off to a place I hope will have a better climate than Buffalo. At the same time, I, who am used to thinking of physicians as fatherly figures of authority, find it a mite difficult to take a person much younger than I altogether seriously.

But then I have never taken doctors as seriously as did the generation of my parents, for whom they were as gods. I have some inkling of how ill-educated the contemporary physician tends to be, having gone to university with many of them. The reason for this, I realize, is that he had to concentrate all his mental energies on life's only important goal—getting into medical school—and this was a goal, for the aspiring physician, not compatible with even a narrow liberal education. Not, you understand, that I wish to discuss the *Meno* with a urologist, but I should just as soon that he didn't talk to me about "quality time" or "bonding." The physician treating me for Me Troubles, I am pleased to report, said at one point that, in my case, he hoped to be able to "avoid the barbarity of surgery," a phrase and sentiment that earned my appreciative attention.

I went to school with a young man whose family physician was William Carlos Williams. I am not sure why, but I do not think I would have wanted Williams for my physician; perhaps it is because he has written too many insignificant poems—sheer aesthetic snobbery on my part. I am not even sure that I would prefer to have had Chekhov as my physician. I rather doubt that so productive a writer, adding to world literature, would have had time to keep up with medical literature, which, in my selfishness, I should be eager that he do. Then, too, Chekhov saw too much in the way of true medical disasters, on Sakhalin Island and over the many years that he treated (often for nothing) the multitudes of Russian peasants, who came to him with their horrendous ailments and ghastly injuries, to be greatly sympathetic to my relatively minor affliction. No, a famous physician, especially one famous for extra-medical reasons, does not seem the answer.

What is wanted is a physician with great competence, considerable sympathy, and perhaps a touch of the philosopher. Lord Moran, Winston Churchill's personal doctor, was such a physician. He was always available and had a fine sense of his responsibilities, as the following passage from *Churchill,* the book drawn from his diary, makes clear:

In a sense Winston is tough, yet he is hardly ever out of my hands. His eyes, his ears, his throat, his heart and lungs, his digestion and his diverticulitis have given him trouble at different times. Some little thing goes wrong and apprehension and impatience do the rest. And if his doctor cannot bring relief, well, he ought to.

Better still, Lord Moran shared, in a qualified sense, my own views of the arbitrariness of good health, especially beyond a certain age:

When a man begins to grow old his future becomes guess-work. His faculties may be unimpaired, his health by all appearances sound, yet any day, without warning, a coronary thrombosis may strike him dead, or leave him an invalid, who remains a tenant of this world only by courtesy, well knowing that another arrow from the same quiver will get him in the end.

Arrows and darts, darts and arrows—it is, I tell you, a jungle out there.

I am up at four-thirty on a below-zero morning. I have had a bad night, failing to recapture sleep after a disturbing dream about surgery. I look out the window, and on the street below a fellow padded in heavy clothes is running down the middle of the road, risking frostbite to stay in shape, the damn fool. The physician treating me for Me Troubles had told me only the day before that he and I are likely to have a longtime relationship. I like him well enough, but the news, somehow, did not elate me. I do not have much talent for being a patient.

The word *patient*, which means "suffering or enduring without complaint," derives, of course, from the word *patience*, which, the etymologist C. T. Onions reports, means "endurance with calm." So far I have felt the suffering but not withheld the complaint; obviously, I shall endure, but don't ask me to be calm. Since learning of Me Troubles, I seem to have volleyed back and forth emotionally between rage and depression. Sitting in a hospital corridor, awaiting X-rays of my entrails, in one of those silly green gowns, wearing underneath only shorts and shoes and black socks, I feel vaguely put-upon, humiliated, and depressed. Death didn't seem so bad at the time, I recall thinking, though no one had actually mentioned my dying.

I have heard it said that people who are generally gloomy, who go about expecting the worst, take life's setbacks better than those with rosier views. Apparently, I have been one of those people with rosier views; evidently life, which has been very easy on me, has made me so. Beneath the reader of Kierkegaard, Dostoyevsky, and Nietzsche, a Rotarian has all along been living, for I had optimistically assumed that life would continue to issue me a free pass. I recognized that Me Troubles, as troubles go, were minor. I was not in danger of dying; I did not lose the function of any part of my body or facet of my mind; I was not disfigured; I was in fact not even suffering now that I had been put on a drug regimen. (Send no get-well cards.) Why, then, the rage? Why the depression?

Intimations of bloomin' mortality is why. I owe to this little disease of mine the first real intimation that there are some losses in life that cannot be recouped, that health is not endlessly regainable, that one is not going to live forever. Before now I knew all this without quite believing it. Now I believe it. "Every day you get older," says Butch Cassidy, "and that's a law." Although Butch was too polite to say it, eventually you run out of days, and then not even your "personal exercise physiologist," or your "total fitness plan," or your "non-punitive eating program" can come to your aid. I have never had a personal physiologist, plan, or program, but I did have a belief in my own invincibility. I now feel rather more vincible, if still far from defeated. Hitherto, I have been dancing in the dark; henceforth, as I am keenly aware, I shall be dancing in the darts, as we all are. But the great thing—all right, Maestro, hit it!—is to keep on dancing.